ST BERNARD OF CLAIRVAUX'S LIFE OF ST MALACHY OF ARMAGH

By H. J. LAWLOR, D.D.

LIVES OF THE CELTIC SAINTS

SOCIETY FOR PROMOTING CHRISTIAN KNOWLEDGE

Irish Classics

Printed in Great Britain by Richard Clay & Sons, Limited, BRUNSWICK ST.,
STAMFORD ST., S.E. 1, AND BUNGAY, SUFFOLK.

CONTENTS

PRINCIPAL AUTHORITIES REFERRED TO

A. T.C.D. MS. F. 4, 6, containing the *Vita S. Malachiae* and a portion of *Sermo* ii. imbedded therein. Cent. xiii.; copied from a much earlier exemplar.

AA.SS. *Acta Sanctorum.*

A.F.M. *Annals of the Kingdom of Ireland by the Four Masters*, ed. J. O'Donovan, 1851.

A.I. Annals of Inisfallen, in O'Conor, *Rerum Hibernicarum Scriptores*, 1814-1826, vol. ii.

A.L.C. *Annals of Loch Cé*, ed. W. M. Hennessy (R.S.), 1871.

A.T. *Annals of Tigernach* (so called: see J. MacNeill in *Eriu*, vii. 30), ed. W. Stokes, in *Revue Celtique*, xvi.-xviii.

A.U. *Annals of Ulster, otherwise Annals of Senat*, ed. W. M. Hennessy and B. MacCarthy, 1887-1901.

Adamnan. The Life of St. Columba, written by Adamnan, ed. W. Reeves (Irish Archæological and Celtic Society), 1857.

Archdall. M. Archdall, *Monasticon Hibernicum*, 1786: the earlier part ed. by P. F. Moran, 1873.

C.M.A. *Chartularies of St. Mary's Abbey, Dublin*, ed. J. T. Gilbert (R.S.), 1884.

Cant. S. Bernardi Sermones in Cantica, in *P.L.* clxxxiii. 779 ff. (1879): English Translation by S. J. Eales, *The Life and Works of St. Bernard*, vol. iv., 1896.

Colgan, *A.S.H.* J. Colgan, *Acta Sanctorum Hiberniae*, Lovanii, 1645, tom. i.

D.A.I. The Dublin Annals of Inisfallen, Royal Irish Academy MS. 23, F. 9.

De Cons. S. Bernardi *De Consideratione Libri V.*, in *P.L.* clxxxii. 727 ff. (1879): English Translation by G. Lewis, 1908.

De Dil. S. Bernardi *De Diligendo Deo* in *P.L.* clxxxii. 973 ff. (1879). English Translations by M. C. and C. Patmore, second ed., 1884, and E. G. Gardner, 1916.

Dugdale. W. Dugdale, *Monasticon Anglicanum*, ed. J. Caley, H. Ellis and B. Bandinel, 1817-30.

Eadmer. Eadmeri *Historia Novorum in Anglia*, ed. M. Rule (R.S.), 1884.

Ep. S. Bernardi Epistolæ in *P.L.* clxxxii. 67 ff. (1879): English Translation in S. J. Eales, *The Life and Works of St. Bernard*, vols. i.-iii. (1889-1896).

Giraldus, *Expug.*; *Gest.*; *Top.* Giraldi Cambrensis Opera, ed. J. S. Brewer, J. F. Dimock and G. F. Warner (R.S.), 1861-1901. *Expugnatio Hibernica*, vol. v. p. 207 ff.; *De Rebus a se Gestis*, vol. i. p. 1 ff.; *Topographia Hibernica*, vol. v. p. 1 ff.

Gorman. *The Martyrology of Gorman*, ed. W. Stokes (Henry Bradshaw Society), 1895.

Gougaud. L. Gougaud, *Les Chrétientés Celtiques*, 1911.

Gwynn. The Book of Armagh, ed. J. Gwynn, 1913.

J.R.S.A.I. *Journal of the Royal Society of Antiquaries of Ireland*: references to volumes according to the consecutive numbering.

Jaffé. *Regesta Pontificum Romanorum*, ed. P. Jaffé, 1851.

John of Hexham. *Historia Johannis Prioris Hagustaldensis Ecclesiae*, in *Symeonis Monachi Dunelmensis Opera Omnia*, ed. T. Arnold (R.S.), ii. (1885), 284 ff.

K. Codex Kilkenniensis; Marsh's Library, Dublin, MS. Z. 1.5, containing the *Vita S. Malachiae*. Cent. xv.

Keating. G. Keating, *History of Ireland*, ed. D. Comyn and P. S. Dinneen (Irish Texts Society), 1902-1914.

L.A.J. *County Louth Archæological Journal.*

L.B. Leabhar Breac, Royal Irish Academy MS. (Facsimile ed. 1876.)

Lanigan. J. Lanigan, *An Ecclesiastical History of Ireland ... to the Beginning of the Thirteenth Century*, 1829.

M.G.H. *Monumenta Germaniae Historica.*

Mansi. *Sacrorum Conciliorum nova et amplissima Collectio*, ed. J. D. Mansi, 1759-1798.

O.C.C. *The Book of Obits and Martyrology of the Cathedral Church of the Holy Trinity, commonly called Christ Church, Dublin*, ed. J. C. Crosthwaite and J. H. Todd (Irish Archæological Society), 1844.

Oengus. *The Martyrology of Oengus the Culdee*, ed. W. Stokes (Henry Bradshaw Society), 1905.

O'Hanlon. J. O'Hanlon, *The Life of Saint Malachy O'Morgair*, 1859.

O'Hanlon, *Saints*. J. O'Hanlon, *Lives of the Irish Saints*, vols. i.-ix., 1875-1901.

P.L. *Patrologiæ Cursus Completus, Series Latina*, ed. J. P. Migne.

Petrie. G. Petrie, *The Ecclesiastical Architecture of Ireland ... comprising an Essay on the Origin and Uses of the Round Towers of Ireland*, 1845.

Plummer. *Vitae Sanctorum Hiberniae*, ed. C. Plummer, 1910.

Plummer, *Bede. Venerabilis Baedae Opera Historica*, ed. C. Plummer, 1896.

R.I.A. *Proceedings of the Royal Irish Academy*, Archæology, Linguistic and Literature. References to volumes according to the consecutive numbering.

R.I.A. *Trans. Transactions of the Royal Irish Academy.*

R.Q.H. *Revue des Questions Historiques.*

R.T.A. *Register of the Abbey of St. Thomas, Dublin*, ed. J. T. Gilbert (R.S.), 1889.

Reeves. W. Reeves, *Ecclesiastical Antiquities of Down, Connor and Dromore*, 1847.

Reeves, *Churches*. W. Reeves, *Ancient Churches of Armagh*, 1860.

Richard of Hexham. *Historia Ricardi prioris Haugustaldensis*, in *Chronicles of Stephen*, etc., ed. Howlett (R.S.), iii. (1886), 137 ff.

Theiner. A. Theiner, *Vetera Monumenta Hibernorum et Scotorum, 1216-1547*, Romae, 1864.

Todd. J. H. Todd, *St. Patrick Apostle of Ireland*, 1864.

Trias. J. Colgan, *Triadis Thaumaturgae seu divorum Patricii, Columbae et Brigidae Acta*, Lovanii, 1647 (vol. ii. of his *Acta Sanctorum Hiberniae*).

Trip. W. Stokes, *The Tripartite Life of Patrick with other Documents relating to that Saint*, ed. W. Stokes (R.S.), 1887.

Tundale. *Visio Tnugdali lateinisch und altdeutsch*, ed. A. Wagner, 1882.

Ussher. J. Ussher, *Veterum Epistolarum Hibernicarum Sylloge*, in Works, ed. C. R. Elrington, 1847-1864, vol. iv., pp. 383 ff.

V.P. *S. Bernardi Vita Prima*, in *P.L.* clxxxv., 225 ff.

Vacandard. *Vie de Saint Bernard Abbé de Clairvaux* par l'Abbé E. Vacandard, 4e édition, 1910.

NAMES OF IRISH PERSONS AND PLACES

Form used
in this volume. Form used
by St. Bernard. Irish Form. Antrim Oenthreb Oentreb Armagh Ardmacha Ard Macha

Bangor Benchor Benchor Cashel Caselensis Caisel Catholicus Catholicus Catlac
Cellach Celsus Cellach Christian Christianus Gilla Crist Coleraine Culratim Cúl Rathin
Columbanus Columbanus Columbán Comgall Congellus Comgall Connor Connereth
Coindire Conor Conchobar Cork Corcagia Corcach Dermot Diarmicius Diarmait Derry
Daire Desmond Mumonia australis Desmuma Donnell Domnall Donough \'7bDonnchad
\'7bDonngus Down Dunum Dún dá Lethglas Edan Edanus Aedh Faughart Fochart
Fochart Gelasius Gelasius Gilla meic Liag Gilbert Gillebertus Gilla espuig Imar Imaru
Imar Inispatrick Inis Pátraic Iveragh Ibracensis Ui Ráthach
 Leinster Laginia Laigin Limerick Luimneach Lismore Lesmore Lis Mór Lugadh
Luanus \'7bLugaid
 \'7bMolua MacCarthy Mac (meic) Carthaig Maelisa \'7d
 Malchus \'7d Malchus Mael Ísa Malachy Malachias Máel Máedóc Moriarty Ua
Muirchertaig Munster Mumonia Muma Murrough Murchadh Murtough Mauricius
Muirchertach Nehemiah Nehemias Gilla na Naem Niall Nigellus Niall O'Boyle Ua
Baigill O'Brien Ua Briain O'Carroll Ua Cerbaill O'Conor Ua Conchobair O'Hagan Ua
hAedacain O'Hanratty Ua hIndrechtaig O'Hanley Ua hAingli O'Kelly Ua Cellaig
O'Loughlin Ua Lochlainn Oriel Oirgialla O'Rorke Ua Ruarc Patrick Patricius Pátraic
Rory Ruaidhri Saul \'7bSaballum \'7d
 \'7bSaballinum\'7d Sabal Phátraic Shalvey Ua Selbaig Teague Tadhg Thomond
Tuathmuma Turlough Toirdelbach Ulaid Ulydia Ulaid Usnagh Uisnech Waterford Port
Láirge

INTRODUCTION

        The main purpose of this Introduction is to give an account of a movement which
changed the whole face of the Irish Church, and to the advancement of which St.
Malachy devoted his life. In default of a better word we may call the movement a
Reformation, though it might perhaps be more accurately described as an ecclesiastical
revolution. Without some knowledge of its aims and progress it is impossible to assign to
Malachy his true place in the history of his native country.
        That such a movement actually took place in the twelfth century is beyond doubt.
From about the year 1200 on it is certain that the organization of the Church of Ireland
was similar to that of the other Churches of western Christendom. The country was
divided into dioceses; and each diocese had a bishop as its ruler, and a Cathedral Church
in which the bishop's stool was placed. The Cathedral Church, moreover, had a chapter of
clergy, regular or secular, who performed important functions in the diocese. But up to
the end of the eleventh century all these things were unknown among the Irish. The
constitution of the Church was then of an entirely different type, one that had no exact
parallel elsewhere. The passage from the older to the newer organization must have taken
place in the twelfth century. During that century, therefore, there was a Reformation in
the Irish Church, however little we may know of its causes or its process. But this
Reformation was no mere re-modelling of the hierarchy. It can be shown that it imposed
on the members of the Church a new standard of sexual morality; if we believe
contemporary writers, it restored to their proper place such rites as Confession,
Confirmation and Matrimony; it substituted for the offices of divine service previously in
use those of the Roman Church; it introduced the custom of paying tithes; it established

in Ireland the monastic orders of Latin Christendom1; and it may have produced changes in other directions.2 But I propose to confine myself to the change in the constitution of the Church, which was its most striking feature. The subject, even thus narrowed, will give us more than can be satisfactorily treated in a few pages.

First, I must emphasize the assertion made a moment ago that the constitution of the Irish Church in the eleventh century was *sui generis*. Let us begin by reminding ourselves what it was from the sixth to the eighth century. It was then essentially monastic in character. The rulers of the Church were the abbots of the monasteries, commonly known as the coarbs or successors of their founders. These abbots were sometimes bishops; but whether they were bishops or of lower rank in the ministry, their authority was inherent in their office of coarb. At this period bishops were numerous— more numerous than in later medieval or modern times; and certain functions were reserved for bishops, for example, ordination. No ecclesiastic, of whatever status, could perform such functions, unless he was of the episcopal order. But no bishop, as such, had jurisdiction. The bishops were often subordinate officers in monasteries, reverenced because of their office, but executing their special functions at the command of the abbots. Sometimes a bishop was attached to a single tribe. Sometimes a group of bishops —often seven in number—dwelt together in one place. But in no case, I repeat, had they jurisdiction. Thus ecclesiastical authority was vested in the abbots. The episcopate was bestowed on certain individuals as a personal distinction. Thus the bishops, if they were not also abbots, had only such influence on the affairs of the Church as their sanctity, or their learning, might give them.

It may surprise some that so anomalous a system of government should have persisted as late as the eleventh century, in other words for a period of over 500 years. But we must take account of the Danish—or as we should rather call it, the Norse— invasion of Ireland. Danish ships first appeared off the Irish coasts about the year 800. From that time for two centuries Ireland was to a large extent cut off from intercourse with the rest of Europe. The aim of the northern hordes, as it seems, was not mere pillage, but the extinction of Christianity. Ecclesiastical institutions were everywhere attacked, and often destroyed. And these institutions were centres of scholarship. Heretofore Ireland had been the special home of learning, and had attracted to itself large numbers of foreign students. But in those disastrous centuries its culture was reduced to the lowest point. In such circumstances it was not possible that the organization of the Church should be developed or strengthened. The Danish domination of the country must have tended to stereotype the old hierarchical system. It might, indeed, suffer from deterioration: it probably did. But it could not be assimilated to the system which then prevailed on the Continent. We should expect that the constitution of the Church in the eleventh century, whatever abuses may have crept into its administration, would in principle be identical with that of the pre-Danish period.

There can in fact be no doubt that it was. We have in our hands writings of Lanfranc, Anselm, St. Bernard and Giraldus Cambrensis which picture the state of the Irish Church at that time. They speak of it in terms which are by no means complimentary. But when they come to details we discover that the irregularities in its hierarchical arrangement which shocked them most went back to the days of St. Columba. Quotations cannot be given here. But the reader will probably find in the Life printed below, and the authorities referred to in the notes, sufficient proof that the constitution of the Irish Church in 1100 was in the main a following, though perhaps a corrupt following, of that of the sixth century.3

There was indeed one abuse in the Irish Church of the tenth and eleventh centuries of which few traces are found before the Danish invasion. We learn from St. Bernard that the abbots of Armagh were the representatives of a single family, and held office, as of right, by hereditary succession.4 There is reason to believe that this evil custom was not peculiar to Armagh.5 According to St. Bernard, it was the gravest departure from Catholic tradition of which the Irish Church was guilty, and the parent of many evils. We shall hear more of it in the sequel. For the moment it is sufficient to note that it existed.

I.—The Beginnings of the Movement

But before the eleventh century ended forces were at work in Ireland which prepared the way for the introduction of a new order. They were set free by the conversion of the Norsemen to Christianity, and by their final defeat at the battle of Clontarf. The date of the conversion cannot be fixed: it was probably a gradual process. And we do not know from what source the Danes derived their Christianity. The victory of Clontarf was won on Good Friday, 1014.

Now a study of the Annals reveals the fact that in the seventh and eighth centuries there was a goodly, and on the whole an increasing, body of scholars in Ireland. Under the Norse domination, as we might expect, the number was greatly diminished. But already in the tenth century there was a notable increase: in the eleventh century the number was doubled. In the tenth century, moreover, and still more in the eleventh, scholars began to congregate at special centres, which became permanent homes of learning, the most prominent of these schools being at Armagh and Clonmacnoise. And during the same period we find frequent mention of an official, unknown before the arrival of the Norsemen, who is styled *fer légind* or professor. Between 925 and 1000 the obits of twenty-three professors are recorded; in the eleventh century of more than fifty. In the greater number of cases the *fer légind* is associated with one of those seats of learning which is known to have been most prolific of scholars.

Thus it appears that gradually, as the onslaughts of the Danes became less frequent, Irish men of learning tended more and more to become teachers rather than mere students, and to gravitate towards a few great centres of study. The climax of this movement towards organization and the eminence of special places was reached about the middle of the eleventh century (1030-1063), when mention is made of thirty-three persons who held the office of *fer légind*, and when the principal schools seem to have been those of Clonmacnoise, Armagh, Kildare and Kells.6

The Reformation of the twelfth century, like that of the sixteenth, was prepared for by a revival of learning.

But further, the defeat of the Danes removed the barrier which had hindered communication between Ireland and the rest of Europe. Students once more came to Ireland from other lands to pursue their studies. The most remarkable of these was perhaps Sulien, the future bishop of St. David's. Sulien the Wise was born shortly before the date of the battle of Clontarf in the district of Cardigan. In early youth he displayed much aptitude for learning, and in middle life, about 1058, "stirred by the example of the fathers," he paid a visit to the Irish schools in order to perfect his studies. He spent thirteen years in that country, and then established a famous school at Llanbadarn Fawr in Wales. In the library of Trinity College, Dublin, there is a precious relic of the work of this school. It is a beautiful manuscript of St. Jerome's Latin version of the Psalter according to the Hebrew, once the property of Bishop Bedell.7 The manuscript was written by a member of the school, a Welshman named Ithael. It is adorned with excellent illuminations by John, one of Sulien's sons, and was presented to Ricemarch, another son of Sulien. A valuable copy of the Hieronymian Martyrology prefixed to it gives sundry indications that it was transcribed from an Irish exemplar. At the end of the volume are some verses composed by Ricemarch, and perhaps written there by his own hand. They display considerable Biblical and patristic learning. Another relic of the school is a copy of St. Augustine's *De Trinitate* in Corpus Christi College, Cambridge.8 It was written and illuminated by John, and contains excellent Latin verses from his pen. In the British Museum there is also a poem of Ricemarch describing the horrors of the Norman invasion of Wales.9 And finally we have a *Life of St. David*, by the same author. It relates many incidents culled from the lives of Irish saints who had in one way or another been brought into contact with David; all of them reminiscent of Sulien's studies in the Irish Schools.10

I have dwelt on these things because they illustrate in a striking way the revival of Irish learning in the eleventh century. But just at the time when Sulien, and doubtless many other foreigners, were coming to Ireland to study, Irish scholars were beginning to renew their ancient habit of travelling to other countries. By way of example I may mention two, both of whom were known by the same name, Marianus Scotus. One of these, a native of the north of Ireland, whose real name was Muiredach Mac Robartaich, founded the monastery of St. Peter at Ratisbon about 1070; and he was succeeded there by six abbots of north Irish birth. He wrote a commentary on the Pauline Epistles, which is still preserved in the Imperial Library at Vienna. The other, Mael Brigte by name, left Ireland in 1056, and after some wanderings established himself at Mainz in 1069. He compiled a chronicle, which is of considerable value.11 Hereafter I shall have to mention other Irish men of travel; and it will be seen that from some of them, who returned home, came the main impulse to the reform of the Irish Church.

The battle of Clontarf broke the power of the Danes in Ireland; but it did not secure their departure from the country. Those that remained were mainly settled in the four cities of Dublin, Wexford, Waterford and Limerick. In due time these four Danish colonies adopted the Christian Faith, and before long they became organized churches, each presided over by a bishop. In Dublin this took place a quarter of a century after the battle of Clontarf, the first bishop being Dunan, in whose episcopate the Danish king, Sitric, founded the Cathedral of the Holy Trinity about 1040. Of the early ecclesiastical history of Wexford practically nothing is known; but the first bishop of Waterford was consecrated in 1096,12 and the first bishop of Limerick eight or ten years later.13 These were the first churches in Ireland ruled by bishops who were not abbots; and it seems that each of the bishops had a defined diocese. The dioceses of Dublin, Waterford, and perhaps Wexford, were very small, extending only a little way, if at all, beyond the walls of the Cathedral city. The diocese of Limerick, on the other hand, was extensive; rather larger than the present diocese of the same name. But whether large or small each of these dioceses presented to the eyes of the Irish a model of Church government similar to that in vogue on the Continent, and utterly different from that to which they were accustomed.

This might prove a potent factor in the Reformation, once a tendency developed among the Irish to bring their ecclesiastical machinery into conformity with that of the rest of the world. But it is manifest that by itself it would not induce them to re-model their hierarchy. It was not to be expected that they would cast aside the tradition of centuries, moved merely by a desire to imitate their late enemies. If, as is commonly held, the Danish dioceses, without exception, held themselves aloof from, or were hostile to, Irish Christianity, such a result could hardly have been attained, at any rate until the coming of the Anglo-Normans. These later invaders would doubtless have forced diocesan episcopacy on the Irish Church. But that it was established in Ireland before the country came, even in part, under English rule, is certain. So we must ask the question: What was the connecting link which bound the Church of the Danish colonists to that of Celtic Ireland? By way of answer I point to the remarkable fact, often overlooked, that all the earliest bishops of the Danish dioceses were of Irish birth. Why Danish Christians should have elected Irishmen as their bishops I do not attempt to explain. But the evidence for the fact is clear.

The first two bishops of Dublin, Dunan and Patrick (Gilla Pátraic), had unmistakably Irish names. So too had their immediate successors Donough O'Hanley and his nephew Samuel O'Hanley; and of these two the latter is stated by the English chronicler Eadmer[14] to have been "natione Hibernensis." The next bishop, Gregory—the first archbishop of Dublin—was likewise "natione Hibernensis" according to the continuator of Florence of Worcester.[15] He was followed by St. Laurence O'Toole, of whose nationality it is unnecessary to give proof.

Malchus, the earliest bishop of Waterford, was an Irishman;[16] so also was Gilbert, the first bishop of Limerick. And when Gilbert resigned his see, after an episcopate of thirty-five years, he was succeeded by Patrick, whose name tells its own tale.[17]

Most of the Irish rulers of Danish dioceses whom I have mentioned were men of travel. Patrick of Dublin, to whose learning Lanfranc bears testimony, "was nourished in monastic institutions from his boyhood,"[18] and certainly not, in an Irish religious house. Donough O'Hanley, before his consecration, was a monk of Canterbury; Samuel O'Hanley was a monk of St. Albans;[19] Malchus was called to Waterford from Walkelin's monastery at Winchester;[20] Gilbert of Limerick had visited Normandy,[21] and at a later date we find him assisting at the consecration of a bishop in Westminster Abbey.[22] Such men had had training which familiarized them with Roman methods of Church Government. They were well fitted to organize and rule their dioceses. And if they desired to imbue the Celtic Church with the principles which they had learnt, and on which they acted, their nationality gave them a ground of appeal which no Dane could have had. It is of course not to be assumed that all of them were so disposed. The Danish Christians of Dublin not only stood aside from the Celtic Church; for reasons which will appear later they were inimical to it, and it to them. Their bishops, with the possible exception of the first, made profession of canonical obedience to the English Primates. Not only so: they gloried in their subjection to Canterbury. "We have always been willing subjects of your predecessors," wrote the burgesses and clergy of Dublin to Ralph, archbishop of Canterbury, when the see was vacant in 1121. And then, after a reference to the great jealousy of Cellach of Armagh against them, they proceed to declare, "We will not obey his command, but desire to be always under your rule. Therefore we beseech you to promote Gregory to the episcopate if you wish to retain any longer the parish which we have kept for you so long."23 It was clearly impossible that this diocese could directly influence the Irish in the direction of reform. But no such obstacle barred the path of the first bishops of Limerick and Waterford. Gilbert owed no allegiance to Canterbury; Malchus was consecrated at Canterbury, but he soon escaped his profession of obedience to Anselm.24 Both became leaders of the romanizing movement in Ireland.

But the influence of the Danish dioceses on the Irish Church was not limited to the personal action of their bishops. Indirectly all of them, including Dublin, had a share in promoting the Reformation. Archbishop Lanfranc, as early as 1072, claimed that his primacy included Ireland as well as England.25 The claim, curiously enough, was based on Bede's *History*, in which there is not a single word which supports it. But the arrival two years later of Patrick, elect of Dublin, seeking consecration at his hands, gave him his opportunity to enforce it. When Patrick returned to take possession of his see he carried with him two letters from Lanfranc. One was addressed to Gothric, the Manx prince who for the moment was king of Dublin. Lanfranc, with tactful exaggeration, dubs him "glorious king of Ireland," and tells him that in consecrating Patrick he had followed the custom of his predecessors in the chair of St. Augustine. The other letter was more important. It was directed to Turlough O'Brien, grandson of Brian Boroimhe, who is also styled, inconsistently, and not altogether truly, "magnificent king of Ireland": he was doubtless king of Ireland in hope, but in fact he never extended his sway beyond the southern half of the island. Turlough's attention is called to the irregularities of the Irish Church. He is urged to call a council of bishops and religious men for the extirpation of those evil customs, and to be present at it in person. This letter evidently produced an impression, and not only on Turlough O'Brien. For a few years later Lanfranc wrote another letter, this time to a bishop named Donnell and others, who had sought his advice on a difficult question concerning the sacrament of baptism.26

Anselm followed in the footsteps of Lanfranc. Not long after his consecration (1093) he wrote to Donnell, Donough O'Hanley and the rest of the bishops of Ireland, begging the aid of their prayers, and urging them to consult him in all cases of difficulty. Almost immediately afterwards came the election of Malchus, bishop of Waterford, in 1096. Among those who signed the petition for his consecration were Bishop Donnell, Samuel O'Hanley, whom Anselm had consecrated for Dublin earlier in the same year, and O'Dunan, bishop of Meath (*Idunan episcopus Midiae*), whose name we shall do well to remember. But most notable of all were Murtough O'Brien, son of Turlough, then the strongest of Irish kings, soon to be *ardrí*, and his brother Dermot O'Brien.27 It is clear that Lanfranc had won the O'Briens to the Romanizing side; and Anselm was determined to hold them fast. Within the next few years there was a fairly regular correspondence between him and Murtough, of which some letters have been preserved.28 The relation between the two men was evidently most friendly. And the archbishop fully exploited his opportunity. Again and again he reminded the king of his duty to repress abuses, the most important of which in his eyes were lax sexual morality, and the consecration of bishops by single bishops, without fixed sees or defined dioceses.

So Lanfranc and Anselm schooled the O'Briens in the principles of Rome. And from one point of view their efforts were completely successful. The O'Briens became staunch friends of the Reform movement in Ireland. But from another point of view they failed. We must remember that their aim was not only to purify the Irish Church, but to bring it into subjection to Canterbury. That they did not succeed in doing. The Reformation, which they taught the O'Briens to support, meant, in the end, a repudiation of the pretensions of the English primates.

I have mentioned among those who were concerned in the election of Malchus of Waterford, O'Dunan, bishop of Meath. He is unquestionably Máel Muire Ua Dunáin, whom the annalists describe as "learned bishop of the Goidhil, and head of the clergy of Ireland, and steward of the almsdeeds of the world," and who died on Christmas Eve, 1117, at the age of seventy-six. He is mentioned in a charter in the Book of Kells, the date of which is apparently about 1100, as Senior of Leath Chuinn (*i.e.* the north of Ireland).29 He was fifty-five when Malchus was elected, and had probably already attained the eminence throughout Ireland which is attested by the high-flown phrases of the Annals. That he was then bishop of Meath in the modern sense is impossible; the title at that period would mean no more than that he was a bishop who lived within the borders of the Kingdom of Meath. But the *Annals of Tigernach* tell us that he died at Clonard, from which it may perhaps be inferred that his see was at that place. His importance for us just now is that he is the only adherent of the Reform movement whom we have yet discovered in the north of Ireland.

II.—The First Stage

Before proceeding further in our investigation of the origin and course of the Reformation, it may be well to recall how far we have already advanced. We started from the fact that a Reformation of the Irish Church was actually accomplished in the twelfth century, and we proceeded to look for the causes which may have brought it about. We have found that the first of these was the revival of learning consequent on the cessation of the ravages of the Norsemen. We have noted also the restoration at the same period of communication between Ireland and the rest of Europe—the coming of students to the Irish schools, and the wanderings of Irish scholars in other lands. We have seen that the establishment of the Danish dioceses gave to the Irish a model of diocesan episcopacy, and that among the Irish-born bishops of those dioceses there were men capable of leading a Reform movement. And we have learned that Lanfranc and Anselm, through their relation with the Danish dioceses, found means to induce the more conspicuous civil and religious leaders of the Celtic population to undertake the work of reconstituting the Church. Finally, we have been able to name some persons who might be expected to take a prominent place in the early stages of the Reformation. They are Gilbert of Limerick, Malchus of Waterford, O'Dunan of Meath, and the princes of the O'Brien family. The best proof that we have rightly conceived the origin of the movement will come before us when we study the share which these persons severally had in promoting it.

We must now trace, as far as it can be done, the first steps in the process by which, under the influences which I have indicated, the Church of Ireland passed from its older to its later hierarchical system.

The earliest attempt to give concrete form to the principles of the Reformers seems to have been made in the Kingdom of Meath, about the year 1100. But the primary evidence for the fact is of much later date. There are extant some constitutions of Simon Rochfort, bishop of Meath, put forth at a synod of his diocese held at the monastery of SS. Peter and Paul at Newtown, near Trim, in 1216. The first of them recites an ordinance of the papal legate, Cardinal John Paparo, at the Council of Kells in 1152, which is of great importance.

Paparo ordered that as the bishops of the weaker sees died off, arch-priests, or, as we call them, rural deans, should succeed to their place, and take charge of the clergy and people within their borders.[30]

The inference which this enactment suggests is that the weaker sees to which it refers were the centres of small dioceses, which Paparo desired to be converted into rural deaneries. In accordance with the ordinance of Paparo, Rochfort's synod enjoined that rural deans should be placed in the five sees of Trim, Kells, Slane, Skreen and Dunshaughlin, each of whom should supervise the churches in his own deanery. These, with Clonard, which had long been the see of Rochfort's diocese, are six of the twelve rural deaneries into which the present diocese of Meath is divided.[31] I conclude that they, and probably the remaining six, coincided [Pg xxviii]more or less closely with dioceses ruled by bishops in the first half of the twelfth century.[32]

Let us now call to our aid a much earlier witness. The annalists inform us that in the year 1111 there was an assembly at Usnagh in Meath. It decreed that "the parishes[33] of Meath" should be equally divided between the bishops of Clonmacnoise and Clonard. We may infer that Clonmacnoise and Clonard, two of the present rural deaneries, were then dioceses. It is not likely that the dioceses of Meath would have been formed into two groups, each to constitute the diocese of a bishop who had already no diocese of his own. But however that may be, we have here proof that before 1111 Meath had been parted into a number of small dioceses ruled by bishops.

If the question be asked, By whose authority or influence this division of Meath into dioceses was made? I can suggest no one more likely than Máel Muire Ua Dunáin, the "bishop of Meath" to whom reference has already been made.[34] He was a Meath man, and probably bishop of Clonard: he was an ecclesiastic of great repute, especially in the north; and he was a devoted adherent of the Reform movement. His action, if indeed it was his, was premature and ill-advised. As we shall see, his work had to be slowly undone. But it is remarkable, as the first attempt known to us to establish diocesan episcopacy among the Irish. I shall have more to say about it hereafter; but now I must follow the main stream of events.

Gilbert,[35] the first bishop of Limerick, as has already been noted, was an Irishman. Indeed, we may venture to describe him as one of the most remarkable Irishmen of his time, in spite of the fact that the Annals pass him by in almost complete silence. He was at any rate a staunch supporter, or, as we should rather say, the leader of the Reformation movement in its earliest course. In a letter written in 1107 Anselm exhorted him, in virtue of their mutual friendship, to make good use of his episcopal office by correcting that which was amiss, and planting and sowing good customs, calling to aid him in the work his king (Murtough O'Brien), the other Irish bishops, and all whom he could persuade.[36] That, assuredly, Gilbert was forward to do.

No sooner had he taken possession of his see than he began to organize a diocese. Its boundaries seem to have been fixed with care. It was exactly co-extensive with the modern diocese of Limerick, except on the north, where it stretched across the Shannon and included part of the present diocese of Killaloe.37 Moreover he made the Church of St. Mary his Cathedral Church; indeed it is not unlikely that he built it to serve that purpose.

A few years later he was appointed Legate of the Holy See. It is manifest that his new office gave him a unique opportunity of moulding the fortunes of the Irish Church. In Ireland Gilbert was now virtually the chief prelate and head of the Church. He was the representative and embodiment of the authority of the Holy See. The whole Romanizing party would naturally circle round him as their leader, and many waverers would be attracted to the new movement in the Irish Church, by the claim which he could make to speak in the name of the head of the Church Catholic.

It was after he became legate, and no doubt in virtue of his legatine commission, that he issued a treatise which may be regarded as the programme of the Reformation. It is entitled *De Statu Ecclesiae*. Of this a fragment, including its earlier chapters, is still in our hands.38

Before giving a slight summary of its contents I must mention that it is addressed "to the bishops and presbyters of the whole of Ireland," and that Gilbert declares that he wrote it at the urgent request of many of them. In this statement there may lurk an element of exaggeration. But behind it there lies at least so much truth as this. A considerable body of the clergy had approached the newly made legate, and requested his instruction regarding the proper constitution of the Church—for such is the subject of his tract; and that implies that the Romanizing movement was no longer in its infancy. There were many bishops and presbyters who had become dissatisfied with the old Irish method of Church government. They desired to bring it into conformity with that of the Roman Church. But they were in some uncertainty as to the nature of the changes that should be made, and so they asked Gilbert to give them authoritative counsel.

In reply to their petition, with the aid of an elaborate diagram, he sketched as follows the organization of a properly ordered Church.

The bishops, he tells us, and others of higher rank in the ministry belong to the general Church, as distinct from particular churches. The priest is the highest officer in a particular church. It is the primary duty of every priest to serve and obey his bishop with all humility. For by the bishops particular churches are ruled. To each bishop are subject all the churches within his jurisdiction. And this applies as well to monastic establishments as to parishes. The head of each parish is a priest, the head of each monastery is an abbot, who is himself a priest. The bishop has a pontifical church, in which is his see (*sedes*), and of which he is the head. From it he governs the inferior churches. A bishop can perform all the offices of a priest, but he has seven functions peculiar to himself: to confirm, to bless, to absolve, to hold synods, to dedicate churches and altars, to consecrate the ornaments of churches, to ordain abbots and abbesses and the secular clergy. Gilbert's diagram represented the bishop as ruling two churches; but he explains that this is to be interpreted figuratively. A bishop may have as many as a thousand churches within his jurisdiction: he must have at least ten.

A bishop is himself subject to authority. His immediate superior is the archbishop. An archbishop has a sphere of immediate jurisdiction, like any other bishop, but he also rules a number of subject bishops. Of these there must be at least three; but an archbishop is not permitted to have more than twenty subject bishops—an important point, as we shall see. Above the archbishop is the primate. It is the special privilege of the primate to ordain and crown the king. He too has his sphere of immediate jurisdiction, and he must have at least one subject archbishop, but not more than six.

Primates and archbishops must be consecrated at Rome by the Pope, or at least must receive the pall39 from him. Without the pall they are not raised above their fellow-bishops.

Finally, the primates are subject to the Pope, and the Pope to Christ.

The higher members of the hierarchy have their analogues in the civil order. The Pope corresponds to the emperor, the primate to the king, an archbishop to a duke, a bishop to an earl, a priest to a knight. But all these are merely grades of the order of priests. There are but seven orders of the ministry—priests, deacons, sub-deacons, acolytes, exorcists, readers and door-keepers. [Pg xxxiii]Of the laity Gilbert says little. They are of two classes; husbandmen and soldiers. Their duties are to attend church, to pay first-fruits, tithes and oblations, to avoid evil and do good, and to obey their pastors.

There is nothing original in all this; and some parts of it must have been very puzzling to stay-at-home Irishmen. For example, what were they to make of Gilbert's comparison of primates, archbishops, bishops and priests to kings, dukes, earls and knights? They knew as little of dukes and earls in the civil order as they did of primates and archbishops in the ecclesiastical; and they had far more kings than suited Gilbert's scheme. But the tract is important, both as a summary of the teaching which Gilbert had no doubt been inculcating far and wide for years, and as a permanent record, for future use, of the aims of the Reformers.

However unintelligible the treatise may have been in parts, it brought out with startling clearness one or two essential points. First the Church must be ruled by bishops. Even the monasteries are subject to them. How amazing such a statement must have sounded to men who had inherited the tradition, many centuries old, that the abbots of monasteries were the true ecclesiastical rulers, bishops their subordinate officials.

Moreover, bishoprics and dioceses could not be set up at random. The number of bishops and by consequence the size of dioceses must be carefully considered. The puny bishoprics of Meath, for example, could form no part of a scheme such as Gilbert adumbrated.

It was manifest that if his guidance were to be followed, no mere modification of existing arrangements would suffice. The old hierarchy must be torn up by the roots, and a new hierarchy planted in its place.

We shall meet Gilbert again in the course of our story. But we may now turn aside from him to make the acquaintance of a new actor in the drama of the Reformation. Like O'Dunan he was a Northern.

Cellach was born in 1080. He was an Armagh man, sprung from the family which for centuries past had provided abbots for the monastery of that city, the grandson of a former abbot. He first appears on the scene in 1105, when on the death of Abbot Donnell he became coarb of Patrick and abbot of Armagh. He was elected, we may assume, in the customary way. He was then under twenty-six years of age, and was apparently still a layman. But his subsequent action shows that he was already a convinced disciple of the new movement. Doubtless he had fallen under the spell of Gilbert of Limerick. Six weeks after his election he abandoned the tradition of a century and a half, and received holy orders. But in other respects he trod in the footsteps of his predecessors. In the following year he went on a circuit of the Cenél Eoghain, and "took away his full demand: namely, a cow for every six, or an in-calf heifer for every three, or a half ounce of silver for every four, besides many donations also." Next he proceeded to Munster, with similar results. But his circuit of Munster is important for other reasons. There he had opportunities of intercourse with his Munster friends, Gilbert of Limerick and Malchus of Waterford. And with that circuit we may connect two incidents of the highest significance. In 1106, apparently in the latter part of the year, Caincomrac Ua Baigill, bishop of Armagh, died. The news of his death probably reached Cellach while he was in the south. Certainly in Munster Cellach was consecrated bishop. It is impossible not to connect the latter event with the former. He was consecrated to fill the vacancy created by the death of O'Boyle. Thus he was now bishop of Armagh as well as coarb of Patrick. In his own person he united the two lines of coarbial and episcopal succession, which had parted asunder in 957, when the first of a series of lay coarbs had been elected, and the first of the six contemporary bishops had been consecrated.40 This was a great gain for the Reformers. The old anomaly of a ruler of the Church who was not a bishop had, so far as Armagh was concerned, disappeared for the time. And Armagh was the principal ecclesiastical centre in Ireland. Cellach might now call himself archbishop of Armagh, though he had not fulfilled the condition laid down by Gilbert, that an archbishop must receive the pall at the hands of the Pope. The title was actually accorded to him by so rigid a papalist as St. Bernard.41

But there was more to come. In the year 1101 there had been held at Cashel a great assembly of the clergy and people of Ireland. Bishop O'Dunan, whom we already know, was at their head. To it came also Murtough O'Brien, who earlier in the year, after an expedition in force through Connaught and Ulster, had entered Tara as *ardrí* of Ireland.42 In the presence of the assembly he surrendered Cashel, the royal city of the kings of Munster, to the Church, as an offering to God and St. Patrick.43 When we consider the persons who were concerned in this transaction we find good ground for the suspicion that the gift was intended in some way to benefit the movement for reform. Now St. Bernard informs us that Cellach created a second archiepiscopal see in Ireland in subordination to Armagh.44 After his manner he does not tell us where it was situated. It is certain, however, that it was at Cashel, which was the seat of an archbishop in 1110.45 It was probably surrendered for this very purpose by O'Brien. And if it be asked when Cellach erected it into an archbishopric the answer is scarcely doubtful. Only once, so far as we know, did Cellach enter Munster before 1110. It was on the occasion of his circuit. In the year of the circuit, therefore, 1106, the archbishopric of Cashel was founded. In that same year, or shortly afterwards, Malchus of Waterford was translated to the new see, and became its first archbishop. There is no evidence that a new bishop was consecrated for Waterford in succession to Malchus: this indeed is unlikely. But it should be noted that by his acceptance of an archbishopric subject to Armagh, Malchus was released from the profession of obedience which he had made to Anselm ten years earlier. He was now a bishop of the Church of Ireland, with undivided allegiance.

The reason for the creation of a second archbishopric is not difficult to guess. By this time the plans of the Reformers must have been in some degree matured: before long, as we shall see, they were set forth in minute detail. Already Cellach was archbishop of Armagh. His suffragan sees, indeed, apart from those formed by O'Dunan, if their bishops acknowledged themselves as his suffragans, were *in nubibus*. But suffragan sees he must have, according to the theory of Gilbert, each with a diocese attached to it. They must be at least three in number, but *not more than twenty*. Now it was a foregone conclusion that if the Reformers had their way there would be more than twenty dioceses in Ireland. Hence, by Gilbert's rule, there must be a second archbishop. Moreover, by making the archbishopric of Cashel subject to Armagh, [Pg xxxvii]Cellach secured for himself and his successors a title yet more imposing than that of archbishop. He was now Primate of Ireland; for it sufficed, if Gilbert spoke truly, that a primate should have one subject archbishop. As coarb of Patrick Cellach's authority ranged over the whole country; as primate his sway would be no less extensive. He actually claimed the title, if not then, at least a few years later.46

We may now for a while leave Gilbert and Cellach and Malchus and O'Dunan. With Gilbert as legate, and Cellach and Malchus as archbishops; with dioceses already formed at Limerick and Waterford and in Meath, probably also at Armagh and Cashel and Wexford; with the great extension of the movement, and its spread from Munster to Meath and Ulster, all was ready for the meeting of the Synod whose ordinances should give definite shape to the policy to be pursued in the future.

III.—The Synod of Rathbreasail

Geoffrey Keating quotes from the lost *Annals of Clonenagh* an account of a national Synod or Council held at Rathbreasail in the year 1110.47 The existing Annals record that a national Council met at Fiadh meic Oengusa in 1111. With the exception of the *Annals of Inisfallen*, none of them mention Rathbreasail; but the Inisfallen annalist tells us that it is another name for Fiadh meic Oengusa.48 I shall assume therefore that there were not two national Synods in successive years, [Pg xxxviii]but one; and, following the *Annals of Clonenagh*, I shall call it the Synod of Rathbreasail, and date it in 1110.

The Synod of Rathbreasail marks the beginning of the second stage of the Reformation movement. It was convened by the papal legate; its purpose was the Romanizing of the Irish Church, and, in particular, the establishment in it of diocesan episcopacy. Fortunately Keating's excerpts from its Acts give us ample information concerning the canons which dealt with this matter.

The annalists, as I have said, describe the council as a national assembly. But we can hardly claim so much for it. It is much more probable that it was in reality a meeting of the Reforming party. The first signature appended to its canons was that of Gilbert, who presided as legate of the Holy See. He was followed by Cellach, "coarb of Patrick and Primate of Ireland," and Malchus, "archbishop of Cashel," whom we have known as bishop of Waterford. The signatures of many bishops followed, but they have not been preserved. We know, however, that Bishop O'Dunan was present, as was also Murtough O'Brien, king of Ireland. These were all leaders of the Reforming party; and it is evident that they guided the deliberations of the Council. Moreover there were no representatives of the provinces of Connaught and Leinster, in which as yet, it appears, the Reform movement had not established itself. That is made clear by notes appended to canons which specially concerned those provinces. One of them begins thus: "If the Connaught clergy agree to this ... we desire it, and if they do not"—in that case they may do as they please, with certain limitations. The clergy of Leinster are accorded a similar liberty. It is obvious that if among the members of the Council there had been men who could speak with authority for the provinces mentioned such notes need not, and therefore could not, have been written. The Council represented Munster, Ulster and Meath. It was national, not because it could speak for all Ireland, but because it made laws for all Ireland.

I must now give an account of those laws, so far as they relate to the organization of the Church. I follow the *Annals of Clonenagh*, as reported by Keating: but in two or three places I have been obliged to amend his text.49

The fathers began by appealing to English precedent. "Just as twelve bishops were fixed under Canterbury in the south of England, and twelve bishops in the north under the city of York," so it was ordained that there should be twelve bishops in the south of Ireland, and twelve in the north. The constitution of the Irish Church was henceforth, it would seem, to be a copy of that of the English Church. But, as it happens, neither in 1110 nor in any other year of its history, had the Church of England twelve sees under Canterbury and twelve under York. How then can we explain the statement of the Synod? The answer is simple. Bede50 preserves a letter of Pope Gregory the Great, written in 601, in which St. Augustine of Canterbury was directed to consecrate twelve bishops as his own suffragans. He was also ordered to consecrate a bishop for York, who, if his mission proved successful, was likewise to consecrate twelve suffragans, and to be promoted to the dignity of a metropolitan. It is clear that the Synod found its precedent in this letter, not observing that Pope Gregory's ordinance was never carried into effect. But they made another mistake. For Gregory intended that there should be twelve bishops in the north of England, and twelve in the south, exclusive of the archbishops, twenty-six in all; while it is evident that the Council of Rathbreasail intended that there should be twelve bishops in the north of Ireland, and twelve in the south, including the archbishops, twenty-four in all. Some one whose lead the Synod followed—probably the papal legate —had read his Bede with little care. But that is not surprising. Lanfranc had misread Bede, when on his authority he claimed to be Primate of Ireland; why should not Gilbert have gone astray in like fashion? The point to be noticed and emphasized is that the first act of the Synod was to fix the number of the Irish sees, on the curious principle that what the wisdom of Pope Gregory held to be good for England would suit Ireland also.

Apparently the next step in the procedure was to determine the distribution of the dioceses among the provinces, and to fix the see of each prospective diocese. Ireland was divided into two portions by a line running, approximately, from Dublin to Galway. The part to the north of that line was known as Leath Chuinn, the part to the south as Leath Mogha. In Leath Chuinn were the provinces of Ulster and Connaught and the kingdom of Meath; in Leath Mogha were the provinces of Munster and Leinster. The Synod decreed that there should be five sees in Ulster, five in Connaught, and two in Meath, making twelve bishoprics for Leath Chuinn; there were to be seven in Munster and five in Leinster—twelve bishoprics for Leath Mogha. The names of all these sees were given in the Acts of the Synod.

Finally the Synod defined the boundaries of the dioceses to which the sees severally belonged. It is not my purpose to give a minute description of these boundaries. That would involve an excursus on Irish topography, which would be, to say the least, out of place. It will suffice to indicate roughly those of the five dioceses of Ulster. To the west was what was called the "parish" (*fairche*)51 of Derry or Raphoe. It was nearly identical with our diocese of Raphoe. The only important difference is that it included

Inishowen, the district between Lough Swilly and Lough Foyle, which now belongs to the diocese of Derry. Next to the parish of Derry or Raphoe the Synod placed the parish of Ardstraw.52 Ardstraw never became the see, and the diocese was subsequently known as "of Derry." It extended eastward to the Carntougher Mountains, and coincides pretty closely with the present diocese. It subsequently gained Inishowen from its western neighbour, and the strip between the Carntougher Mountains and the Bann from its eastern neighbour. But otherwise it remains much as the Synod of Rathbreasail determined. Next to it was to be the parish of Connor or Down. When the portion of it to the west of the Bann was transferred to Derry, it coincided almost exactly with the modern Down, Connor and Dromore. On the other hand the parish of Armagh seems originally to have included the modern county of Monaghan: it has shrunk to little more than half its size. The parish of Clogher, at first very small, has extended east and west, and is three times as large as it was intended to be. On the whole the work of the Synod has stood well the test of many centuries of history.

It is indeed wonderful that it should have done so. For the method of the Synod—fixing the number of the dioceses before their boundaries were discussed—was unstatesmanlike. Always, and necessarily, ecclesiastical divisions have coincided with civil divisions. We may find the germ of the rule in the Acts of the Apostles.53 If this was inevitable in other lands it was even more inevitable in Ireland in pre-Norman days. The Irish people was a collection of clans, having, it is true, certain common institutions, but bound together by no sort of national constitution, and often at war with each other. If ecclesiastical divisions were to be permanent in Ireland, they must take account of the tribal divisions of the country. The primary ecclesiastical unit must be the territory of a tribe, just as it was the primary civil unit.54 But to base the limits of dioceses, consistently and in every case, on tribal boundaries was impossible when the number of dioceses was arbitrarily fixed beforehand. It could not be that exactly the same number of dioceses would suit Ulster as suited Leinster and Connaught. In one province the tribes would be more or less numerous, and more or less mutually antagonistic, than in another. By reason of its method, therefore, the Synod was doomed to fall short of complete success in its work.

We have instances in Ulster of the soundness of the principle that I have stated. Take the diocese of Raphoe. It was designed to include Inishowen. But from a tribal point of view Inishowen (Inis Eoghain) belonged to the next diocese, which included the tribeland of Tír Eoghain. Its inhabitants were of the same stock as the Cenél Eoghain, and were known as the Cenél Eoghain of the Island. So the natural result followed. Inishowen broke off from the diocese of Raphoe and became part of the diocese of Derry. When this happened the diocese of Raphoe was stabilized. It consisted of the land of a single tribe, the Cenél Conaill; and so henceforth its limits were never altered.

We can easily understand, therefore, that the disregard of tribal boundaries, forced on it in many cases by its method, was an element of weakness in the Rathbreasail scheme. And yet it was natural that special stress should be laid on the arbitrary limitation of sees which was its main cause. Ireland was overrun with bishops. It is said that over fifty of them attended the Synod of Rathbreasail; and they represented only part of the country. But Gilbert had laid down the rule that an archbishop could not have more than twenty suffragans. On this principle, if all the existing bishops had been provided with dioceses, or all the larger tribes had been given bishops, Ireland would have had not two, but six or seven archbishops: and this would have been a travesty of Catholic Church order, as it was then understood. It was essential that the number should be ruthlessly cut down.

But the legislators of Rathbreasail did not entirely ignore tribal boundaries. On the contrary, so far as the numerical basis of their scheme permitted, they took them into account. And here we find that the Synod was confronted with another difficulty. The territories of tribes were fluctuating quantities. Hence, even if a diocese was the district of a single tribe, with very definite boundaries, no one could be sure that in the course of years its limits would not change. Again I take an example from Ulster. The Synod selected the Carntougher Mountains as the boundary between the dioceses of Derry and Connor. And wisely. For between those mountains and the Bann there dwelt a sept—the Fir Li—whose affinities were altogether with the people to the east of the river. But only a few years after the Synod that territory was overrun by the O'Kanes of the Roe Valley, and the Fir Li retreated across the Bann, never to return. The result followed which might have been expected. Their territory was transferred from Connor to Derry, and the Bann to this day is the boundary of the two dioceses.55

It may be well, before I pass to another subject, to call attention to some special features of the Rathbreasail canons.

First, let us note the prominence which is given to Limerick, the diocese of Gilbert, the president of the Synod. Usually a diocese is somewhat vaguely defined by four places on its borders. But here no less than thirteen are named. So full are the indications that a fairly exact map of the diocese could be drawn. Further, in this diocese alone mention is made of a Cathedral Church: "The Church of Mary in Limerick is its principal church."56 Note the present tense: "The Church of Mary is"—not shall be—"its principal church." We remember that Gilbert insisted in the *De Statu Ecclesiae* that a diocese should have a "pontifical church." Again, the boundaries of this one diocese are protected by a clause which has no parallel elsewhere: "Whosoever shall go against these boundaries goes against the Lord, and against Peter the Apostle, and St. Patrick and his coarb and the Christian Church." Who but the legate of the Pope would have thus invoked St. Peter?

Surely this portion of the ordinances of the Synod must have been penned by Gilbert himself. And the whole passage—by the minuteness of its description of the diocese, by the strength of the terms in which it is expressed, by the reference to the Cathedral Church as already existing—suggests that the diocese was formed and organized before the Synod met, as I have already assumed. We may even suspect that an attempt had been made to invade it, which Gilbert stoutly resisted, relying on his legatine authority.

In the list of dioceses there is an omission which demands explanation. No mention whatever is made of Dublin, the oldest diocese in Ireland. Not only so; the northern limit of the diocese of Glendalough is marked by Lambay Island and Greenogue, which lies due west of it in the County Meath. Thus the diocese of Glendalough, as contemplated by the Synod—and, it may be added, as it was in fact forty years later57—included the whole of the actually existing diocese of Dublin. The Danish Christians of Dublin and their Irish bishop are treated as interlopers; they are absolutely ignored. It may be said that this was due to the mutual hostility which divided the diocese of Dublin from the native Church, and to the fact that the bishops of Dublin had always been subject to Canterbury. But it is not enough to say this; for the estrangement of Dublin from the Irish is the very thing that has to be accounted for.

It had its root in the growing prosperity of the Danish city. The Irish had no towns. Town life was introduced among them by the Norsemen. And of their towns Dublin was always the chief. By this time it had become so important that it had good right to be called the metropolis of the country. And its citizens were thoroughly aware of this. As early as 1074 the burgesses of Dublin and their bishop, Patrick, claimed for it that title.58 Now in all reason a metropolis should have a metropolitan as its bishop; and no doubt the bishops of Dublin thought themselves *de facto*, if not *de jure*, superior to the other bishops of Ireland. In fact we find one of them playing the archbishop. We have two interesting letters of Anselm, written apparently about 1100. One of them is addressed to Malchus, bishop of Waterford, directing him to rebuke Samuel O'Hanley, bishop of Dublin, for various irregularities, in particular for having his cross carried before him like an archbishop; the other is addressed to Samuel himself, and complains of the same actions.59 These proceedings are not likely to have been brought to an end by Anselm's letters; and we may assume that they were continued as long as Samuel held the see of Dublin. It was but natural that Cellach should strongly resent them, for they were disrespectful both to himself and to the archbishop of Cashel. We are not surprised, therefore, to find that on the death of Samuel in 1121, eleven years after Rathbreasail, Cellach tried to get possession of the Church of Dublin,60 most probably with the intention of bringing it under the jurisdiction of the bishop of Glendalough. Nor are we surprised that the men of Dublin at once replied by electing another bishop and bidding Ralph of Canterbury to consecrate him if he desired to retain the suffragan see which they had so long preserved for him.61 We shall see hereafter how the bishops of Dublin were at length induced to look with favour on the Irish Church. Meanwhile we learn that they were not very obedient suffragans of Canterbury; and we cease to wonder that they were ignored in the Rathbreasail decrees.

Another feature of the canons of the Synod is worth noting. In several instances the see of a diocese was not absolutely fixed. Two places were named, and it was apparently left to the bishop of the future to select that one of the two which he preferred to be his city. Thus we have a diocese of Derry or Raphoe, a diocese of Connor or Down, another of Wexford or Ferns, and so forth. The meaning of this is best seen by taking a single example. To one of the dioceses of Munster was assigned the area now occupied by the two dioceses of Waterford and Lismore. It consisted of the original Danish diocese of Waterford, together with a much more extensive non-Danish area. Alternative sees were named; it was described as the parish of Lismore or Waterford. Now Lismore was the most sacred spot in the enlarged diocese. It was the site of a monastery founded by St. Mochuta. It was an ideal place for a bishop's see. But it was doubtless ruled at the moment by an abbot, the coarb of Mochuta. Unless he was prevailed on to accept episcopal orders, or was deprived of his authority, a diocesan bishop could not be established there. On the other hand, Waterford had no sacred traditions; but it was already the see of a diocese. In default of Lismore it would be a convenient place for the see. Between Lismore and Waterford the circumstances of the future must decide. Ultimately, it appears, Malchus retired from the archbishopric of Cashel, and became bishop of his older diocese, now so much greater than it had been. He placed his stool, however, not at Waterford but at Lismore.62 A similar, [Pg xlviii]but not always identical course was followed in other such cases.

What the Synod of Rathbreasail actually accomplished was this. It gave to Ireland a paper constitution of the approved Roman and Catholic type. But by doing this it had not achieved the purpose of its existence. In the years that followed, its enactments had to be carried into effect. And here was the real crux. Before the Church came to be ruled by diocesan bishops, the existing rulers—the coarbs of church founders—must be dispossessed of their authority; the numerous bishops of the old Irish type must be got rid of; the jurisdiction of the new bishops must be fixed by common consent, or enforced without it; and revenues must be provided for them. A mere synodal decree could not accomplish all this. The diocesan system could become a fact throughout the whole Church, and the last vestiges of the ancient constitution be made to disappear, only after determined effort, and probably bitter contention. And when all was done it would certainly be found that the scheme of dioceses arranged at Rathbreasail had been largely departed from.

I can best illustrate the nature of the difficulties which had to be encountered, and the length of time which might be required to overcome them, by giving a short outline of the history of the forming of the dioceses of the kingdom of Meath.

In Meath, as we have seen, there were dioceses ruled by bishops before Rathbreasail. But these dioceses were of small size. It may be doubted whether most of them fulfilled the condition laid down by Gilbert, that a bishop should have not less than ten churches within his jurisdiction. They had therefore to be grouped under a smaller number of prelates. What had to be accomplished in this case was not so much the clipping of the wings of the abbots, as the extirpation of the more recently appointed diocesan bishops. The Synod determined that the kingdom should be divided into two dioceses, one in the west, the other in the east. The western see was to be at Clonard, at the moment, as it seems, the see of O'Dunan, and famed as the site of the great monastery of St. Finnian, founded in the sixth century; the eastern see was to be at Duleek, near Drogheda. Now a few months after the Synod of Rathbreasail there was held at Usnagh a local synod of the men of Meath, at which the king and many notable persons were present.63 This synod ordained that the parishes of Meath should be equally divided between the bishops of Clonmacnoise and Clonard. It will be observed that the principle of the Rathbreasail decree was accepted, that there should be two, and only two, dioceses in Meath. But the change made in the sees is significant. The Synod of Rathbreasail intended that Clonard should be the see of the western diocese, which would include Clonmacnoise. The Synod of Usnagh demanded that Clonmacnoise, founded by one of the most noted of Irish saints, St. Ciaran, should be one of the surviving sees, and that Clonard should be the see, not of the western, but of the eastern half of the kingdom. Thus the Synod of Rathbreasail was at once met with strenuous and, as it proved, successful opposition in Meath.

And here I may mention another fact. A few years after the Synod we have proof of the existence of a diocese in the north of the kingdom, which has not hitherto been mentioned, and which is not named in the Rathbreasail canons. We know it as the diocese of Kilmore.64 It may have been one of O'Dunan's dioceses, or it may have been founded later. One thing is certain. The diocese formed the territory of a strong tribe. Consequently it had in it the element of stability. It was never suppressed: it exists to this day. So far as it was concerned the canons of Rathbreasail were a dead letter from the beginning.

But let us return to Clonard. It was the business of its successive bishops, in accordance with the decrees of Usnagh, to annex the small neighbouring bishoprics of east Meath. They had considerable success. We possess a list of churches granted by Eugenius, the last Irish bishop of Clonard, to the monastery of St. Thomas the Martyr, Dublin.65 They are scattered over the three deaneries of Dunshaughlin, Skreen and Trim. Thus Eugenius had absorbed into his diocese the bishoprics of those three places. Another document tells us that this same Eugenius consecrated the church of Duleek;66 which implies that the diocese of Duleek was also suppressed. Thus by 1191, the year of Eugenius's death—within eighty years of the Synod of Rathbreasail, and before the Anglo-Normans had captured the ecclesiastical domination of Meath—the diocese of Clonard had expanded to four times its original size. Its bishop ruled the whole area of the modern county of Meath which lies south of the Boyne and Blackwater.

Simon Rochfort, the first English bishop, stretched his arm further. We have a charter of his, which may be dated before 1202, confirming to St. Thomas's Abbey a number of churches in his diocese.67 It includes most, if not all, of the churches granted by his predecessor, but adds others. Among these are some in the deanery of Slane. The bishopric of Slane had been absorbed.

The rapid extension of his diocese towards the north suggested to Rochfort the desirability of having for his headquarters a more central place than Clonard. So in 1202 he translated the see to Newtown, near Trim,68 and began to call himself Bishop of Meath. Ten years later, as we know, this "impudent bishop" captured the diocese of Kells.69 The bishop of Meath (no longer of Clonard) from his see at Newtown had the oversight of nearly the whole of the modern county. Within the confines of his diocese were the seven older dioceses of Clonard, Dunshaughlin, Skreen, Trim, Duleek, Slane and Kells. This was probably the whole of the eastern diocese as designed by the Synod of Usnagh.

But the policy of annexation still went forward apace. Another document enables us to measure the progress of half a century. It is a concordat concerning metropolitical visitations, between the archbishop of Armagh and Rochfort's third successor, Hugh de Tachmon. It is dated 9th April, 1265.70 The tenor of the concordat does not concern us: it is important for our purpose because it proves that in 1265 there were eleven rural deaneries in the diocese of Meath. Four more petty dioceses had been suppressed, Mullingar, Loxewdy, Ardnurcher and Fore. The diocese was co-extensive with that of the present day, except that the diocese of Clonmacnoise—as small in 1265 as it had been in 1100—was not yet brought in.

Clonmacnoise preserved its independence three centuries longer. It was incorporated with Meath in 1569. Thus at length the dream of the fathers of Rathbreasail was fulfilled. There were two dioceses in the ancient kingdom of Meath—Meath and Kilmore. But neither Duleek nor Clonard nor Clonmacnoise was a see. From that day to this, in fact, the diocese of Meath has had no see. And the boundary which parts Meath from Kilmore is very different from the line which the fathers of Rathbreasail drew between the dioceses of Clonard and Duleek, or that which the assembly of Usnagh drew between Clonmacnoise and Clonard.

IV.—St. Malachy's Part in The Reformation

It is not possible, within the limits of this Introduction, to follow the later stages of the Reformation movement in detail. In the present section I confine myself to the part which St. Malachy played in its development.

Malachy was born at Armagh in 1095. He was therefore a mere boy when the Synod of Rathbreasail met. At the dawn of his manhood he became the disciple of the recluse Imar O'Hagan. Imar was in sympathy with the aims of the reformers, and it was probably through his influence that Malachy became imbued with their principles. He soon attracted the notice of Cellach, and was by him ordained deacon. He was advanced to the priesthood about 1119. Shortly afterwards Cellach made the young priest his vicar. For the next year or two it was Malachy's duty to administer the diocese of Armagh; and he did so in the most effective—indeed revolutionary—fashion. He evidently let no man despise his youth. His purpose, as his biographer tells us, was "to root out barbarous rites, to plant the rites of the Church." "He established in all the churches the apostolic sanctions and the decrees of the holy fathers, and especially the customs of the Holy Roman Church." He introduced the Roman method of chanting the services of the canonical hours. "He instituted anew Confession, Confirmation, the Marriage contract, of all of which those over whom he was placed were either ignorant or negligent." In a word, Malachy showed himself an ardent reformer.71

One wonders how, even with the assistance of Cellach and Imar, a young man who had never left Armagh could have already become sufficiently acquainted with the usages of other churches to carry out these sweeping measures. Perhaps his zeal was not always according to knowledge. But he soon became aware of his limitations, and determined to seek instruction. With the consent of Cellach and Imar he betook himself to Malchus, who had by this time retired from the archbishopric of Cashel and was settled at Lismore. There Malachy spent three years. During that period he doubtless increased his knowledge of Roman customs and principles. But he did more. Cormac MacCarthy, son of the king of Desmond, was then a refugee in the monastery of Malchus. Between Cormac and Malachy there grew up a friendship, which proved in later years of much advantage to the reforming cause.72

But at length Malachy's presence was urgently needed in the north, and he was recalled by Cellach and Imar. What had happened was this. The coarb of St. Comgall at Bangor, the principal religious site in the north-east of Ireland, had lately died. Since he ended his days at Lismore, it may be assumed that he was a friend of Malchus, and of the movement with which he was identified. At any rate his successor, who was Malachy's uncle, expressed his willingness to surrender his office and the site of the monastery to his nephew.73 Here was an opportunity to carry into effect one of the canons of Rathbreasail, which had hitherto been a dead letter, by establishing the diocese of Connor. Cellach, duly elected coarb of Patrick, and consecrated bishop, had no doubt been able to organize the diocese of Armagh in accordance with the Rathbreasail scheme. In like manner such a man as Malachy, enjoying the prestige which belonged to the coarb of Comgall, if consecrated bishop, would probably succeed in organizing the diocese of Connor. So in 1124 Malachy journeyed to Bangor, was installed as abbot, and was made bishop by Cellach.74 He administered his diocese with the same vigour which had already characterized his work at Armagh. But it is interesting to observe how closely he conformed to the old Irish type of bishop, in spite of his Roman proclivities. At heart he was far less bishop of Connor than coarb of Comgall, abbot of Bangor. Indeed, in strictness, he had no right to the title "bishop of Connor"; for Connor was not his see. He made Bangor his headquarters.75 Doubtless Malachy preferred Bangor to the nominal see, because it was consecrated by centuries of sacred memories, and because as yet he could not place the office of bishop above that of abbot. He ruled his great newly formed diocese, or as much of it as he succeeded in ruling, from its remotest corner on the sea shore, as Aidan ruled Northumbria from Holy Island. There he lived among his brethren, of whom he gathered a great company. There was no provision for his mensa, for he was "a lover of poverty." He practised austere asceticism. Yet he was an active missionary. He travelled incessantly through the diocese, but always on foot, visiting the towns, and roaming about the country parts, surrounded by his disciples. He preached to the people whom he met on his way.76 Nothing could be more unlike a medieval bishop of the ordinary kind. At every point we are reminded of the labours of Aidan and Ceadd and Cedd as they are described by Bede. But we may be sure that it was precisely because Malachy was coarb of Bangor, because he lived according to the ancient Irish ideal of sainthood, that he secured the obedience of the people of his diocese.

In such work as I have mentioned Malachy was engaged from 1124 to 1127. In the latter year he was driven out of Bangor by Conor O'Loughlin, king of the north of Ireland, and a second time betook himself to Lismore. There he again met Cormac MacCarthy, for that unfortunate prince was once more taking sanctuary with Malchus. He had succeeded a little while before to the throne of Desmond, but had been driven out by Turlough O'Conor, who made his brother king in his stead. But after a few months, persuaded by the entreaties of Malchus and Malachy, and aided by the arms of Conor O'Brien, king of Thomond, a nephew of Murtough, Anselm's correspondent, he made a successful attempt to regain his kingdom.77 Then Malachy moved on to Iveragh in the County Kerry, and there, under Cormac's patronage, he founded a new monastery for his community.78 Once again Cormac has friendly intercourse with Malachy, and another O'Brien is on good terms with the reformers.

It was at Iveragh, two years later, that Malachy received news of the death of Archbishop Cellach.79 It was an announcement which must have caused great anxiety to him and his friends. Who was to succeed to the primacy?

The importance of the question will become manifest if we recall the progress which had already been made at Armagh, and what still remained to be done. When Cellach was elected abbot in 1105, and in the following year was consecrated bishop, a great point had been gained. For the first time for 150 years the church of Armagh had a bishop as its ruler. We may suppose that Cellach soon organized the diocese, the limits of which were fixed at Rathbreasail. But whatever Gilbert or Malchus might hold as to the source of his authority, we cannot imagine that the members of the Church in the diocese based their allegiance to him on any other ground than the fact that he was their abbot and the coarb of Patrick. That he was a bishop added nothing, in their view, to his claims. Moreover Cellach belonged to the family which had long supplied Armagh with abbots. The abuse of hereditary succession had not disappeared with his appointment.80 If his successor was chosen in the time-honoured way, a member of the coarbial family would certainly be selected, and in all probability he would be a layman, who would not accept episcopal orders. In a word, all that had been achieved by the reformers at the most important ecclesiastical centre in Ireland would be undone.

Cellach had foreseen this, and accordingly he determined to nominate Malachy as his successor. "With the authority of Patrick" he laid upon the nobles, and especially upon "the two kings of Munster," the obligation of securing that his wish should be carried into effect. The two kings who were thus charged with a difficult duty were Conor O'Brien, king of Thomond, the principal representative of the O'Briens, and Cormac MacCarthy, king of Desmond, Malachy's friend.

From Cellach's point of view the choice of a successor which he had made was a wise one. Malachy was as zealous a reformer as himself. He was a man of unusual ability and force of character. Besides, he was possessed of a personal charm which might in time disarm opposition. He was already a bishop; therefore, if he were once seated in the chair of Patrick, the question whether the new coarb should be consecrated would not arise. More important still, he was not of the coarbial stock; with his entry into the see the scandal of hereditary succession would come to an end.

But it was not to be expected that the appointment would be accepted without strong protest; and at the moment there seemed little prospect that the scheme of Cellach would attain fruition. There is no need to enter into the details of the fierce struggle that ensued. It is dealt with elsewhere.[81] Suffice it to say that by 1137, with the aid of O'Brien and MacCarthy, and apparently with assistance also from Donough O'Carroll, king of Oriel, he was undisputed coarb of Patrick and archbishop of Armagh. The victory was won, and an immense stride had been made in the Reformation movement.

But Malachy had no mind to spend the rest of his life at Armagh. Five years before, as the condition of his entry into the fray, he had stipulated that as soon as he had been accepted as archbishop he should resign the see and return to his beloved Bangor. So in 1137 he nominated and consecrated Gelasius as his successor in the primacy, and "returned to his former parish, but not to Connor." Let me explain this enigmatical statement. Malachy had had some years' experience of the people of the diocese of Connor, whom St. Bernard gently describes as "not men but beasts." He had doubtless discovered that the district which it included could not be ruled by a single bishop. In fact it consisted of two tribal territories, Dál Araide in the north, and Ulaid in the south; and the two tribes which inhabited them were usually engaged in mutual war. He decided that it should be divided into two dioceses. He consecrated a bishop for Dál Araide, with his see at Connor, and himself resumed the oversight of Ulaid, with his see at Bangor.[82] Thus originated the present dioceses of Down and Connor. In Malachy's time the boundary between them seems to have run west from Larne. In the course of centuries it has shifted further south.

This division was a direct violation of the letter of the ordinance of Rathbreasail; but it did not contravene its spirit. In the letter, which ignored the civil divisions of the country, the ordinance could not be obeyed. Malachy adopted a scheme which secured the permanent rule of diocesan bishops in the district.

Malachy was now, and continued to be till his death, bishop of Down, or more strictly of Bangor; in the current Irish phrase bishop of Ulaid. But his activities already extended beyond his diocese. Within the next two years he succeeded in establishing in actual fact another diocese which till now had existed only on paper. It was that which the Synod of Rathbreasail had called the diocese of Clogher, and which we know by the same name; but which for sixty years or more bore the name of the diocese of Oriel.

That we may understand his action let us return for a moment to the five Ulster dioceses as planned at Rathbreasail. In four of them regard was paid to tribal boundaries. The diocese of Raphoe corresponded to Tír Conaill, Derry to Tír Eoghain, Armagh to Oriel, while Connor comprehended the two territories of Dál Araide and Ulaid. The diocese of Clogher was of necessity the remainder of the province. If it coincided with a tribal district, that could only happen by chance. In fact it did not. It was much smaller than the other dioceses. It embraced only the present barony of Clogher in the county of Tyrone, and the portion of Fermanagh lying between it and the Erne waterway. It had within it no element of cohesion. It was most unlikely that it could ever constitute an ecclesiastical unit, governed by a bishop.

Nevertheless an attempt seems to have been made to consolidate it as a diocese a few years after Rathbreasail; as might have been expected, without success. A bishop of Clogher, who apparently had no diocese, died in 1135. He was succeeded by Christian O'Morgair, brother of Malachy. He was probably nominated and consecrated by his brother, who was then titular archbishop of Armagh. Now about this time Donough O'Carroll, king of Oriel, joined the ranks of the reformers, as we may suppose under the influence of Malachy. His kingdom included the little diocese of Clogher; but the main part of it consisted of the present counties of Monaghan and Louth. Accordingly a bold stroke of policy was conceived and carried out. The diocese of Clogher was enlarged so as to cover the greater part of O'Carroll's kingdom. For this purpose the archbishop of Armagh surrendered a large part of his diocese—the whole of Monaghan and Louth. Then Christian moved his see from Clogher to the spot now occupied by the village of Louth. Thus there was constituted a new diocese, which included the Rathbreasail diocese of Clogher, but was four times its size, and had its see at Louth. It was known as the diocese of Oriel. In all this we see plainly the hand of Malachy. Not long after the removal of the see Christian died, and Malachy selected and consecrated his successor, one Edan O'Kelly. O'Kelly had a long episcopate, from 1139 to 1182; and with the help of O'Carroll he organized his diocese, and gave it a cathedral at Louth with a chapter of Augustinian canons.83 Once again Malachy was the maker of a diocese; and once again, in the interest of stability, he transgressed the letter of the Rathbreasail canons, while fulfilling their spirit. It was not till after the coming of the Anglo-Normans that the see was brought back to Clogher. Subsequently the county of Louth reverted to Armagh, and the diocese extended to the west. About the year 1250 its boundaries came to be what they now are.84

In 1139, after settling the affairs of the diocese of Oriel, Malachy left Ireland on an important mission. It will be remembered that Gilbert had declared that no archbishop could exercise his functions till the Pope had sent him the pall. That was the current doctrine of the age. Now neither Cellach, nor Malachy, nor Gelasius, nor Malchus, nor his successor at Cashel, had received that ornament. They had therefore, in the strict sense, no right to the title of archbishop. Malachy resolved to make request to the Pope in person for palls for the two Irish metropolitans. So he set out from Bangor for Rome.85 Of his journey it is unnecessary to say anything here.86

At Rome Malachy was received by Pope Innocent II. with great honour. He confirmed the erection of the metropolitan see of Cashel. But he politely declined to grant the palls. They must be demanded, he said, by a council of the bishops, clergy and magnates; and then they would be given.

But if the Pope refused Malachy's request, he bestowed on him an office, the securing of which we may conjecture to have been one of the purposes of his visit to Rome, though St. Bernard does not say so. Gilbert, now old and infirm, had resigned the see of Limerick, and with it his legatine commission. Innocent made Malachy papal legate in his stead.87

Thus Malachy returned to Ireland, still bishop of Down indeed, but virtually chief prelate of the Irish Church. For the following eight years he laboured with zeal and vigour. St. Bernard unfortunately gives little information concerning the details of his administrative work as legate. But he relates one incident which suggests that in this period Malachy was instrumental in founding another diocese. He nominated and consecrated the first known bishop of Cork,88 not improbably with the intention that he should unite in his own person the two offices of coarb of Barre, founder of Cork, and diocesan bishop.

And in this connexion it is worth noticing that he was evidently on friendly terms with Nehemiah, the first known bishop of the neighbouring diocese of Cloyne.89 If that diocese was also founded by him he once again violated the letter of the Rathbreasail canons, for by them Cloyne was included in the diocese of Emly.

In 1148 Malachy convened a synod at Inispatrick, an island opposite Skerries, Co. Dublin. This synod demanded the palls in due form, and sent Malachy to obtain them. But he got no further on his journey than Clairvaux. There, after celebrating Mass on St. Luke's Day, he was taken ill of a fever; and there a fortnight later he died in the arms of St. Bernard, on All Souls' Day, 2nd November, 1148.90

Nevertheless the palls came. They were brought to Ireland by a legate specially commissioned by Pope Eugenius III., John Paparo, cardinal priest of St. Laurence. A synod was held at Kells to receive them in March 1152,91 of which the joint presidents were Paparo, as *legatus a latere*, and Christian, first abbot of Mellifont, and now bishop of Lismore, who had lately succeeded Malachy as *legatus natus*.

Of this synod Keating gives a short account, abridged from the *Annals of Clonenagh*,92 from which he had also derived his knowledge of the proceedings at Rathbreasail. He preserves a list of the bishops who attended. It includes twenty-two names, if we count two vicars who represented absent bishops. There were besides, as Keating informs us, five bishops-elect. And there was certainly one bishop of a diocese who was neither present nor represented, Edan O'Kelly, bishop of Oriel. So it appears that in 1152 there were at least twenty-eight dioceses in Ireland—a number considerably larger than was contemplated at Rathbreasail. The increase in number is partly accounted for by the presence of the bishop of the recently formed diocese of Kilmore, the division of the diocese of Connor into Connor and Down, and, a most striking addition, the inclusion of Gregory, bishop of Dublin, among the assembled prelates. It is remarkable that the bishop of Kells is not mentioned, though the synod was held in his own city. How was the bishop of Dublin induced to throw in his lot with the Irish Church? We shall see in a moment.

Much business was transacted at this Synod. But that which concerns us most nearly is the giving of the palls. Cardinal Paparo brought the Irish bishops more than they had asked for; more indeed than they desired. He presented, not two palls but four, Dublin and Tuam, as well as Armagh and Cashel, being recognized as archiepiscopal sees. This excessive generosity caused much displeasure among the Irish bishops. "For

Ireland," says Keating, apparently paraphrasing the *Annals of Clonenagh*, "thought it enough to have a pall in the church of Armagh and a pall in Cashel; and particularly it was in spite of the church of Armagh and the church of Down that the other palls were given." The cause of this discontent is not far to seek. The chief gravamen no doubt was that Dublin was included among the four. The constant friction which had subsisted for many years between the diocese of Dublin and the Irish Church sufficiently explains the indignation of the archbishop of Armagh, aggravated by the fact that the creation of new archbishops imposed a limit upon his authority. It also enables us to understand why his displeasure was shared by the Irish generally. That a see whose bishops had behaved so haughtily in the past should, at the very moment of its entrance into the Irish Church, receive so signal an honour, long denied to Armagh and Cashel, and that in the person of its bishop it should be given jurisdiction over bishops whom till now it had treated with contempt, could not but be regarded as unreasonable, or even insulting. But on the other hand, recalling the early history of the Church in Dublin, we can comprehend why, in spite of all this, special favour was bestowed upon it. Dublin, as we have seen, was a not too submissive suffragan of Canterbury. Its ambition was that its bishop should have the status of a metropolitan. The opportunity had come for gratifying its desire, and at the same time bringing it under the Irish ecclesiastical régime. The pall at once separated it from Canterbury and united it with Ireland. It was the price paid for its submission to the Primacy of Armagh. Gregory therefore became archbishop of Dublin, and had the right—which his predecessor had long before illegally assumed—to have the cross carried before him. With the gift of the pall Paparo bestowed upon him "the principal part of the bishopric of Glendalough as his diocese," promising him the remainder on the death of the bishop who then ruled it. All this was done, we are told, because it was fitting that the place "in which from ancient time had been the royal seat and head of Ireland," should be made a metropolitan see.93

There was at last one Church in Ireland, which embraced within it not only the Celtic parts of the island, but all the Danish dioceses as well. And the whole Church was ruled by the bishops. The Reformation may not have been complete in every detail—there was indeed much left for the Anglo-Normans to do—but the Synod of Kells had set the crown on the work of the Irish reformers. And this consummation was mainly due to the wisdom and the untiring zeal of St. Malachy of Armagh.

A few words more will suffice to complete this too lengthy introduction. The *Life of Malachy* was certainly written before the Synod of Kells met in March 1152; for Christian, who attended the Synod as bishop of Lismore, is spoken of in the *Life* as abbot of Mellifont.94 Its earliest possible date is a couple of months after Malachy's death. The ignorance displayed in § 6995 of the movements of the Pope in 1148 is so inexplicable on the assumption of a later date that it may be assigned to January 1149.96 In the following translation the text printed by de Backer97 is used, with the exception of a few sentences which have been emended. It does not differ to any great extent from that of Mabillon.98 Following de Backer I have divided the text into chapters, in accordance with the MSS.; but Mabillon's sections have been retained, as more convenient for reference, the numbers of de Backer's sections being added within brackets.

By way of illustration four letters of St. Bernard and his two sermons on St. Malachy have been added. They are translated from Mabillon's edition,99 with some corrections. The dates of these documents are discussed below.100

St. Bernard's numerous quotations from the Bible and other sources are printed in italics, so far as I have recognized them. The scriptural allusions are given as nearly as possible in the words of the Authorized (in the Apocryphal books the Revised) Version, though at times they do not agree with the Vulgate Latin. Where it has been found necessary to depart from their renderings, the symbol "vg." follows the references in the footnotes.

I desire to make grateful acknowledgement of help received from my friends, of whom I must specially mention Dr. L. C. Purser, Senior Fellow of Trinity College, Dublin, Mr. R. I. Best, the Rev. J. E. L. Oulton, the Rev. Dr. J. M. Harden and the Rev. Canon C. P. Price. My wife assisted me in the preparation of the index.

St. Patrick's Day, 1920.

[1] See *Life*, §§ 6 (end), 7, 16, 17, 39 with notes, and Additional Note A.

[2] *E.g.* in the doctrine of the Eucharist and of Baptism. See *Life*, § 57, and Lanfranc's letter to Donnell in Ussher, 495; *P.L.* cl. 532.

[3] See p. 46, note 1, and Additional Note B.

[4] *Life*, § 19.

[5] R. King, *Memoir Introductory to the Early History of the Primacy of Armagh*, 1854, p. 22.

[6] See Lawlor, *Psalter and Martyrology of Ricemarch*, vol. i., pp. ix-xii.

[7] MS. A. 4. 20.

[8] MS. 199.

[9] Cotton MS. Faustina, C. 1, f. 66.

[10] Lawlor, *op. cit.*, pp. xii.-xvii.

[11] Lanigan, vol. iii. p. 446; vol. iv. pp. 2-8; Reeves, *On Marianus Scotus*, extracted from the *Natural History Review and Quarterly Journal of Science*, July, 1860. B. MacCarthy, *The Codex Palatino-Vaticanus, No. 830*, 1892, pp. 4 ff.

[12] Below, p. 18, note 6.

[13] See below, p. 47, note 3.

[14] p. 73.

[15] *Chronicle of John of Worcester*, ed. J. R. H. Weaver, 1908, p. 16.

[16] p. 18, note 6.

[17] p. 47, note 3, p. 73, note 1. I can name only three bishops of Danish sees who were apparently of Danish extraction; and they all lived at a time when the Reformation was far advanced. They are Erolbh (Erulf?), bishop of Limerick, who died in 1151, and Tostius of Waterford and Turgesius of Limerick, who were in office in 1152. *A.F.M.* 1151, and *Annals of Clonenagh* quoted in Keating, iii. 317.

[18] Ussher, 491.

[19] Ware, *Bishops*, ed. Harris, p. 309; Eadmer, p. 73.

[20] Ussher, 518; and below, *Life*, § 8.

[21] See p. 47, note 3.

[22] 1115. Eadmer, p. 236. Gougaud (p. 358) infers from this passage that Limerick was at that time a suffragan see of Canterbury. But this seems impossible in view of Gilbert's share in the proceedings of the Synod of Rathbreasail five years earlier. Eadmer is not a very good witness in such matters, and his language is hardly decisive for two reasons. (1) It is not clear that he includes Gilbert among the suffragans who co-

operated in the consecration: "Huic consecrationi interfuerunt et cooperatores extiterunt suffraganei ecclesiae Cantuariensis, episcopi videlicet hi, Willelmus Wintoniensis, Robertus Lincoliensis, Rogerus Serberiensis, Johannes Bathoniensis, Urbanus Glamorgatensis, Gislebertus Lumniensis de Hibernia." (2) The word "suffragan" is often used as meaning merely an assistant bishop. Thus in the fifteenth century several bishops of Dromore were "suffragans" of the archbishop of York; but Dromore was certainly not regarded as one of his suffragan sees.

[23] Ussher, 532.

[24] See p. xxxvi.

[25] Ussher, 567; *Beati Lanfranci Opera*, ed. J. A. Giles, Oxon., 1844, vol. i. p. 24.

[26] See Ussher, 490-497; *P.L.* cl. 532, 535, 536. This Donnell was probably Donnell O'Heney (Ua hEnna), a Munster bishop who died in 1098 (*A. U.*).

[27] Ussher, 515-519. The letter to Donnell is also in *P.L.* clix. 262.

[28] Ussher, 520-527; *P.L.* clix. 173, 178, 243.

[29] *Miscellany of Irish Archælogical Society*, vol. i. (1846), p. 136.

[30] Wilkins, *Concilia*, i. 547. In the form in which Rochfort quotes it the ordinance applies to the whole of Ireland. But we have no evidence of the transformation of dioceses into deaneries outside Meath; and it is quite probable that a synod held in Meath would have in view, in such a decree, only the conditions which prevailed in that district.

[31] The deanery of Dunshaughlin is now named Ratoath. The deanery of Kells has been divided into Upper and Lower Kells.

[32] The cogency of this argument is enhanced when we observe that there is strong independent evidence for the existence in the twelfth century of one of the six dioceses—the diocese of Kells. (*a*) Up to the latter part of the sixteenth century (1583) there was an archdeacon of Kells, as well as an archdeacon of Meath; the jurisdiction of an archdeacon (at any rate in Ireland) seems to have been always originally co-extensive with a diocese. The first known archdeacon of Kells was Adam Petit who was in office in 1230 (*R.T.A.* 279; *C.M.A.* i. 101); but it is unlikely that he had no predecessors. (*b*) Among the prelates who greeted Henry II. at Dublin in 1171 was Thaddaeus, bishop of Kells (Benedict of Peterborough (R. S.), i. 26). (*c*) In the time of Innocent III. (1198-1216) the question was raised in the papal curia whether the bishop of Kells was subject to the archbishop of Armagh or the archbishop of Tuam (Theiner, p. 2). (*d*) The bishop of Kells is mentioned in a document of the year 1202 (*Cal. of Docts. Ireland*, i. 168). (*e*) A contemporary note records the suppression of the bishopric: "When a Cistercian monk ... had been elected and consecrated bishop of Kells by the common consent of the clergy and people, and had been confirmed by the Pope, the impudent bishop of Meath cast him out with violence and dared to [add] his bishopric to his own" (*C.M.A.* ii. 22). This statement implies that the dispossessed bishop ruled over a diocese. Moreover, when we remember that the see was certainly suppressed before Rochfort's Synod of 1216, that Rochfort was the first person who assumed the title "bishop of Meath" in the modern sense, and that a bishop of Kells died in 1211 (*A.L.C.*), we need not hesitate to conclude that the "impudent bishop" was Rochfort himself, and that the suppression was accomplished about 1213.

[33] *I.e.* dioceses. This synod is mentioned in *A.T.*, *A.I.* and the *Annals of Boyle*.

Particulars of its Acts and of the persons present at it are given in *C.S.* and *D.A.I. C.S.* has "parish" in the singular. But this does not seem to yield good sense; for the whole extent of the kingdom of Meath could scarcely have been called a "parish" in the twelfth century. I therefore read "parishes." The singular may have been substituted for the plural at a later time, when the kingdom (or the greater part of it) included only the dioceses of Meath and Clonmacnoise, and their earlier history was forgotten. Cp. the unhistorical statement of St. Bernard about Down and Connor in *Life*, § 31. *D.A.I.* have an anomalous form (*faircheadh*), which may have come from either the singular (*fairche*) or the plural (*faircheadha*) in the exemplar, but more probably from the latter.

[34] p. xxiv. f.

[35] See p. 47, note 3.

[36] Ussher, 513.

[37] A small portion of the present diocese of Limerick lies north of the Shannon.

[38] Ussher, 501 ff.; *P.L.* clix. 995.

[39] See p. 65, note 1.

[40] See Additional Note B, pp. 164, 166. The events of Cellach's life are gathered from *A. U.*

[41] *Life*, § 19.

[42] See MacCarthy's Note in *A. U.* 1101.

[43] *A.F.M.*, Keating, iii. 297. Keating seems to confuse the events of 1101 with those of 1106.

[44] *Life*, § 33.

[45] See p. 18, note 6.

[46] See next page.

[47] Keating, iii. 299 ff. The date is there misprinted 1100.

[48] I formerly disputed this identification, on the ground that the archbishop of Cashel who was present at Fiadh meic Oengusa was O'Dunan (G. T. Stokes, *Ireland and the Celtic Church*, ed. 6, 1907, p. 372). I am now convinced that he was archbishop of Cashel. I was not then aware that all MSS. of Keating date the Synod of Rathbreasail in 1110.

[49] On p. 298 read *no* (*or*) for *is* (*and*) before *Dun dá Leathghlas*; and on p. 306 *chathar* for *chuigear ar fhichid* (i.e. *twenty-four* for *twenty-five*). On p. 306 a portion of the note on the Leinster diocese has evidently dropped out, which should be restored to bring it into conformity with the corresponding passage on p. 302.

[50] *H.E.* i. 29.

[51] *I.e.* diocese.

[52] The parish (using the word in its modern sense) in which is Newtown Stewart, co. Derry.

[53] Ramsay, *Paul the Traveller* (1907), p. 173.

[54] Some changes of phraseology might have been made here and elsewhere if Professor MacNeill's *Phases of Irish History* (1919) had come into my hands before this volume went to press. But they would not have affected the argument.

[55] See *Irish Church Quarterly*, vol. x. p. 234.

[56] Agus is é teampull Muire i Luimneach a príomheaglais.

[57] When Cardinal Paparo came to Ireland in 1151 he found "a see constituted at Dublin in the diocese of Glendalough."—*Crede Mihi* (ed. Gilbert), p. 11.

[58] Ussher, 488 (*P.L.* cl. 534), 564.

[59] *Ibid.* 528, 530; *P.L.* clix. 109, 216.

[60] See p. 20, note 3.

[61] See p. xxii.

[62] See p. 18, note 6.

[63] See above, p. xxviii.

[64] There was a bishop of Breifne (*i.e.* Kilmore) in 1136 (*A.T.*).

[65] *R.T.A.* p. 269.

[66] *Ibid.* p. 259.

[67] *Ibid.* p. 241.

[68] *Cal. of Papal Letters*, v. 75. For date see *Cal. of Documents, Ireland*, i. 168.

[69] See p. xxviii, note 1.

[70] *R.T.A.* p. 71.

[71] *Life*, §§ 4-7.

[72] *Life*, §§ 8 f., and p. 21, note 1.

[73] See *Life*, § 12, and p. 27, note 1.

[74] See *Life*, § 16, and notes.

[75] p. 33, note 1.

[76] *Life*, §§ 16, 17.

[77] See *Life*, § 9, and notes.

[78] *Life*, § 18.

[79] *Ibid.* § 19.

[80] See p. xv, and Additional Note B.

[81] *Life*, §§ 20-31, with notes, and Additional Note C.

[82] §§ 31, 32.

[83] See *Life*, § 34 and notes.

[84] For a fuller account of the beginnings of the diocese of Clogher see *L.A.J.* vol. iv. pp. 129-159. To the reasons there given for believing that Christian transferred the see from Clogher to Louth should be added the fact that in Tundale (p. 54) he is called *Lugdunensis episcopus*.

[85] *Life*, §§ 33, 34.

[86] *Ibid.* §§ 35-41. The reader may be reminded, however, that the two visits of Malachy to Clairvaux, in the course of this journey, produced the friendship between him and St. Bernard, which had its twofold issue in the composition of the important documents included in this volume, and the introduction of the Cistercian Order into Ireland.

[87] *Life*, § 38.

[88] § 51.

[89] § 47.

[90] *Life*, §§ 67-75.

[91] There was no unnecessary delay on the part of the Pope in sending the palls. After the death of Malachy a deputation was sent from Ireland to Rome to demand them. Paparo set out to confer them, and reached England in 1150; but King Stephen would not allow him to proceed to Ireland except on terms which he could not accept. (John of Hexham, p. 326; *Historia Pontificalis* in *M.G.H.* xx. 539 f.)

[92] Vol. iii. p. 313 ff.

[93] See Letter of Pope Innocent III. to Henry of London, 6 Oct. 1216, in *Crede Mihi* (ed. Gilbert), p. 11.

[94] §§ 14, 52.

[95] See p. 122, note 1.

[96] Cp. *R.I.A.* xxxv. 258 ff. This conclusion is corroborated by Tundale's Vision, which seems to have been written early in 1149 (see Friedel and Meyer, *La Vision de Tondale*, 1907, pp. vi-xii; *Rev. Celt.* xxviii. 411). The writer speaks of the *Life of Malachy* as already written, and in course of transcription (Tundale, p. 5, 'cuius uitam ... Bernhardus ... transscribit'). He may have derived his erroneous statement (*ibid.*) that Pope Eugenius went *to Rome* in the year of Malachy's death from St. Bernard: see p. 122, note 1.

[97] *AA.SS.*, Nov., xii. 1., 143-146.

[98] *Sancti Bernardi Abbatis Claræ-vallensis Opera Omnia*, ed. J. Mabillon, 1839, vol. i. 2, cols. 1465-1524. Reprinted *P.L.* clxxxii. 1073-1118.

[99] *Op. cit.* i. 2, 2221-2231; i. 1, 341, 356, 357, 374; reprinted in *P.L.* clxxxiii. 481-490; clxxxii. 545 f., 558 f., 579 f.

[100] See notes on pp. 131, 133 f., 137, 141, 157.

THE LIFE OF ST. MALACHY

PREFACE

1. It is indeed always worth while to portray the illustrious lives of the saints, that they may serve as a mirror and an example, and give, as it were, a relish to the life of men on earth. For by this means in some sort they *live* among us, even *after death*,101 and many of those who *are dead while they live*102 are challenged and recalled by them to true life. But now especially is there need for it because holiness is rare, and it is plain that our age is lacking in men. So greatly, in truth, do we perceive that lack to have increased in our day that none can doubt that we are smitten by that saying, *Because iniquity shall abound the love of many shall wax cold*;103 and, as I suppose, he has come or is at hand of whom it is written, *Want shall go before his face*.104 If I mistake not, Antichrist is he whom famine and sterility of all good both precedes and accompanies. Whether therefore it is the herald of one now present or the harbinger of one who shall come immediately, the *want* is evident. I speak not of the crowd, I speak not of the vile multitude of *the children of this world*:105 I would have you lift up your eyes upon the very *pillars*106 of the Church. Whom can you show me, even of the number of those who seem to be *given for a light to the Gentiles*,107 that in his lofty station is not rather a smoking wick than a blazing lamp? And, says One, *if the light that is in thee be darkness, how great is that darkness!*108 Unless perchance, which I do not believe, you will say that they shine who *suppose that gain is godliness*;109 who in the Lord's inheritance *seek not the things which are* the Lord's, but rather *their own*.110 Why do I say *their own*? He would be perfect and holy, even while he seeks his own and retains his own, who should restrain his heart and hands from the things of others. But let him remember, who seems to himself to have advanced perhaps thus far, that the same degree of holiness is

demanded even of a gentile.111 Are not *soldiers* bidden to *be content with their wages* that they may be saved?112 But it is a great thing for a doctor of the Church if he be as one of the soldiers; or, *if*, in truth (as the prophet speaks to their reproach), *it be as with the people so with the priest*.113 Hideous! Is it so indeed? Is he rightly to be esteemed highest who, falling from the highest rank can scarce cleave to the lowest, that he be not engulfed in the abyss? Yet how rare is even such a man among the clergy! Whom, likewise, do you give me who is content with necessaries, who despises superfluities? Yet the law has been enjoined beforehand by the Apostles on the successors of the Apostles, *Having* food *and* raiment, *let us be therewith content*.114 Where is this rule? We see it in books, but not in men. But you have [the saying] about the righteous man, that *the law of his God is in his heart*,115 not in a codex. Nor is that the standard of perfection. The perfect man is ready to forgo even necessaries. But that is beside the mark.116 Would that some limit were set on superfluous things! Would that our desires were not infinite! But what? Perhaps you might find one who can achieve this. It would indeed be difficult; but [if we find him] see what we have done. We were seeking for a very good man, a deliverer of many; and lo, we have labour to discover one who can save himself. The very good man to-day is one who is not utterly bad.

2. Wherefore, *since the godly man has ceased*117 from the earth, it seems to me that I do not employ myself to no purpose when I recall to our midst, from among those *who were redeemed from the earth*,118 Bishop Malachy, a man truly holy, and a man, too, of our own time, of singular wisdom and virtue. *He was a burning and a shining light*;119 and it has not been quenched, but only removed. Who would with good right be angry with me if I move it back again? Yes indeed, neither the men of my own age, nor any succeeding generation should be wanting in gratitude to me if by my pen I recall one whom the course of nature has borne away; if I restore to the world one *of whom the world was not worthy*;120 if I preserve for the memory of men one *whose memory may be blessed*121 to all who shall deign to read; if while I rouse my sleeping friend, *the voice of the turtle be heard in our land*122 saying, *Lo, I am with you alway, even unto the end of the world*.123 Then again, he was buried among us;124 this duty is eminently ours. Nay, is it not mine, inasmuch as that holy man included me among his special friends, and in such regard that I may believe that I was second to none *in that respect of glory*?125 Nor do I find that intercourse with holiness so eminent misses its reward; I have already received the first-fruits. He was near the end; nay, rather, near the beginning, according to the saying, *when a man hath finished then is he but at the beginning*.126 I ran to him that *the blessing of him that was ready to* die might *come upon me*.127 Already he could not move his other limbs; but, mighty to give blessing, he raised his hands upon my head and blessed me.128 I have *inherited the blessing*;129 how then can I be silent about him? Finally, you enjoin me to undertake this task, Abbot Congan,130 my reverend brother and sweet friend, and with you also (as you write from Ireland) *all* that *Church of the saints*131 to which you belong.132 I obey with a will, the more so because you ask not panegyric but narrative. I shall endeavour that it may be chaste and clear, informing the devout, and not wearying the fastidious. At any rate the truth of my narrative is assured, since it has been communicated by you;133 and beyond doubt you assert nothing but things of which you have most certain information.

Here ends the Prologue.

[101] Ecclus. xlviii. 12 (vg.).

[102] 1 Tim. v. 6. Cp. Rev. iii. 1.

[103] Matt. xxiv. 12.

[104] Job xli. 22 (vg.).

[105] Luke xvi. 8.

[106] Gal. ii. 9.

[107] Isa. xlix. 6.

[108] Matt. vi. 23.

[109] 1 Tim. vi. 5.

[110] Phil. ii. 21; 1 Cor. xiii. 5.

[111] Cp. Matt. v. 47.

[112] Luke iii. 14.

[113] Isa. xxiv. 2; Hos. iv. 9 (inexact quotation).

[114] 1 Tim. vi. 8 (inexact quotation).

[115] Ps. xxxvii. 31.

[116] *Gratis.*

[117] Ps. xii. 1.

[118] Rev. xiv. 3.

[119] John v. 35.

[120] Heb. xi. 38.

[121] Ecclus. xlv. 1.

[122] Cant. ii. 12. For the meaning compare Cant. lix. 3: The voice of the turtle "is a sign that winter is past, proclaiming nevertheless that the time of pruning has come.... The voice, more like one who groans than one who sings, admonishes us of our pilgrimage." After Eugenius III. had visited Clairvaux St. Bernard wrote, "The voice of the turtle has been heard in our chapter. We had great joy and delight." (*Ep. 273.*)

[123] Matt. xxviii. 20.

[124] That is, at Clairvaux. See § 75.

[125] Apparently a confused reference to 2 Cor. iii. 10; xi. 17 (vg.).

[126] Ecclus. xviii. 7 (inexact quotation).

[127] Job xxix. 13.

[128] See § 73, end.

[129] 1 Pet. iii. 9.

[130] This abbot, to whom the *Life* is dedicated, belonged to the Cistercian Order, as the words "reverend brother" imply. He may therefore be identified with Congan, abbot of the Cistercian monastery of the Suir, mentioned in § 64. That he was personally known to St. Bernard is clear; and it is probable that he was one of the Irishmen who by Malachy's desire were instructed at Clairvaux (§ 39). Thady Dowling (*Annals, s.a.* 1147) identifies him with "Cogganus," abbot of Killeshin, near Carlow, stating on the authority of Nicholas Maguire that he wrote the *gesta* of Malachy and Bernard. Though this statement is probably not accurate, it is possible that our Congan was abbot of Killeshin before he became a Cistercian.

[131] Ecclus. xxxi. 11 (vg.).

[132] *Vestra illa omnis ecclesia sanctorum.* We should perhaps render, "the whole church of holy persons over which you preside," *i.e.* Congan's convent. Elsewhere in the *Life, ecclesia* is used for a local community, such as the church of Armagh (§ 20, etc).

But see Serm. i. § 3. Vacandard understands the phrase to mean "the Cistercian communities of Ireland" (*R.Q.H.* lii. 48).

[133] *Vobis* (pl.); *i.e.* Congan and others in Ireland.

Here begins the life of Malachy the Bishop

CHAPTER I

The early life of Malachy. Having been admitted to Holy Orders he associates with Malchus

1095.   1. Our Malachy, born in Ireland,134 of a barbarous people, was brought up there, and there received his education. But from the barbarism of his birth he contracted no taint, any more than the fishes of the sea from their native salt. But how delightful to reflect, that uncultured barbarism should have produced for us so worthy135 *a fellow-citizen with the saints and member of the household of God.*136 He who brings *honey out of the rock and oil out of the flinty rock*137 Himself did this. His parents,138 however, were great both by descent and in power, *like unto the name of the great men that are in the earth.*139 Moreover his mother,140 more noble in mind than in blood, took pains, *in the very beginning of his ways,*141 *to show* to her child *the ways of life,*142 esteeming this knowledge of more value to him than the empty knowledge of the learning of this world. For both, however, he had aptitude in proportion to his age. In the schools *he was taught* learning, at home *the fear of the Lord,*143 and by daily progress he duly responded to both teacher and mother.144 For indeed he was endowed from the first with a *good spirit,*145 in virtue of which he was a docile boy and very lovable, wonderfully gracious to all in all things. But he was [now] drinking, instead of milk from the breast of a mother, *the waters of saving wisdom,*146 and day by day he was increasing in discretion. In discretion, shall I say, or in holiness? If I say both, I shall not regret it, *for I should say the truth.*147 He behaved as an old man, a boy in years without a boy's playfulness. And when because of this he was regarded with reverence and astonishment by all, he was not found on that account, as commonly happens, more arrogant, but rather quiet and subdued in *all meekness.*148 Not impatient of rule, not shunning discipline, not averse from reading, not, therefore, eager for games—so especially dear to the heart of boys of that age. *And he advanced beyond all of his own age*149 in that learning, at least, which suited his years. For in discipline of morals and advance in virtues in a short time he even outshone *all his instructors*.150 His *unction*,151 however, rather than his mother, was his teacher. Urged by it he exercised himself not slothfully also in divine things, to seek solitude, *to anticipate vigils*,152 to *meditate in the law*,153 to eat sparingly, to pray frequently, and (because on account of his studies he had not leisure to frequent the church, and from modesty would not) to *lift up holy hands everywhere*154 to heaven; but only where it could be done secretly—for already he was careful to avoid vainglory, that poison of virtues.155

2. There is a hamlet near the city in which the boy studied,156 whither his teacher was wont to go often, accompanied by him alone. When they were going there both together, as he related afterwards, he would *step back, stop a moment*,157 and standing behind his teacher, when he was not aware of it, *spread forth his hands toward heaven*,158 and quickly send forth a prayer, as if it were a dart; and, thus dissembling, once more would follow the teacher. By such a pious trick the boy often deceived him who was his companion as well as teacher. It is not possible to mention all the qualities which adorned his earlier years with the hue of a good natural disposition; we must hasten to greater and more useful matters. One further incident, however, I relate because, in my judgement, it yielded a sign, not only of good, but also of great hope in the boy. Roused once on a time by the reputation of a certain teacher, famous in the studies which are called liberal, he went to him desiring to learn. For indeed he was now grasping after the last opportunities of boyhood, and was longing eagerly for such learning. But when he went into the house he saw the man playing with an awl, and with rapid strokes making furrows in the wall in some strange fashion. And shocked at the bare sight, because it smacked of levity, the serious boy dashed away from him, and did not care even to see him from that time forward. Thus, though an avid student of letters, as a lover of virtue he esteemed them lightly in comparison with that which was becoming. By such preliminary exercises the boy was being prepared for the conflict which awaited him in more advanced159 age; and already in his own person he was challenging the adversary. Such, then, was the boyhood of Malachy. Moreover he passed through his adolescence with like simplicity and purity; except that as *years* increased, there *increased* also for him *wisdom and favour with God and man*.160

3. From this time, that is, from his early adolescence, *what was in the man*161 began to appear more plainly, and it came to be seen that *the grace of God which was in him was not in vain*.162 For the *industrious young man*,163 seeing how *the world lieth in wickedness*,164 and considering what sort of spirit *he had received*, said within himself, "It is *not the spirit of this world*.165 What have the two in common?166 One has no *communion* with the other any more than *light with darkness*.167 But my spirit *is of God*, and *I know the things that are freely given me*168 in it. From it I have innocence of life till now, from it the ornament of continence, from it hunger for *righteousness*,169 from it also that *glory of mine*, by so much more secure because it is more secret, *the testimony of my conscience*.170 None of these is safe for me under *the prince of this world*.171 Then, *I have this treasure in an earthen vessel*.172 I must take heed lest it should strike against something and be broken, and the *oil of gladness*173 which I carry be poured out. And in truth it is most difficult not to strike *against something amid* the stones and rocks *of this* crooked and winding *way and life*.174 Must I thus in a moment lose together all *the blessings of goodness with which* I have been *prevented*175 from the beginning? Rather do I resign them, and myself with them, to Him from whom they come. Yea, and I

am His. I *lose my* very *soul*176 for a time that I may not lose it for ever. And what I am and all that I have, where can they be as safe as in the hand of their Author? Who so concerned to preserve, so powerful to hold, so faithful to restore? He will preserve in safety. He will restore in good time. Without hesitation I give myself to serve Him by His gifts. I cannot lose aught of all that I spend on my labour of piety. Perchance I may even hope for some greater boon. He who gives freely is wont to repay with usury. So it is. He will even heap up and *increase virtue in my soul*."177

So he thought—and did; *knowing that* apart from deeds *the thoughts of man are vanity*.178

c. 1112.   4. (3) There was a man in the city of Armagh,179 where Malachy was brought up—a holy man and of great austerity of life, a pitiless *castigator of his body*,180 who had a cell near the church.181 In it he abode, *serving God with fastings and prayers day and night*.182 To this man Malachy betook himself to receive a rule183 of life from him, who had condemned himself while alive to such sepulture. And note his humility. From his earliest age he had had God as his teacher—there is no doubt of it—in the art of holiness; and behold, he became once more the disciple of a man, himself a man *meek and lowly in heart*.184 If we did not know it, by this one deed he himself gave us proof of it. Let them read this who attempt to teach what they have not learned, *heaping to themselves* disciples,185 though they have never been disciples, *blind leaders of the blind*.186 Malachy, *taught of God*,187 none the less sought a man to be his teacher, and that carefully and wisely. By what better method, I ask, could he both give and receive a proof of his progress? If the example of Malachy *is* for them *a very small thing*,188 let them consider the action of Paul. Did not he judge that his *Gospel*, though he had *not received it of man but* from *Christ*,189 *should be discussed* with men, *lest by any means he was running or had run in vain*?190 Where he was not confident, neither am I. If any one be thus confident191 let him take heed lest it be not so much confidence as rashness. But these matters belong to another time.

5. Now, however, the rumour of what had happened went through the city, and it was universally stirred by this new and unexpected event. All were amazed, and wondered at his virtue, all the more because it was unusual in a rude people. You would see that then *thoughts were being revealed out of the hearts of many*.192 The majority, considering the act from a human standpoint, were lamenting and grieving that a youth who was an object of love and delight to all had given himself up to such severe labours. Others, suspecting lightness on account of his age, doubted whether he would persevere, and feared a fall. Some, accusing him of rashness, were in fact highly indignant with him because he had undertaken a difficult task, beyond his age and strength, without consulting them. But without counsel he did nothing; for he had counsel from the prophet who says, *It is good for a man that he bear the yoke in his youth*, and adds, *He sitteth alone and keepeth silence because he hath borne it upon him*.193 The youth sat at the feet of Imar (for that was the man's name) and either *learned obedience*194 or showed that he had learnt it. He sat as one that was at rest, as meek, as humble. *He sat and kept silence*,195 knowing, as the prophet says, that *silence is the ornament of righteousness*.196 *He sat* as one that perseveres, *he was silent* as one that is modest, except that by that silence of his he was speaking, with holy David, in the ears of God: *I am a youth and despised, yet do not I forget thy precepts*.197 And for a time *he sat alone*, because he had neither companion nor example; for who before Malachy even thought of

attempting the most severe discipline inculcated by the man? It was held by all indeed to be wonderful, but not imitable. Malachy showed that it was imitable by the mere act of sitting and keeping silence. In a few days he had imitators not a few, stirred by his example. So he who at first *sat alone*198 and the only son of his father, became now one of many, from being *the only-begotten*199 became *the firstborn among many brethren*.200 And as he was before them in conversion,201 so was he more sublime than they in conversation; and he who came before all, in the judgement of all was eminent above all in virtue. And he seemed both to his bishop202 and to his teacher,203 worthy to be promoted to the degree of deacon. *And they constrained him.*204

6. (4) From this time onwards the Levite205 of the Lord publicly girded himself to every work of piety, but more especially to those things in which there seemed some indignity. In fact it was his greatest care to attend to the burial of the dead poor,206 because that savoured not less of humility than of humanity. Nor did *temptation* fail to test our modern Tobit,207 and, as in the old story, it came from a woman,208 or rather from the serpent through a woman.209 His sister,210 abhorring the indignity (as it seemed to her) of his office, said: "What are you doing, madman? *Let the dead bury their dead.*"211 And she attacked him daily with this *reproach*.212 But he *answered the foolish* woman *according to her folly*,213 "Wretched woman, you preserve the sound of the *pure word*,214 but you are ignorant of its force." So he maintained with devotion, and exercised unweariedly the ministry which he had undertaken under compulsion. 1119(?)For that reason also they215 deemed that the office of the priesthood should be conferred upon him. And this was done. But when he was ordained priest he was about twenty-five years old.216 And if in both his ordinations the rule of the Canons seems to have been somewhat disregarded—as indeed does seem to have been the case, for he received the Levitical ministry before his twenty-fifth, and the dignity of the priesthood before his thirtieth year217—it may well be ascribed to the zeal of the ordainer and the merits of him who was ordained.218 But for my part, I consider that such irregularity should neither be condemned in the case of a saint, nor deliberately claimed by him who is not a saint. 1120.Not content with this the bishop also committed to him his own authority219 *to sow the* holy *seed*220 in a *nation* which was not *holy*,221 and to give to a people rude and living *without law*,222 the law of life and of discipline. He received the command with all alacrity, even as he was *fervent in spirit*,223 not hoarding up his talents, but eager for profit from them.224 And behold he began to *root out* with the hoe of the tongue, *to destroy, to scatter*,225 day by day making *the crooked straight and the rough places plain*.226 *He rejoiced as a giant to run* everywhere.227 You might call him a consuming *fire* burning *the briers* of crimes.228 You might call him *an axe* or *a mattock casting down*229 evil plantings.230 He extirpated barbaric rites, he planted those of the Church. All out-worn superstitions (for not a few of them were discovered) he abolished, and, wheresoever he found it, every sort of malign influence *sent by evil angels*.231

7. In fine whatsoever came to his notice which was irregular or unbecoming or perverse his *eye did not spare*;232 but as the hail scatters the *untimely figs* from *the fig-trees*,233 and as *the wind the dust from the face of the earth*,234 so did he strive with all his might to drive out before his face and destroy entirely such things from his people. And in place of all these the most excellent legislator delivered the heavenly laws. He made regulations full of righteousness, full of moderation and integrity. Moreover in all

churches he ordained the apostolic sanctions and the decrees of the holy fathers, and especially the customs of the holy Roman Church.235 Hence it is that to this day there is chanting and psalmody in them at the canonical hours after the fashion of the whole world. For there was no such thing before, not even in the city.236 He, however, had learnt singing in his youth, and soon he introduced song into his monastery,237 while as yet none in the city, nor in the whole bishopric, could or would sing. Then Malachy instituted anew238 the most wholesome usage of Confession,239 the Sacrament of Confirmation, the Marriage contract—of all of which they were either ignorant or negligent.240 And let these serve as an example of the rest, for [here] and through the whole course of the history we omit much for the sake of brevity.

8. (5). Since he had a desire and a very great zeal for the honouring of the divine offices and the veneration of the sacraments, lest by chance he might ordain or teach anything concerning these matters otherwise than that which was in accordance with the rite of the universal Church, it came into his mind to visit Bishop Malchus,241 that he might give him fuller information on all points. He was *an old man, full of days*242 and virtues, and *the wisdom of God was in him*.243 He was of Irish nationality, but had lived in England in the habit and rule of a monk in the monastery of Winchester, from which he was promoted to be bishop in Lismore,244 a city of Munster, and one of the noblest of the cities of that kingdom. There so great grace was bestowed upon him from above that he was illustrious, not only for life and doctrine, but also for signs. Of these I set down two as examples, that it may be known to all what sort of preceptor Malachy had in the knowledge of holy things. He healed a boy, who was troubled with a mental disorder, one of those who are called lunatics, in the act of confirming him with the holy unction. This was so well known and certain that he soon made him porter of his house, and the boy lived in good health in that office till he reached manhood. He restored hearing to one who was deaf; in which miracle the deaf person acknowledged a wonderful fact, that when the saint put his fingers into his ears on either side he perceived that two things like little pigs came out of them. For these and other such deeds, his fame increased and he won a great name; so that Scots245 and Irish flowed together to him and he was reverenced by all as the one father of all.

1121 When therefore Malachy, having received the blessing of Father Imar, and having been sent by the bishop,246 came to him, after a prosperous journey, he was kindly received by the old man; and he remained with him for some years,247 in order that by staying so long he might draw fuller draughts from his aged breast, knowing that which is written, *With the ancient is wisdom.*248 But I suppose that another cause of his long sojourn was that the great Foreseer of all things would have His servant Malachy become known to all in a place to which so many resorted, since he was to be useful to all. For he could not but be dear to those who knew him. In fact one thing happened in that period, by which in some measure he made manifest to men what had been known to God as being in him.

1127 9. A conflict having taken place between the king of South Munster249—which is the southern part of Ireland—and his brother,250 and the brother being victorious, the king, driven from his kingdom, sought refuge with Bishop Malchus.251 It was not, however, in order that with his help he should recover the kingdom; but rather the devout prince *gave place unto wrath*252 and made a virtue of necessity,253 choosing to lead a private life. And when the bishop was preparing to receive the king with due honour, he declined it, saying that he preferred to be as one of those poor brothers who consorted with him, to lay aside his royal state, and to be content with the common poverty, rather to await the will of God than to get back his kingdom by force; and that he would not for his earthly honour *shed man's blood*,254 since it would *cry unto* God against him *from the ground*.255 When he heard this the bishop rejoiced greatly, and with admiration for his devotion satisfied his desire. Why more? The king is given a poor house for his dwelling, Malachy for his teacher, bread with salt and water for his food. Moreover for dainties, the presence of Malachy, his life and doctrine, were sufficient for the king; so that he might say to him, *How sweet are thy words unto my taste, yea, sweeter than honey to my mouth*.256 Besides, *every night he watered his couch with his tears*,257 and also with a daily bath of cold water he quenched the burning lust for evil in his flesh. And the king prayed in the words of another king, *Look upon my affliction and my pain; and forgive all my sins*.258 And *God did not turn away his prayer nor His mercy from him*.259 *And his supplication was heard*,260 although otherwise than he had desired. For he was troubled about his soul; but God, the avenger of innocence, willing to show men *that there is a remainder for the man of peace*,261 was preparing meanwhile *to execute a judgement for the oppressed*,262 which was utterly beyond his hope. And God *stirred up the spirit* of a neighbouring *king*:263 for Ireland is not one kingdom, but is divided into many. This king therefore seeing what had been done, was filled with wrath; and indignant, on the one hand, at the freedom of the raiders and the insolence of the proud, and on the other, pitying the desolation of the kingdom and the downfall of the king, he went down to the cell of the poor man; urged him to return, but did not succeed in persuading him. He was instant, nevertheless, pledged himself to help him, assured him that he need not doubt the result, promised that God would be with him, *whom all his adversaries would not be able to resist*.264 He laid before him also the oppression of the poor and the devastation of his country; yet he prevailed not.

10. But when to these arguments were added the command of the bishop265 and the advice of Malachy—the two men on whom he wholly depended—at length, with difficulty, he consented. A king followed a king, and according to the word of the king,266 *as was the will in heaven*,267 the marauders were driven out with absolute ease, and the man was led back to his own, with great rejoicing of his people, and was restored to his kingdom. From that time the king loved and always reverenced Malachy; so much the more because he had learned more fully in the holy man the things that were worthy of reverence and affection. For he could not be ignorant of the holiness of him with whom he had enjoyed so much intimacy in his adversity. Therefore he honoured him the more in his prosperity with constant acts of friendship, and faithful services, *and he heard him gladly, and when he heard him did many things*.268 But enough of this. Nevertheless I suppose it was not without purpose that the Lord so magnified him then *before kings*,269 but *he was a chosen vessel unto Him*, about *to bear His name before kings* and princes.270

[134] Malachy was born in 1095, before November. See below, p. 130. n. 2.

[135] *Urbanum*, citizen-like.

[136] Eph. ii. 19.

[137] Deut. xxxii. 13.

[138] *A.T.* make the curious statement that "Mael Maedoc o Mongair and his

father Mughron" died in 1102. This is perhaps sufficient evidence that Malachy's father was Mughron Ua Morgair, who according to *A.U.* was *ard fer légind* (chief professor) at Armagh, and died at Mungret, Co. Limerick, on October 5, 1102. Malachy was then only seven or eight years of age. Thus we may account for the large part taken by his mother in his early education. But a poem attributed to Malachy (*L.B.* 88) calls his father Dermot. The form of the surname varies. It is usually written Ua Morgair; but *A.T.*, *A.I.* (Ua Mongain), *L.B.* (*l.c.*), and the Yellow Book of Lecan (T.C.D. ms. H. 2. 16, p. 327 c), have Ua Mongair. The form Ua Morgair is certainly right, for it appears in the contemporary Book of Leinster (*R.I.A.* xxxv. 355-360); and Ua Mongair obviously arose out of it through confusion of the similar letters *r* and *n*. The name must have been unfamiliar, if it had not died out, when the mistake was made. Therefore we may accept Colgan's statement that the family was known as O'Dogherty in his day (*Trias*, p. 299). If so, they had probably only resumed an earlier surname: for according to MacFirbis (Royal Irish Academy ms. 23 P. 1, p. 698) Malachy was of the same stock as St. Mael Brigte, son of Tornan. The latter, as well as the O'Doghertys, were of the race of Conall Gulban (Adamnan, Genealogy opp. p. 342).

[139] 2 Sam. vii. 9.

[140] It is interesting to note the emphasis laid by St. Bernard on the influence of Malachy's mother on his life. How much he himself owed to his mother Aleth is well known. See *V.P.* i. 1, 2, 9, 10. Malachy's mother was probably a member of the family of O'Hanratty. See below, p. 27, n. 2.

[141] Prov. viii. 22.

[142] Ps. xvi. 11.

[143] Ps. xxxiv. 11.

[144] The description of Malachy's boyhood by St. Bernard may be compared with that given of his own boyhood in *V.P.* i. 3. It was written before the *Life of Malachy*.

[145] Neh. ix. 20; Ps. cxliii. 10.

[146] Ecclus. xv. 2, 3 (vg.).

[147] 2 Cor. xii. 6.

[148] Eph. iv. 2.

[149] Gal. i. 14.

[150] Ps. cxix. 99.

[151] 1 John ii. 20.

[152] Ps. lxxvii. 4 (vg.).

[153] Ps. i. 2.

[154] 1 Tim. ii. 8.

[155] *Virus uirtutum.*

[156] Armagh. See § 4.

[157] Cp. Virg. *Aen.* vi. 465.

[158] 1 Kings viii. 22, 54.

[159] *Fortiori.*

[160] Luke ii. 40, 52.

[161] John ii. 25.

[162] 1 Cor. xv. 10.

[163] 1 Kings xi. 28.

[164] 1 John v. 19.

[165] 1 Cor. ii. 12.

[166] Cp. John ii. 4 (vg.).

[167] 2 Cor. vi. 14.

[168] 1 Cor. ii. 12.

[169] Cp. Matt. v. 6.

[170] 2 Cor. i. 12 (vg.).

[171] John xiv. 30, etc.

[172] 2 Cor. iv. 7.

[173] Ps. xlv. 7.

[174] Collect of Mass for Travellers.

[175] Ps. xxi. 3.

[176] Matt. x. 39.

[177] Ps. cxxxviii. 3 (vg.).

[178] Ps. xciv. 11.

[179] His name was Imar (§ 5). He was no doubt Imar O'Hagan, who founded the monastery of St. Paul and St. Peter at Armagh, and built a stone church for it which was consecrated on October 21, 1126. It was placed, either at its foundation or subsequently, under the rule of the regular canons of St. Augustine. Imar died on pilgrimage at Rome in 1134, and is commemorated in Gorman on August 13, and in Usuard on November 12. He was at this time evidently leading the life of an anchoret. Reeves (*Churches*, p. 28) inferred from his Christian name that he had some Danish blood in his veins. There is no certain indication of Malachy's age when he became his disciple. But he had reached adolescence (§ 3), and was old enough to choose his own teachers (§ 2). In 1112 he was seventeen years of age. We shall see that he long acknowledged Imar as his master: §§ 5, 6, 8, 12, 14, 16.

[180] 1 Cor. ix. 27 (vg.).

[181] That is, apparently, the great stone church (*daimliac mór*), on which Cellach put a shingle roof in 1125. According to Reeves (*Churches*, pp. 14, 28) it was probably on the site of the present Cathedral, from which the Abbey of St. Paul and St. Peter was distant 130 yards to the north. It was the principal church of Armagh till 1268. For an account of the life of such recluses as Imar the reader may be referred to B. MacCarthy, *Codex Palatino-Vaticanus No. 830*, p. 5 f.

[182] Luke ii. 37.

[183] *Formam.* The word, as used by St. Bernard, seems to include the two notions of rule and example. It would seem that Malachy received some sort of monastic rule from Imar. Cp. § 7, "his monastery," and the reference to "the first day of his conversion" in § 43. Both passages imply that he belonged to a religious order. So in § 5 he is said to have been before the other disciples of Imar "in conversion." On later occasions he was subject to Imar's "command" (§§ 14, 16). It is not improbable that the disciples who gathered round Imar were the nucleus of the community which he founded at Armagh (note 1). If so, the inference is reasonable that Malachy became a regular canon of St. Augustine.

[184] Matt. xi. 29.

[185] Cp. 2 Tim. iv. 3.

[186] Matt. xv. 14.

[187] Isa. liv. 13; John vi. 45.

[188] 1 Cor. iv. 3.

[189] Gal. i. 11, 12.

[190] Gal. ii. 2.

[191] Printed text, *hoc scit.* I read *sit* with K (*hec sit*), and two of de Backer's MSS.

[192] Luke ii. 35.

[193] Lam. iii. 27, 28 (inexact quotation).

[194] Heb. v. 8.

[195] The rule of silence was very strictly observed by the Cistercians. This explains the stress laid by St. Bernard, here and elsewhere, on Malachy's practice. Cp. the Preface of Philip of Clairvaux to *V.P.* vi.: "In truth I have learned nothing that can more effectively deserve the riches of the grace of the Lord than to sit and be silent, and always to condescend to men of low estate."

[196] Isa. xxxii. 17 (vg.).

[197] Ps. cxix. 141 (vg.).

[198] Lam. iii. 28.

[199] John i. 14, 18.

[200] Rom. viii. 29.

[201] The technical word for entry into a religious order.

[202] Cellach, archbishop of Armagh (§ 19), son of Aedh, and grandson of Maelisa, who was abbot of Armagh 1064-1091. He was born early in 1080. Of his childhood and youth we know nothing, for the statement of Meredith Hanmer (*Chron. of Ireland* (1633), p. 101) that he is said to have been "brought up at Oxford" is probably as inaccurate as other assertions which he makes about him. Cellach was elected abbot of Armagh in August, 1105, and in the following month (September 23) he received Holy Orders. In 1106, while engaged on a visitation of Munster, he was consecrated bishop. Thus he departed from the precedent set by his eight predecessors, who were without orders (§ 19). He was one of the leaders of the Romanizing party in Ireland, and attended the Synod of Rathbreasail in 1110 (Keating, iii. 307). He died in his fiftieth year, at Ardpatrick, in co. Limerick, on April 1, 1129, and was buried on April 4 at Lismore. These facts are mainly gathered from the Annals. For more about Cellach, see p. xxxiv.

[203] Imar. See above p. 11, n. 1.

[204] Luke xxiv. 29.—Malachy can hardly have been more, he was probably less, than twenty-three years of age at this time. See p. 16, n. 2.

[205] *I.e.* deacon.

[206] It does not appear that deacons as such were specially concerned with the burial of the dead. The present passage, indeed, implies the contrary. Malachy was made deacon against his will; his care for the dead poor is mentioned as a work of piety, voluntarily superadded to the duties of his office. His sister (see below) would have been unlikely to ask him to abandon a practice which he could not decline. But there was ancient precedent for a deacon engaging in such work, of which Malachy may have been aware. At Alexandria throughout the persecution of Valerian, one of the deacons, Eusebius by name, not without danger to himself, prepared for burial the bodies of "the perfect and blessed martyrs" (Eus., *H.E.* vii. 11. 24).

[207] *Tobiae.* The Greek of the Book of Tobit, followed by the English versions, calls the father Tobit, and the son Tobias; the Vulgate calls both Tobias. The text of chap.

ii. is longer in the Vulgate than in the Greek and English, and neither of the verses (Vulg. 12, 23) from which St. Bernard here borrows words is represented in the latter.

[208] Tobit ii. 12 (vg.).

[209] Cp. Gen. iii. 12 f.

[210] She is mentioned again in § 11.

[211] Matt. viii. 22.

[212] Tobit ii. 23 (vg.).

[213] Prov. xxvi. 5.

[214] Ps. xii. 6.

[215] Cellach and Imar.

[216] Malachy completed his twenty-fifth year in 1120. See p. 130, n. 2. For the date of his ordination to the priesthood see p. 16, n. 2.

[217] For the canons of councils which regulated the minimum age of deacons and priests reference may be made to the article "Orders, Holy," by the late Dr. Edwin Hatch in the *Dictionary of Christian Antiquities*, vol. ii. p. 1482 f. From a very early date they were respectively twenty-five and thirty years, in accordance with the statement of the text, though there were some exceptions in remote places. The eighth-century Irish Canons, known as the *Hibernensis*, prescribe the same minimum ages for the diaconate and presbyterate, and add a clause, the gist of which seems to be that a bishop at the time of his consecration must be thirty or forty years of age (Wasserschleben, *Irische Kanonesammlung*, 1885, p. 8). As late as the year 1089, at the Council of Melfi, presided over by Pope Urban II., it was decreed (can. 5, Mansi, xx. 723) that none should be admitted deacon under twenty-four or twenty-five years of age, or priest under thirty. But at the Council of Ravenna, 1315 (can. 2, *ibid.* xxv. 537), the ages were lowered to twenty and twenty-five respectively.

[218] Cellach would hardly have understood the need for this apology. It is more than probable that he was ignorant of the canons referred to. He himself was ordained, apparently to the priesthood, in 1105, when he was under twenty-six, and consecrated bishop in 1106, when he was under twenty-seven years of age. St. Bernard himself seems to have been ordained priest when he was about twenty-five years old (Vacandard, i. 67).

[219] In other words he made him his vicar. This may well have been in 1120; for the Annals record that in that year Cellach made a visitation of Munster. It was quite natural that during a prolonged absence from his see he should leave its administration in the hands of one who had proved himself so capable as Malachy. And we shall see that this date harmonizes with other chronological data. If, then, we place the beginning of Malachy's vicariate in 1120, his ordination as priest, which appears to have been not much earlier, may be dated in 1119, when he was "about twenty-five years of age," *i.e.* probably soon after his twenty-fourth birthday. His admission to the diaconate may be placed at least a year earlier, *i.e.* in 1118. Indeed, if we could be sure that in Ireland the normal interval between admission to the diaconate and to the priesthood was at all as long as in other countries we might put it further back.

[220] Luke viii. 5.

[221] 1 Pet. ii. 9.

[222] Rom. ii. 12.

[223] Rom. xii. 11.

[224] Cp. Matt. xxv. 24 ff.

[225] Jer. i. 10 (vg.).

[226] Isa. xl. 4.

[227] Ps. xix. 5.

[228] Cp. Isa. x. 17.

[229] Ps. lxxiv. 6 (vg.).

[230] Cp. Ignatius, *Trall.* 11.

[231] Ps. lxxviii. 49 (vg.: inexact quotation).

[232] Ezek. v. 11, etc.

[233] Cp. Rev. vi. 13.

[234] Ps. i. 4 (vg.).

[235] Malachy acted in accordance with the aims of Gilbert, bishop of Limerick, who about the year 1108, wrote these words (*De Usu Ecclesiastico*, in Ussher, 500): "I have endeavoured to describe the canonical custom in saying the hours and performing the office of the whole ecclesiastical order ... to the end that the various and schismatical orders, with which almost the whole of Ireland has been deluded, may give place to the one Catholic and Roman office."

[236] Armagh.

[237] This was probably the monastery of SS. Peter and Paul. See p. 11, n. 5. J. de Backer's suggestion (*AA.SS.*, Nov. ii. 1, p. 147), that "his monastery" was Bangor is negatived by the whole context, which refers only to Armagh.

[238] The word "anew" (*de nouo*) seems to indicate St. Bernard's belief that it was only in comparatively recent times that the usages to which he refers had fallen into desuetude.

[239] It is interesting to observe that Confession is here not ranked as a sacrament.

[240] For the statements in this section see Additional Note A.

[241] Mael Isa Ua hAinmire, who is always called Malchus in Latin documents, though a native of Ireland, had been a monk of Winchester, as we are here told. He was elected first bishop of the Danish colony of Waterford in 1096, and was consecrated by Anselm, assisted by the bishops of Chichester and Rochester, at Canterbury on December 28, having previously made his profession of obedience to the archbishop as one of his suffragans (Eadmer, p. 76 f.; Ussher, pp. 518, 565). He signed the Acts of the Synod of Rathbreasail in 1110 as archbishop of Cashel (Keating, iii. 307). He had probably been translated to that see shortly after its foundation in 1106 (see below, p. 65, n. 4). The Synod of Rathbreasail enlarged the Danish diocese of Waterford by adding to it an extensive non-Danish area, which included the ancient religious site of Lismore, on which St. Carthach or Mochuta had founded a community in the early part of the seventh century (Lanigan, ii. 353). The Synod decreed that the see of this diocese should be either at Lismore or at Waterford, apparently giving preference to the former (see p. xlvii). It would seem that after organizing the diocese of Cashel Malchus retired to his former "parish," just as at a later date Malachy retired from Armagh to Down (§ 31), placing his see at Lismore. There, at any rate, he was established when Malachy visited him, and there he died in 1135 "after the 88th year of his pilgrimage" (*A.F.M.*). An attempt has been made to distinguish Mael Isa Ua hAinmire from the Malchus of the text (Lanigan, iv. 74), but without success. It is interesting to observe that both *A.F.M.* and *A.T.* style him bishop of Waterford in the record of his death.

[242] Gen. xxxv. 29; 1 Chron. xxiii. 1; Job xlii. 16.—Malchus was in his 75th year when Malachy visited him in 1121. See preceding note, and p. 20, n. 3.

[243] 1 Kings iii. 28.

[244] An error for Waterford. It is explained by, and confirms, the suggestion that Malchus transferred the see to Lismore.

[245] Throughout the *Life*, *Scotia* is used, in its later sense, for the country now called Scotland; and here the Scots are evidently its inhabitants. But traces of earlier usage remain in § 14, "a Scotic (*i.e.* Irish) work," § 61 "We are Scots," and § 72 where Ireland is called "further Scotland" (*ulterior Scotia*).

[246] Cellach. Note Imar's share in the matter, and cp. p. 11, n. 1.

[247] Malachy must have been the archbishop's vicar for a considerable time if the account of his labours in that capacity (§ 7) is not grossly exaggerated. Hence, if his vicariate began in 1119 or 1120 his departure for Lismore can hardly have been earlier than 1121; and as he spent "some years" there before he was raised to the episcopate (1124; see § 16), it cannot have been later. Samuel O'Hanley, bishop of Dublin, died on July 4, 1121, and Cellach at once made an attempt, which proved unsuccessful, to take possession of the vacant see. Samuel's successor, Gregory, was duly elected, and was consecrated at Lambeth on October 2. (*O.C.C.* p. 31; *A.U.* 1121; John of Worcester, ed. J. H. R. Weaver, 1908, p. 16; Ussher, 532). It may have been in August or September, on the return of Cellach from Dublin, that Malachy was released from his office and went to Lismore.

[248] Job xii. 12.

[249] I read *rex australis Mumoniae*, for *rex Mumoniae* in the printed text, restoring the word *australis* from two of de Backer's MSS. The king is said in § 18 to have been Cormac, *i.e.* Cormac Mac Carthy, son of Teague Mac Carthy, who succeeded his father as king of Desmond (South Munster) in 1124. He was never king of the whole of Munster. That he went to Lismore in 1121 is very probable. For the Annals tell us that in that year Turlough O'Conor, king of Connaught, invaded Desmond, and "arrived at the termon of Lismore" (*A.I.* say that he destroyed Lismore, which can hardly be true). What more likely than that one of the sons of Teague, the reigning monarch of Desmond, should fly before that formidable warrior to the sanctuary of Mochuta? But St. Bernard errs in supposing that he was then king of Desmond. On Cormac, see also p. 43, n. 5.

[250] Donough Mac Carthy. See next note. There is a brief notice of him in Tundale, p. 42.

[251] That the narrative of this and the following section is historical, but that St. Bernard has misplaced it, is proved by the following extract from *A.T.* under the year 1127: "A hosting by Toirdelbach, king of Ireland [really of Connaught], till he reached Corcach, he himself on land and his fleet at sea going round to Corcach, ravaging Munster by sea and by land so that he drove Cormac mac meic Carthaig into Lismore in pilgrimage. And Toirdelbach divided Munster into two parts, the southern half [Desmond] to Donnchad mac meic Carthaig; and the northern half [Thomond] to Conchobar o Briain.... Cormac mac meic Carthaig came from his pilgrimage, and made an alliance with Conchobar o Briain and with all the men of Muma, save those of Tuathmuma. Donnchad mac meic Carthaig came from them—for he was not in the alliance—with 2000 men."

The other Annals have notices to the same effect. These events occurred in 1127, three years after Malachy returned from his long stay at Lismore, and was made bishop of Connor (§ 16). If he had the part which is ascribed to him in the restoration of Cormac, he must therefore have paid two visits to Lismore, which St. Bernard has confounded. That he was in the south of Ireland for a considerable time prior to 1129 will appear later (p. 40, n. 2).

[252] Rom. xii. 19.

[253] *Necessitatem in uirtutem conuertit.* Apparently a proverbial expression. Cp. Quintilian *Declam.* iv. 10: "Faciamus potius de fine remedium, de necessitate solatium"; Jer. *Adv. Rufin.* iii. 2: "Habeo gratiam quod facis de necessitate uirtutem"; *Ep.* 54. 6 (Hilberg): "Arripe, quaeso, occasionem et fac de necessitate uirtutem." Chaucer's "To maken vertu of necessitee" is well known (*Knightes Tale*, 3042, *Squieres Tale*, 593, *Troilus and Criseyde*, iv. 1586).

[254] Gen. ix. 6.

[255] Gen. iv. 10.

[256] Ps. cxix. 103.

[257] Ps. vi. 6 (vg.).

[258] Ps. xxiv. 18.

[259] Ps. lxvi. 20.

[260] Ecclus. li. 11.

[261] Ps. xxxvii. 37 (vg.).

[262] Ps. cxlvi. 7.

[263] 2 Chron. xxxvi. 22.—Conor O'Brien. See p. 21, n. 3. It appears from the last sentence of the passage there quoted that Donough MacCarthy, to whom Turlough O'Conor had given the kingdom of Desmond, had driven out O'Brien from Thomond. This explains the anxiety of the latter to make alliance with Cormac. His action was less disinterested than St. Bernard represents it.

[264] Luke xxi. 15.

[265] Malchus.

[266] Judas Maccabæus.

[267] 1 Macc. iii. 60.

[268] Mark vi. 20.

[269] Ps. cxix. 46.

[270] Acts ix. 15.

CHAPTER II

Malachy's pity for his deceased sister. He restores the Monastery of Bangor. His first Miracles.

11. (6). Meanwhile Malachy's sister, whom we mentioned before, 271 died: and we must not pass over the visions which he saw about her. For the saint indeed abhorred her carnal life, and with such intensity that he vowed he would never see her alive in the flesh. But now that her flesh was destroyed his vow was also destroyed, and he began to see in spirit her whom in the body he would not see. One night he heard in a dream the

voice of one saying to him that his sister was standing outside in the court, and that for thirty entire days she had tasted nothing; and when he awoke he soon understood the sort of food for want of which she was pining away. And when he had diligently considered the number of days which he had heard, he discovered that it went back to the time when he had ceased to offer the *living bread from heaven*272 for her. Then, since he hated not the soul of his sister but her sin, he began again the good practice which he had abandoned. And not in vain. Not long after she was seen by him to have come to the threshold of the church, but to be not yet able to enter; she appeared also in dark raiment. And when he persevered, taking care that on no single day she should be disappointed of the accustomed gift, he saw her a second time in whitish raiment, admitted indeed within the church, but not allowed to approach the altar. At last she was seen, a third time, gathered in the company of the white-robed, and *in bright clothing.*273 You see, reader, how much *the effectual fervent prayer of a righteous man availeth.*274 Truly *the kingdom of heaven suffereth violence and the violent take it by force.*275 Does not the prayer of Malachy seem to you to have played the part as it were of a housebreaker to the heavenly gates, when a sinful woman obtained by the weapons of a brother what was denied to her own merits? This *violence*, good Jesus, Thou who *sufferest* dost exercise, strong and merciful *to save,*276 *showing* mercy and *strength with thine arm,*277 and preserving it in thy sacrament for *the saints which are in the earth,*278 *unto the end of the world.*279 Truly this sacrament is strong to *consume* sins,280 to defeat opposing powers, to bring into heaven those who are returning from the earth.

12. (7). The Lord, indeed, was so preparing His beloved Malachy in the district of Lismore for the glory of His name. But those who had sent him,281 tolerating his absence no longer, recalled him by letters. When he was restored to his people,282 now better instructed in all that was necessary, behold *a work prepared* and kept by *God*283 for Malachy. A rich and powerful man, who held the place of Bangor and its possessions, by inspiration of God immediately placed in his hand all that he had and himself as well.284 And he was his mother's brother.285 But kinship of spirit was of more value to Malachy than kinship of the flesh. The actual place also of Bangor, from which he received his name,286 the prince287 made over to him, that there he might build, or rather rebuild, a monastery. For indeed there had been formerly a very celebrated one under the first father, Comgall,288 which produced many thousands of monks, and was the head of many monasteries. A truly holy place it was and prolific of saints, *bringing forth* most abundant *fruit to God,*289 so that one of the sons of that holy community, Lugaid290 by name, is said to have been the founder—himself alone—of a hundred monasteries. I mention this in order that the reader may infer from this one instance what an immense number of others there were. In fine, to such an extent did its shoots fill Ireland and Scotland291 that those verses of David seem to have sung beforehand especially of these times, *Thou visitest the earth and blessest it; thou makest it very plenteous. The river of God is full of water: thou preparest their corn, for so thou providest for the earth, blessing its rivers, multiplying its shoots. With its drops of rain shall it rejoice while it germinates;*292 and in like manner the verses that follow. Nor was it only into the regions just mentioned, but also into foreign lands that those swarms of saints poured forth as though a *flood had risen;*293 of whom one, St. Columbanus, came up to our Gallican parts, and built the monastery of Luxovium, and was *made there a great people.*294 So great a people was it, they say, that the choirs succeeding one

another in turn, the solemnities of the divine offices went on continuously, so that not a moment day or night was empty of praises.295

13. (8) Enough has been said about the ancient glory of the monastery of Bangor. This, long ago destroyed by pirates,296 Malachy eagerly cherished on account of its remarkable and long-standing prestige, as though he were about to *replant a paradise*,297 and because *many bodies of the saints slept* there.298 For, not to speak of those which were *buried in peace*,299 it is said that nine hundred persons were slain together in one day by pirates.300 Vast, indeed, were the possessions of that place;301 but Malachy, content with the holy place alone, resigned all the possessions and lands to another. For indeed from the time when the monastery was destroyed there was always someone to hold it with its possessions. For they were both appointed by election and were even called abbots, preserving in name but not in fact what had once been.302 And though many urged him not to alienate the possessions, but to retain the whole together for himself, this lover of poverty did not consent, but caused one to be elected, according to custom, to hold them; the place, as we have said, being retained for Malachy and his followers. And perhaps, as afterwards appeared,303 he would have been wiser to have kept it all; only he looked more to humility than to peace.

14. So, then, by the command of Father Imar, taking with him about ten brethren, he came to the place and began to build. And there, one day, when he himself was cutting with an axe, by chance one of the workmen, while he was brandishing the axe in the air, carelessly got into the place at which the blow was aimed, and it fell on his spine with as much force as Malachy could strike. He fell, and all ran to him supposing that he had received a death-wound or was dead. And indeed his tunic was *rent from the top to the bottom*,304 but the man himself was found unhurt, the skin so very slightly grazed that scarcely a trace appeared on the surface. The man whom the axe had laid low, stood unharmed while the bystanders beheld him with amazement. Hence they became more eager, and were found readier for the work. And *this was the beginning of the miracles*305 of Malachy. Moreover the oratory was finished in a few days, made of smoothed planks indeed, but closely and strongly fastened together—a Scotic work,306 not devoid of beauty.307 And thenceforward God was served in it as in the ancient days; that is, with similar devotion, though not with like numbers. Malachy presided over that place for some time,308 by the ordinance of Father Imar,309 being at once the ruler and the rule of the brethren. They read in his life how they should behave themselves, and he was their leader *in righteousness and holiness before God*;310 save that besides the things appointed for the whole community he did many things of an exceptional kind, in which he still more was the leader of all, and none of the others was able to follow him to such difficult practices.

At that time and place a certain man was sick, and the devil stood by him and suggested in plain speech that he should never heed the admonitions of Malachy, but if he should enter his house, he should attack and kill him with a knife. And when this became known, those who ministered to him, the sick man himself informing them, brought word to Malachy and warned him. But he, seizing his accustomed weapons of prayer, boldly attacked his enemy, and put to flight both disease and demon. *But the* man's *name was Malchus*.311 He is brother according to the flesh of our Christian, abbot of Mellifont.312 For both are still alive, now brothers yet more, in spirit.313 For when he was delivered, immediately he was not ungrateful, but in the same place, having *turned314 to the*

Lord,315 he changed both his habit and his mind. And the brethren knew that the evil one was envious of their prosperity; and they were edified and made more careful henceforth.

15. (9). At the same place he healed a cleric, named Michael, who was suffering from dysentery and despaired of, by sending him something from his table. A second time, when the same person was smitten with a very grave disorder, he cured him both in body and mind. And from that moment *he clave to* God316 and to Malachy His servant, fearing *lest a worse thing should come unto him*,317 if once more he should be found ungrateful for so great a benefit and miracle. And at present, as we have heard, he presides over a monastery in the parts of Scotland; and this was the latest of all Malachy's foundations.318 Through such deeds of Malachy both his reputation and his community increased daily, and his name became great both within and without the monastery, though not greater than the fact. For indeed he dwelt319 there even after he was made bishop, for the place was near the city.320

[271] See § 6. Malachy's sister is here said to have died while he was at Lismore; but whether during his earlier or later visit to that place cannot be determined.

[272] John vi. 51.

[273] Acts x. 30.

[274] Jas. v. 16.

[275] Matt. xi. 12.

[276] Cp. Isa. lxiii. 1.

[277] Luke i. 51.

[278] Ps. xvi. 3.

[279] Matt. xxviii. 20.

[280] Ps vii. 9 (vg.).

[281] Cellach and Imar (§ 8).

[282] That is to Armagh. But see p. 36, n. 5.

[283] Eph. ii. 10 (vg.).

[284] This person was apparently the coarb of Comgall, the founder of Bangor. It would seem that he had been but a short time in office, for Oengus O'Gorman, coarb of Comgall, died at Lismore in 1123 (*A.U.*), probably during Malachy's sojourn there. It is not impossible that the unnamed coarb, mentioned in the text, was Murtough O'Hanratty, who died at Armagh in 1131 (*A.F.M.*). The statement that he gave "himself" to Malachy seems to mean that he placed himself under his rule in the new community.

[285] If the identification suggested in the preceding note is correct, Malachy's mother belonged to the family of O'Hanratty, which in the eleventh and twelfth centuries held the chieftaincy of Ui Méith Macha or Ui Méith Tíre, now the barony of Monaghan, in the county of the same name.

[286] *Cognominabatur.* This verb occurs seventeen times in the Vulgate, and almost always indicates a new or alternative name. In the present passage it certainly applies, not to Malachy's baptismal name, but to its Latin equivalent, Malachias, which he probably assumed when he became abbot of Bangor, or bishop of Down. The remark that he received it from Bangor is to be explained thus. A legend, which has a place in Jocelin's *Life of St. Patrick* (§ 98) and is therefore at least as old as the twelfth century, relates that Patrick, viewing the valley in which the monastery of Comgall was afterwards constructed, perceived that it was "filled with a multitude of the heavenly host." From

this story, no doubt, came the name "Valley of Angels (*Vallis Angelorum*)," by which it was known in the early seventeenth century, and probably long before (Reeves, p. 199). If this name, or the legend on which it was based, was known to Malachy it is quite conceivable that on account of his connexion with Bangor, he adopted, as the Latin alternative of Máel Máedóc, a name which is only the Hebrew for *my angel* with a Latin termination. That St. Bernard was aware of the significance of the name, and liked to dwell upon it, is clear from Sermon ii. § 5. It may be added that the legend just mentioned is connected with a folk-etymology of the word Bangor (*Bennchor*) which explained it as "white choir." For the true etymology see Kuno Meyer, "Zur Keltischen Wortkunde," § 66 (*Preuss. Akad. Sitz.*, 1913).

[287] *Princeps.* This word does not necessarily imply that the donor of Bangor was a secular chieftain. St. Bernard is somewhat arbitrary in his use of such titles; and *princeps* occurs very frequently in *A.U.* up to the tenth century as an equivalent of *abbot.*

[288] Comgall, who was a Pict of Dál Araide (Adamnan, i. 49), was born at Magheramorne, near Larne, co. Antrim (Reeves, p. 269), between 516 and 520. He founded the monastery of Bangor when he was about forty years old, probably in 559, and presided over it till his death in 602 (*A.U.*). According to his Latin Life (§ 13, Plummer, ii. 7), so great a number of monks came to him there that there was not room for them; "he therefore founded very many cells and many monasteries, not only in the district of Ulaid, but throughout the other provinces of Ireland." There were as many as 3000 monks under his rule. On the last leaf of an ancient service book of the monastery, known as the Antiphonary of Bangor (Facsimile edition by F. E. Warren, 1893, vol. ii. p. 33), there is a hymn which gives a complete list of the abbots—fifteen in number—from Comgall to Cronan († 691), in whose period of office it was written. The site of St. Comgall's monastery is beside the Rectory of the parish of Bangor, co. Down, about half-a-mile from Bangor Bay, near the entrance to Belfast Lough.

[289] Rom. vii. 4.

[290] *Luanus.* This is probably Lugaid, or Molua, the founder of Lismore in Scotland, who died in 592 (*A.U.*) and is commemorated on June 25 (Oengus, Gorman). He was a Pict and of the same tribe as St. Comgall, both being descended from Fiacha Araide (*L.B.* 15 c, e); and in later times was the patron saint of the diocese of Argyll (Adamnan, p. 371). He may be the Bishop Lugidus who ordained St. Comgall, and afterwards restrained him from leaving Ireland (Plummer, i. p. lix.; ii. pp. 6, 7). But there is no evidence, apart from the statement of St. Bernard, that either this bishop or Lugaid of Lismore was a member of the community at Bangor. There is a Life of Lugaid of Lismore in the Breviary of Aberdeen (Prop. Sanct. pro temp, aest. ff. 5 *v.* 7; summarized in Forbes, *Kalendars of Scottish Saints*, p. 410). His principal foundation after Lismore was Rosemarkie in Ross. Mr. A. B. Scott (*Pictish Nation*, 1918, p. 347 f.) mentions also Mortlach (Banffshire) and Clova (Aberdeenshire); and Bishop Forbes (*l.c.*) adds other sites with which his name is connected.

[291] St. Comgall himself is said to have been minded in his earlier days to go on pilgrimage to "Britain," and to have been dissuaded therefrom by Lugaid (Latin Life, § 13, Plummer, ii. 7). Seven years after the foundation of Bangor he went to Britain to visit "certain saints" (*ibid.* § 22, p. 11). It was probably on this occasion that he spent some time on the island of Hinba (Eilean-na-naomh?) in the company of SS. Columba, Canice and others (Adamnan, iii. 17). It was somewhat later, apparently, that St. Columba went

with some companions on a mission to Brude, king of the Picts (*ibid.* ii. 35); and we need not question the statement that Comgall and Canice were among those who went with him, though there is reason to doubt that Comgall was the leader of the band, as his Life implies (§ 51, p. 18), and though the *Life of St. Canice*, which frequently refers to his visit, or visits, to Scotland (§§ 17, 19, 21, 23, Plummer, i. 158), never mentions the incident. It is probable, therefore, that the founder of Bangor took part in the evangelization of Scotland; but the memory of very few monasteries founded by him in that country, besides the community in the island of Tiree (*Life*, § 22, p. 11; see Scott, *op. cit.* p. 239), has been preserved to later ages. Mr. Scott credits members of the community of Bangor with the foundation of Paisley, Kingarth and Applecross (*ibid.* p. 337 ff.). See also previous note.

[292] Ps. lxv. 9, 10 (vg., inexact quotation).

[293] Luke vi. 48.

[294] Gen. xii. 2.—St. Columbanus was the greatest of the Irish missionaries on the Continent of Europe. Born in Leinster, according to Bruno Krusch (*Ionae Vitae Sanctorum*, p. 22) in 530, or as others hold in 543, he entered the community of Bangor not long after its foundation, and after spending "many cycles of years" there, he sailed for France about 590. His principal monasteries were Luxeuil (Luxovium) in the department of Haute Saône, and Bobbio in Lombardy. At the latter place he died, November 23, 615. His Life was written by Jonas, about 640. It was critically edited by Krusch in *M.G.H.* (Script. rerum Merovingic., vol. iv. 1-152) and subsequently as a separate volume (*Ionae Vitae Sanctorum Columbani, Vedastis, Iohannis*, 1905). The story of his labours has been told by G. T. Stokes in his *Celtic Church in Ireland*, Lect. vii., and by many other modern writers. See also the collection of documents in Patrick Fleming's *Collectanea* (Lovanii, 1667). Luxeuil is about eighty miles from Clairvaux, and less than seventy from St. Bernard's early home at Dijon. Fifty years after the death of St. Columbanus it adopted the rule of St. Benedict. It was a well-known establishment in St. Bernard's day, though by that time its glory had declined. It was suppressed in 1789 (M. Stokes, *Three Months in the Forests of France*, p. 67).

[295] The Accemetae, founded about the middle of the fifth century, were the first to practise the *laus perennis*, from which they derived their name (*Dict. of Christian Antiquities*, s.v.). It was adopted in the early years of the following century at the monastery of St. Maurice in the Valois, from which it spread to many other religious establishments (*AA.SS.*, Nov., i. 548 ff.).

[296] *A.U.* 823 (*recte* 824): "The plundering of Bangor in the Ards by Foreigners [*i.e.* Norsemen], and the spoiling of its oratory; and the relics of Comgall were shaken out of their shrine." *A.I.* add, "and its learned men and bishops were slain with the sword."

[297] Gen. ii. 8.

[298] Matt. xxvii. 52.

[299] Ecclus. xliv. 14.

[300] This obviously exaggerated statement may refer to the event mentioned in note 2, or to a later occasion (958), when "Tanaidhe, son of Odhar, coarb of Bangor, was killed by Foreigners" (*A.U.*).

[301] "Even at the Dissolution [1539] it was found to be possessed of the temporalities and spiritualities of thirty-four townlands, together with the tithes of nine rectories or chapels" (Reeves, p. 94). The lands included the entire parish of Bangor,

together with part of the adjoining parish of Holywood, and eight outlying townlands (Archdall, ed. Moran, i. 235).

[302] This remark is interesting as showing that the title "abbot of Bangor" was in use in the twelfth century. The last person to whom it is given in the *A.U.* is Indrechtach, who died in 906. From that time onwards "coarb of Comgall" (or in one instance, "coarb of Bangor") is substituted for it. St. Bernard is supported by the Annals when he asserts that so-called abbots were elected down to Malachy's time. *A.U.* preserve the names of twenty abbots or coarbs between 824 and 1123. But St. Bernard leaves the impression that the religious community of Bangor ceased to exist on its destruction by the Norse pirates, and that subsequently the "abbots" merely held the lands that had belonged to it, and exercised no spiritual discipline. There are good reasons, however, for the contrary opinion. Thus Abbot Moengal, who died in 871, was a "pilgrim." Abbot Moenach (died 921) was "the head of the learning of the island of Ireland." Ceile, coarb of Comgall, went on pilgrimage to Rome in 928, and died there in 929: he was a scribe and anchoret, apostolic doctor of all Ireland, and (if *C.S.* can be trusted) a bishop. Dubhinnsi, bishop of Bangor, died in 953. Finally, Diarmait Ua Maeltelcha, coarb of Comgall, whom *C.S.* calls a bishop, died in 1016. It was probably not till after that date, as Reeves (p. 154) assures us, that the monastery began to decline.

[303] See §§ 61, 62.

[304] Matt. xxvii. 51.

[305] John ii. 11.

[306] "Scotic" is obviously to be understood here in its earlier meaning as equivalent to "Irish." From this departure from his ordinary usage (see p. 20, note 1) we may infer that St. Bernard is quoting the words of his authority. The habit of constructing churches of wood prevailed in early times among the Celtic and Saxon tribes in the British Isles, the introduction of stone building for such purposes being due to Roman influence (Plummer, *Bede*, ii. 101). The older custom lingered longer in Ireland than elsewhere; and by the time of Bede it had come to be regarded as characteristically Irish, though wooden churches must still have been numerous in England (Bede, *H.E.*, iii. 25). In a document of much later date, the Life of the Irish Saint Monenna (quoted in Adamnan, p. 177 f.), we read of "a church constructed of smoothed planks according to the custom of the Scottish races"; and the writer adds that "the Scots are not in the habit of building walls, or causing them to be built." Petrie (pp. 138-151) maintained that stone churches were not unusual in early Ireland; but he admits (pp. 341-344) that one type of church—the oratory (in Irish *dairtheach*, *i.e.* house of oak)—was very rarely constructed of stone. The only two passages which he cites (p. 345) as mentioning stone oratories (he says he might have produced others) are not to his purpose. The first is a notice in *A.U.* 788, of a man being killed at the door of a "stone oratory": but another, and apparently better, reading substitutes *lapide* for *lapidei*, thus altering the entry to a statement that the man was killed "by a stone at the door of the oratory." The second is Colgan's rendering (*Trias*, p. 162) of a sentence in *Trip.* iii. 74, p. 232, in which there is in reality no mention of any ecclesiastical edifice. So far as I am aware, there is no indisputable reference in Irish literature to a stone oratory earlier than the one mentioned below, § 61.

[307] Cp. the quatrain of Rummun on an oratory which was in course of construction at Rathen (*Otia Merseiana*, ii. 79):

"O my Lord! what shall I do

About these great materials?
When will these ten hundred planks
Be a structure of compact beauty?"

[308] Evidently until he became bishop. The next sentence implies that the time spent at Bangor was of considerable length, as does also the remark at the end of § 15. St. Bernard, however, seems to have been mistaken in supposing that Malachy resigned the abbacy on his consecration. See p. 36, note 5; p. 40, note 1; p. 80, note 1; p. 104, note 3; p. 112, note 5; p. 113, note 1.

[309] Cp. p. 11, note 1.

[310] Luke i. 75.

[311] John xviii. 10.

[312] For Christian and Mellifont Abbey, see § 39. This Malchus is mentioned again in § 52.

[313] This is not a mere conventional phrase. In a passionate outburst of grief St. Bernard says of his brother Gerard, who had recently died, "He was my brother by blood, yet more my brother in religion" (*Cant.* xxvi. 4).

[314] *Conversus.* Cp. p. 14, note 1. The meaning is that after his recovery Malchus entered the community of Bangor.

[315] Acts ix. 35.

[316] 2 Kings xviii. 6.

[317] John v. 14.

[318] The abbey founded by Malachy at Soulseat. See § 68.

[319] *Demorabatur*, literally, *lingered*, or *tarried*. The fact seems to be that Bangor was Malachy's headquarters for the rest of his life, except the ten years which intervened between his expulsion from it (§ 18), and his resignation of the see of Armagh (§ 31). See p. 33, note 1. St. Bernard was apparently puzzled by the fact that Malachy continued to live at Bangor after his consecration, instead of going to the see-city; and he makes a not very satisfactory apology for it.

[320] The city is evidently Connor; but it is not near Bangor. The two places are twenty-five miles apart, and Belfast Lough lies between them. In Malachy's day they were in different tribal territories.

CHAPTER III

St. Malachy becomes Bishop of Connor; he builds the Monastery of Iveragh.

16. (10). At that time an episcopal see was vacant,321 and had long been vacant, because Malachy would not assent: for they had elected him to it.322 But they persisted, and at length he yielded when their entreaties were enforced by the command of his teacher,323 together with that of the metropolitan.324 It was when he was just entering the thirtieth year of his age,325 that he was consecrated bishop and brought to Connor; for that was the name of the city through ignorance of Irish ecclesiastical affairs St. Bernard misunderstood the information supplied to him, and thus separated Malachy's tenure of the abbacy of Bangor from his episcopate, though the two were in reality

conterminous. For the significance of Malachy's recall to the North, see Introduction, p. liii. f.; and for a fuller discussion, *R.I.A.*, xxxv. 250-254..

1124   But when he began to administer his office, the man of God understood that he had been sent not to men but to beasts. Never before had he known the like, in whatever depth of barbarism; never had he found men so shameless in regard of morals, so dead in regard of rites, so impious in regard of faith, so barbarous in regard of laws, so stubborn in regard of discipline, so unclean in regard of life. They were Christians in name, in fact pagans.326 There was no giving of tithes or first-fruits; no entry into lawful marriages, no making of confessions: nowhere could be found any who would either seek penance or impose it. Ministers of the altar were exceeding few. But indeed what need was there of more when even the few were almost in idleness and ease among the laity? There was no fruit which they could bring forth from their offices among a people so vile. For in the churches there was not heard the voice either of preacher or singer.327 What was *the athlete of the Lord*328 to do? He must either yield with shame or with danger fight. But he who recognized that he was *a shepherd and not a hireling*, elected to stand rather than to *flee*, prepared to *give his life for the sheep* if need be.329 And although all were wolves and there were no sheep, the intrepid shepherd stood in the midst of the wolves, rich in all means by which he might make sheep out of wolves330—admonishing in public, arguing in secret, weeping with one and another; accosting men now roughly, now gently, according as he saw it to be expedient for each. And in cases where these expedients failed he offered for them a *broken and a contrite heart*.331 How often did he spend entire nights in vigil, holding out his hands in prayer! And when they would not come to the church he went to meet the unwilling ones *in the streets and in the broad ways*, and *going round about the city*, he eagerly *sought*332 whom he might gain for Christ.

17. (11). But further afield also, none the less, he very frequently traversed country parts and towns with that holy band of disciples, who never left his side. He went and bestowed even on *the unthankful333 their portion of* the heavenly *meat*.334 Nor did he ride on a horse, but went afoot, in this also proving himself an apostolic man. Good Jesus, *how great things* thy warrior *suffered for Thy name's sake*335 from *crime-stained children*.336 How great things he endured for Thee from those very men to whom, and on whose behalf, he spoke good things. Who can worthily express with how great vexations he was harassed, with what insults he was assailed, with what unrighteous acts provoked,337 how often he was faint with hunger, how often afflicted *with cold and nakedness*?338 Yet *with them that hated peace he was a peacemaker,339 instant*, nevertheless, *in season, out of season*.340 *Being defamed he intreated*;341 when he was dealt with unrighteously he defended himself with the shield of patience and *overcame evil with good*.342 Why should he not overcome? *He continued knocking*,343 and according to the promise, at length, sometimes, *to him that knocked it was opened*.344 How could that not follow which *the Truth*345 had declared beforehand should follow? *The right hand of the Lord brought mighty things to pass*,346 because the *mouth of the Lord spoke*347 the truth. Hardness vanished, barbarity ceased; the *rebellious house*348 began gradually to be appeased, gradually to admit reproof, *to receive discipline*.349 Barbarous laws disappear, Roman laws are introduced; everywhere the ecclesiastical customs are received, their opposites are rejected; churches350 are rebuilt, a clergy is appointed in them; the solemnities of the sacraments are duly celebrated; confessions are made; congregations351 come to the church; the celebration of marriage graces those

who live together.352 In fine, all things are so changed for the better that to-day the word which the Lord speaks by the prophet is applicable to that nation; *those who* before *were not my people are now my people*.353

1127 18. (12). It happened after some years that the city354 was destroyed by the king of the northern part of Ireland;355 for *out of the north* all *evil breaks forth*.356 And perhaps that evil was good for those who used it well. For who knows that God did not wish to destroy by such a scourge the ancient evils of His people? By a necessity so dire Malachy was compelled, and he retired with a crowd of his disciples. Nor was his retirement spent in idleness. It gave opportunity for building the monastery of Iveragh,357 Malachy going there with his brothers, in number one hundred and twenty.358 There King Cormac met him. He it was who at a former time driven out of his kingdom, under the care of Malachy by the mercy of God received consolation;359 and that place was in his kingdom. The king rejoiced to see Malachy, placing at the disposal of him and those who were with him himself and all that he had—as one who was neither ungrateful nor unmindful of a benefit. Many beasts were immediately brought for the use of the brothers; much gold and silver was also supplied, with regal munificence, for the expense of the buildings. He himself also *was coming in and going out with them*,360 busy and ready to serve—in attire a king, but in mind a disciple of Malachy. And the Lord *blessed* that place *for* Malachy's *sake*,361 and in a short time he was made great in goods, possessions and persons. And there, as it were beginning anew, the burden of law and discipline which he laid on others he bore with greater zeal himself, their bishop and teacher. Himself, *in the order of his course*,362 did duty as cook, himself served the brothers while they sat at meat.363 Among the brothers who succeeded one another in singing or reading in church he did not suffer himself to be passed over, but strenuously fulfilled the office in his place as one of them. He not only shared but took the lead in [the life] of holy poverty, being especially zealous for it *more abundantly than they all*.364

[321] Connor: see below. It is clear that after Malachy's consecration it was the see of a diocese which included Bangor (§ 15) and Down, the present Downpatrick (§ 31). The inference is highly probable that it included the whole district which constituted the "parish [*i.e.* diocese] of Connor," according to the decree of the Synod of Rathbreasail in 1110 (Keating, iii. 303: see above p. xli), that is to say, roughly, the present united dioceses of Down, Connor and Dromore. It would seem that Malachy was its first bishop.

[322] Here, again, St. Bernard implies that a long period elapsed between Malachy's return from Lismore and his consecration; for the reason given in § 12 for his recall is inconsistent with the supposition that he had already been elected to a bishopric which Cellach and Imar wished him to accept. They desired to have him with them at Armagh. He must have been "elected" either while he was at Armagh or after he went to Bangor.

[323] Imar.

[324] Cellach. See § 19, where Cellach and his predecessors are called metropolitans.

[325] *Tricesimo ferme aetatis suae anno. A.F.M.* record under the year 1124 that "Mael Maedoc Ua Morgair sat in the bishopric of Connor." This agrees with the date of his consecration as given here. See p. 128, note 1. He was consecrated bishop by Cellach (§ 19).

We have seen (p. 20, note 3) that Malachy probably went to Lismore late in 1121. He spent several years there, and, according to St. Bernard, another long period at Armagh and Bangor before his consecration in 1124. This must be pronounced impossible. The most probable solution of the chronological difficulty is that through ignorance of Irish ecclesiastical affairs St. Bernard misunderstood the information supplied to him, and thus separated Malachy's tenure of the abbacy of Bangor from his episcopate, though the two were in reality conterminous. For the significance of Malachy's recall to the North, see Introduction, p. liii. f.; and for a fuller discussion, *R.I.A.*, xxxv. 250-254.

[326] Cp. Giraldus, *Top.* iii. 19: "It is wonderful that this nation should remain to this day so ignorant of the rudiments of Christianity. For it is a most filthy race, a race sunk in vice, a race more ignorant than all other nations of the rudiments of the faith."

[327] For the statements in the preceding sentences, see Additional Note A.

[328] St. Aug., *De Civ. Dei*, xiv. 9. 2. Cp. Ignatius, *Pol.* 2; *Hero* 1. It may be noted that most of the MSS. of the Latin version of the Ignatian Epistles are Burgundian, and that among them is a Clairvaux MS. of the 12th century. Lightfoot, *Ign. and Pol.*, i. 119.

[329] John x. 11-13.

[330] Compare St. Bernard's words to Pope Eugenius III. about his Roman subjects (*De Cons.*, iv. 6): "I know where thou dwellest, unbelievers and subverters are with thee. They are wolves, not sheep; of such, however, thou art shepherd. Consideration is good, if by it thou mayest perhaps discover means, if it can be done, to convert them, lest they subvert thee. Why do we doubt that they can be turned again into sheep, who were once sheep and could be turned into wolves?"

[331] Ps. li. 17.

[332] Cant. iii. 2; cp. Ps. lix. 6, 14; Luke xiv. 21.

[333] Luke vi. 35.

[334] Luke xii. 42.

[335] Acts ix. 16.

[336] Isa. i. 4 (vg.).

[337] Cp. 2 Pet. ii. 7 f.

[338] 2 Cor xi. 27.

[339] Ps. cxx. 6, 7 (vg.).

[340] 2 Tim. iv. 2.

[341] 1 Cor. iv. 13.

[342] Rom. xii. 21.

[343] Acts xii. 16.

[344] Matt. vii. 8; Luke xi. 10.

[345] John xiv. 6.

[346] Ps. cxviii. 15, 16.

[347] Isa. i. 20.

[348] Ezek. ii. 5, etc.

[349] Lev. xxvi. 23 (vg.).

[350] *Basilicae.*

[351] *Plebes.*

[352] See Additional Note A.

[353] 1 Pet. ii. 10, combined with Hos. ii. 24.

[354] The city was Bangor, though St. Bernard may have taken it to be Connor. The word city (*civitas*), which he no doubt found in his authority, might be applied, like its Irish equivalent, *cathair*, to either place: but to St. Bernard it would naturally suggest an episcopal see. Connor was within the suzerainty of the king of the northern part of Ireland, Bangor was outside it. See next note.

[355] Conor O'Loughlin, who is called king of the north of Ireland in the Annals (s.a. 1136). He succeeded his father Donnell as king of Ailech (Grenan Ely, co. Donegal, the residence of the kings of the northern Ui Neill) in 1121, and the next year he invaded the northern part of Ulaid, the district in which Bangor is situated. He invaded Magh Cobha (Iveagh, co. Down) and Bregha (Meath), with the help of the Dal Araide (the district round Connor, co. Antrim) in 1128. He finally subdued Ulaid in 1130, and "plundered the country as far as the east of Ard [*i.e.* the baronies of the Ards, in which lies Bangor], both lay and ecclesiastical property." He was murdered on May 25, 1136 (*A.U., A.L.C.*). It has been supposed that the expedition of 1130 was the occasion of the destruction of Bangor mentioned in the text. But St. Bernard places it, and the consequent departure of Malachy to the south, before the death of Cellach in 1129 (§ 19), and we have found reason to believe that Malachy was at Lismore in 1127 (p. 21, n. 3). Though no raid by Conor in that year is referred to in the Annals, that fact cannot be regarded as proof that none took place.

[356] Jer. i. 14.

[357] *Ibracense.* That this monastery was in Iveragh, a barony in the county of Kerry, north of the estuary of the Kenmare River, and in Cormac Mac Carthy's kingdom of Desmond, was apparently first suggested by Lanigan (iv. 92). The identification is almost certainly correct. It is more difficult to determine the part of the barony in which the monastery was situated. O'Hanlon suggested Church Island, near Cahirciveen, where there are some ecclesiastical remains, traditionally known half a century ago as "the monastery" (*R.I.A.* xv. 107). But these appear to be of much earlier date than the twelfth century. More plausible is the conjecture of the Rev. Denis O'Donoghue, that the site is on another Church Island, in Lough Currane, near Waterville. On it are the ruins of a church which, in the opinion of Mr. P. J. Lynch, was built in the twelfth century (*J.R.S.A.I.* xxx. 159 f.). Malachy seems to have spent some time at Lismore before going to Iveragh.

[358] This sentence seems to imply that Malachy brought with him the Bangor community, or the greater part of it, and made a new home for it in Iveragh. If so the inference is obvious that up to 1127 Malachy resided at Bangor, and was still abbot.

[359] See §§ 9, 10.

[360] Acts ix. 28 (inexact quotation).

[361] Gen. xxx. 27.

[362] Luke i. 8.

[363] Cp. Luke xii. 37; xxii. 27.

[364] Cp. 1 Cor. xv. 10; 2 Cor. xi. 23.

CHAPTER IV.

Being made Archbishop of Armagh, he suffers many troubles. Peace being made, from being Archbishop of Armagh he becomes Bishop of Down.

1129   19. (12). Meanwhile365 it happened that Archbishop Cellach366 fell sick: he it was who ordained Malachy deacon, presbyter and bishop: and knowing that he was dying he made a sort of testament367 to the effect that Malachy ought to succeed him,368 because none seemed worthier to be bishop of the first see. This he gave in charge to those who were present, this he commanded to the absent, this to the two kings of Munster369 and to the magnates of the land he specially enjoined by the authority of St. Patrick.370 For from reverence and honour for him, as the apostle of that nation, who had converted the whole country to the faith, that see where he presided in life and rests in death371 has been held in so great veneration by all from the beginning, that not merely bishops and priests, and those who are of the clergy, but also all kings and princes are subject to the metropolitan372 in all obedience, and he himself alone presides over all. But a very evil custom had developed, by the devilish ambition of certain powerful persons, that the holy see373 should be held by hereditary succession. For they suffered none to be bishops but those who were of their own tribe and family. And for no short time had the execrable succession lasted, for fifteen generations (as I may call them)374 had already passed in this wickedness. And to such a point had *an evil and adulterous375 generation*376 established for itself this distorted right, rather this unrighteousness worthy of punishment by any sort of death, that although at times clerics failed of that blood, yet bishops never. In a word there had been already eight before Cellach, married men, and without orders, albeit men of letters.377 Hence, throughout the whole of Ireland, all that subversion of ecclesiastical discipline, that weakening of censure, that abandonment of religion of which we have spoken already; hence everywhere that substitution of raging barbarism for Christian meekness—yea, a sort of paganism brought in under the name of Christianity. For—a thing unheard of from the very beginning of the Christian faith—bishops were transferred and multiplied, without order or reason, at the will of the metropolitan, so that one bishopric was not content with one bishop, but nearly every single church had its bishop.378 No wonder; for how could the members of so diseased a head be sound?

 1132   20. Cellach, greatly grieving for these and other like evils of his people—for he was a good and devout man—took all care to have Malachy as his successor, because he believed that by him this evilly rooted succession might be torn up,379 since he was dear to all, and one whom all were zealous to imitate, *and the Lord was with him*.380 Nor was he deceived of his hope; for when he died Malachy was put into occupation in his room. But not soon nor easily. For behold there is one of the evil seed to seize the place—Murtough by name.381 For five years, relying on the secular power,382 this man fastened himself upon the church, not a bishop but a tyrant. For the wishes of the devout had rather supported the claim of Malachy. At last they urged him to undertake the burden according to the ordinance of Cellach. But he, who shunned every high office as nothing else than his downfall,383 thought that he had found good ground of excuse, because at that time it was impossible that he should have a peaceful entry. All were eager for so holy a work and pressed him; especially the two bishops, Malchus384 and Gilbert,385 of whom the former was the elder386 of Lismore mentioned above, the second he who is said to have been the first to exercise the office of legate of the

Apostolic See throughout the whole of Ireland. These, when three years had now passed in this presumption of Murtough and dissimulation of Malachy,387 tolerating no longer the adultery of the church and the dishonour of Christ, called together the bishops and princes of the land,388 and came, in one spirit, to Malachy, prepared to use force. But he refused at first; pleading the difficulty of the project, the numbers, strength and ambition of that noble stock, urging that it was a great venture for him, a poor man and of no account, to oppose himself to men so many, so great, of such sort, so deeply rooted, who now for well-nigh two hundred years had *held* as *by hereditary right the sanctuary of God*,389 and now also had taken possession of it before him; that they could not be rooted out, not even at the cost of human life; that it was not to his advantage that *man's blood should be shed*390 on his account; and lastly, that he was joined to another spouse391 whom *it was* not *lawful for him to put away*.392

21. (14). But when they persisted eagerly in the contrary opinion, and cried out that the *word had come forth from the Lord*,393 and moreover ordered him with all authority to undertake the burden, and threatened him with an anathema, he said, "You are leading me to death, but I obey in the hope of martyrdom; yet on this condition, that if, as you expect, the enterprise has good success, and God frees his *heritage* from *those that are destroying* it,394 all being then at length completed, and the church395 at peace, it may be lawful for me to return to my former spouse and friend, poverty,396 from which I am carried off, and to put in my place there another, if then one is found fit for it." Note, reader, the courage of the man and the purity of his purpose who, for Christ's name, neither sought honour nor dreaded death. What could be purer or what braver than this purpose, that after exposing himself to peril and labour he should yield to another the fruit—peace and security itself in the place of authority? And this he does, retaining for himself according to agreement a free return to poverty when peace and freedom are restored to the church. When they gave the pledge, at length he assented to their will; or rather to the will of God, who, he remembered, had long foreshown to him this occurrence, at the fulfilment of which he was now grieved. For indeed when Cellach was already ailing there appeared to Malachy—far away and ignorant [of Cellach's condition] —a woman of great stature and reverend mien. When he inquired who she was, the answer was given that she was the wife of Cellach.397 And she gave him a pastoral staff which she held in her hand, and then disappeared. A few days later, Cellach, when he was dying, sent his staff to Malachy, indicating that he should succeed him: and when he saw it he recognized that it was the same which he had seen [in vision]. It was the remembrance of this vision which specially put Malachy in fear, lest if he still refused he might seem to *resist* the Divine *will*, which he had ignored long enough.398 But he did not enter the city as long as that intruder lived, lest by such act it should happen that any one of those should die to whom he came rather to minister life. Thus for two years (for so long the other survived), living outside the town, he strenuously performed the episcopal office throughout the whole province.399

1134, Sept. 17   22. (15). When that person, then, had been removed by sudden death,400 again one Niall [*Nigellus*] (in truth *nigerrimus*, very black)401 quickly took possession of the see. And in appointing him as his successor, Murtough, while he was still alive, *made provision for his life*:402 he was going forth to be damned, but in the person of Niall he would go on adding to the works of damnation.403 For he also was of the damned race, a relative of Murtough.404 But the king405 and the bishops and faithful of the land nevertheless came together that they might bring in Malachy. And lo, there was an *assembly of the wicked*406 to oppose them.407 A certain man of the sons of Belial, ready for *mischief, mighty in iniquity*,408 who *knew the place* where they had decided *to come together*,409 gathered many with him and secretly seized a neighbouring high hill opposite to it, intending, when they were engaged with other things, suddenly to rush upon them unawares and *murder the innocent*.410 For they had agreed to butcher the king also with the bishop, that there might be none to *avenge the righteous blood*.411 The plan became known to Malachy, and he entered the church, which was close by, and lifted up his hands in prayer to the Lord. Lo, there came *clouds and darkness*,412 yea also *dark waters and thick clouds of the skies413 changed the day into night*,414 *lightnings and thunderings*415 and *an horrible spirit of tempests*416 presaged the last day, *and all* the elements *threatened* speedy *death*.417

23. But that you may know, reader, that it was the prayer of Malachy that roused the elements, the tempest fell upon those *who sought his life*,418 the *dark whirlwind*419 enveloped only those who had made ready *the works of darkness*.420 Finally, he who was the leader of so great wickedness was struck by a thunderbolt and perished with three others, companions in death as they had been partners in crime; and the next day their bodies were found half-burnt and putrid, clinging to the branches of trees, each where the wind421 *had lifted him up and cast him down*.422 Three others also were found half dead; the rest were all scattered in every direction. But, as for those who were with Malachy, though they were close to the place, the storm *touched them not at all, neither troubled them*.423 In that fact we find fresh proof of the truth of that saying, *The prayer of the righteous pierceth the heavens*.424 It is also a new example of the ancient miracle, by which in former times, when all Egypt was in darkness, Israel alone remained in light, as the Scripture says, *Wheresoever Israel was there was light*.425 In this connexion occurs to me also what holy Elijah did, at one time bringing clouds and rain from the ends of the earth,426 at another, calling down fire from heaven on the revilers.427 And now in like manner *God is glorified in*428 His servant Malachy.

24. (16). In the thirty-eighth year of his age,429 the usurper having been driven out, the poor man, Malachy, entered Armagh, pontiff and metropolitan of all Ireland. But when the king and the others who had brought him in returned home,430 he remained *in the hand of God*;431 and there remained for him *without fightings, within fears*.432 For, lo, the viperous brood, raging and crying out that it was disinherited, aroused itself in full strength, within and without, *against the Lord and against His Anointed*.433 Moreover, Niall, seeing that flight was inevitable,434 took with him certain insignia of that see, to wit, the copy of the Gospels, which had belonged to blessed Patrick,435 and the staff covered with gold and adorned with most costly gems, which they call "the staff of Jesus," because the Lord himself (as report affirms) held it in His hands and fashioned it;436 which are deemed of the highest honour and sanctity in that nation. They are, in fact, very well known and celebrated among the tribes, and so revered by all, that he who is once seen to have them is held by the *foolish and unwise people*437 to be their bishop. That man—a vagabond438 and another *Satan*—*went to and fro in the land and walked up and down in it*,439 bearing round the holy insignia; and, displaying them everywhere, he was for their sake everywhere received, by them winning the minds of all to himself, and withdrawing as many as he could from Malachy. These things did he.

25. But there was a certain prince, of the more powerful of the unrighteous

race,440 whom the king before he left the city, had compelled to swear that he would maintain peace with the bishop, taking from him, moreover, many hostages. Notwithstanding this, when the king left he entered the city, and took *counsel* with his kinsmen and friends *how they might take* the holy man *by subtlety and kill him; but they feared the people*;441 and having conspired to slay Malachy442 they fixed a place and day, and a traitor *gave them a sign*.443 On that very day, when the prelate was now celebrating the solemnity of Vespers in the church with the whole of the clergy and a multitude of the people, that worthless man sent him a message in *words of peace with subtlety*,444 asking him that he would deign to come down to him, so that he might make peace. The bystanders answered that he should rather come to the bishop, and that the church was a more suitable place for establishing peace; for they foresaw guile. The messengers replied that this was not safe for the prince; that he feared for his head, and that he did not trust himself to the crowds who, some days before, had nearly killed him for the bishop's sake. As they were contending in this way, these saying that he should go, those that he should not go, the bishop, desiring peace and not afraid to die, said, "Brethren, let me imitate my Master.445 I am a Christian to no purpose if I do not *follow* Christ.446 Perhaps by humility I shall bend the tyrant; if not, yet I shall conquer by rendering, a shepherd to a sheep, a priest to a layman, that duty which he owed to me. You also, as far as in me lies, I shall edify not a little by such an example. For what if I should chance to be killed? *I refuse not to die*,447 in order that from me you may have an example of life. It behoves a bishop, as the prince of bishops says, not *to be lord over the clergy, but to become an example to the flock*448—no other example449 truly than that which we have received from Him *who humbled himself and became obedient unto death*.450 Who will give me [the opportunity] to leave this [example] to [my] sons, sealed with my blood? Try, at any rate, whether your priest has worthily learnt from Christ not to fear death for Christ." And he arose and went his way, all weeping, and praying that he would not so greatly desire to die for Christ that he should leave desolate so great a flock of Christ.

26. (17). But as for him, *setting his whole hope* in the Lord,451 he went with all speed accompanied only by three disciples who were *ready to die with him*.452 *When he crossed the threshold*453 of the house and suddenly came into the midst of the armed men—himself protected by the *shield of faith*454—the *countenances* of them all *fell*,455 for *dread fell upon them*,456 so that the bishop could say, *Mine enemies which trouble me became weak and fell*.457 This *word is true*.458 You might see the victim standing, the slaughterers surrounding him on all sides, with weapons in their hands; and there was none to sacrifice him. You might suppose their arms were benumbed; for there was none to stretch out a hand. For even that one also, who seemed to be the head of the evil, rose up, not to assail him but to show him reverence. Where is the sign, O man, which you had given for the death of the pontiff? This is a sign rather of honour than death; this postpones, it does not hasten death. Wonderful result! They offer peace who had prepared slaughter. He cannot refuse it who had sought it at the risk of life. Therefore peace was made—a peace so firm that from that day the priest found his foe not merely appeased, but obedient, devoted.459 When they heard this, all the faithful rejoiced, not only because *the innocent blood was saved in that day*,460 but because by the merits of Malachy the souls of many wrongdoers escaped to salvation. And fear took hold on all that were round about when they heard how God had laid low, with sudden power, those

two of His enemies who seemed most ferocious and powerful *in their generation*:461 I refer to him with whom we are now concerned, and the other of whom I spoke above.462 For in a wonderful manner He *took them* both—one terribly punished in the body,463 the other mercifully changed in heart464—*in the devices that they had imagined*.465

1135, July(?) 27. These matters so accomplished, the bishop now began to dispose and order in the city all things pertaining to his ministry with entire freedom, but not without constant risk of his life. For though there was no one now who would harm him openly, yet the bishop had no place that was safe from plotters, and no time when he could be at ease; and armed men were appointed to guard him day and night, though he rather *trusted in the Lord*.466 But his purpose was to take action against the schismatic already mentioned, forasmuch as he was seducing many by means of the insignia which he carried about, persuading all that he ought to be bishop, and so stirring up the congregations467 against Malachy and the unity of the church.468 And thus he did; and without difficulty in a short time he so *hedged up* all *his ways469 through the grace given unto him by the Lord*,470 and which he had toward all, that that evil one was compelled to surrender, to return the insignia,471 and henceforth to be quiet in *all subjection*.472 Thus Malachy, albeit through many perils and labours, prospered day by day and was strengthened, *abounding* more and more *in hope and the power of the Holy Ghost*.473

28. (18). And God swept away, not only those who did evil to Malachy, but also those who disparaged him. A certain man, for example, who was in favour with the princes and magnates, and even with the king himself,474 because he was a flatterer and garrulous and *mighty in tongue*,475 befriended Malachy's opponents in all things, and impudently maintained their contention. On the other hand, when the saint was present, he *withstood him to the face*,476 and when he was absent he disparaged him. Moreover he accosted him rudely everywhere, and especially when he knew that he was engaged in the more frequented assemblies. But he was soon visited with a suitable reward of his impudent tongue. The evil-speaking tongue swelled, and *became putrid and worms swarmed* from it477 and filled the whole blasphemous mouth. He vomited them forth incessantly for well-nigh seven days, and at length with them spued out his wretched soul.

29. Once when Malachy was speaking before the people and exhorting them, a certain unhappy woman dared to interrupt his discourse with evil cries, showing no respect to the priest *and the Spirit which spake*.478 Now she was of the impious race; and having *breath in her nostrils*479 she vomited out blasphemies and insults against the saint, saying that he was a hypocrite, and an invader of the inheritance of another, and even reproaching him for his baldness. But he, modest and gentle as he was, *answered* her *nothing*;480 but the Lord answered for him. The woman became insane by the judgement of the Lord, and crying out many times that she was being suffocated by Malachy, at length by a horrible death she expiated the sin of blasphemy. So this wretched woman, taking up against Malachy the reproach that had been made against Elisha,481 found to her cost that he was indeed another Elisha.

30. Further, because on account of a certain pestilence which arose in the city, he had solemnly led out a multitude of the clergy and people with the memorial of the saints,482 neither is this to be passed over, that when Malachy prayed the pestilence immediately ceased. Thenceforward there was none to murmur against him, for those

who were of the *seed of Canaan483 said, Let us flee from the face of* Malachy, *for the Lord fighteth for him.*484 But it was too late, for the wrath of the Lord, coming everywhere upon them, pursued them *even unto destruction.*485 How, in a few days, *is their memorial perished with resounding noise;486 how are they brought into desolation, they are consumed in a moment, they are punished for their iniquity.*487 A great miracle to-day is the extinction of that generation, so quickly wrought, especially for those who knew their pride and power.488 And *many other signs truly*489 were there by which God glorified His name and strengthened His servant amidst labours and dangers. Who can worthily recount them? Yet we do not omit them all, though we have not ability to describe all. But that the sequence of the narrative may not be interrupted we reserve to the end some that we propose to mention.

1137   31. (19). So then Malachy, when within three years490 *a reward was rendered to the proud*491 and liberty restored to the church, barbarism driven out and the customs of the Christian religion everywhere instituted anew, seeing that all things were at peace, began to think also of his own peace. And mindful of his design he appointed in his own place Gelasius,492 a good man, and worthy of so great an honour, the clergy and people tacitly assenting, or rather supporting him because of the agreement.493 For apart from that it seemed altogether cruel. And when he had been consecrated and earnestly commended to the kings and princes, Malachy himself, renowned for miracles and triumphs, returned to his parish;494 but not to Connor. Hear the cause, which is worth relating. It is said that that diocese in ancient times had two episcopal sees, and that there were two bishoprics; an arrangement which seemed to Malachy preferable to the existing one. Hence those bishoprics which ambition had welded into one,495 Malachy divided again into two, yielding one part to another bishop and retaining the other for himself. And for this reason he did not come to Connor, because he had already ordained a bishop in it;496 but he betook himself to Down, separating the parishes *as in the days of old.*497 O pure heart! O dove-like eye!498 He handed over to the new bishop the place which seemed better organized, which was held to be more important, the place in which he himself had sat. Where are they that fight about boundaries, carrying on perpetual hostilities against one another for a single village? I know not if there is any class of men whom that ancient prophecy touches more than those: *They have ripped up the women with child of Gilead that they might enlarge their border.*499 But this at another place.500

32. When Malachy was made bishop of Down, immediately according to his custom he was at pains to take to himself from his sons, for his comfort, a convent of regular clerics.501 And lo, again he girds himself, as though a new recruit of Christ, for the spiritual conflict; again he puts on the *weapons* that are *mighty through God,*502 the humility of holy poverty, the rigour of monastic discipline, the quietness of contemplation, continuance in prayer. But all these things for a long time he was able to maintain rather in will than in deed. For all men came to him; not only obscure persons, but also nobles and magnates, hastened to commit themselves to his wisdom and holiness for instruction and correction. And he himself meanwhile went about; *he went out to sow his seed,*503 disposing and decreeing with all authority concerning ecclesiastical affairs, like one of the Apostles. And none *said unto him, By what authority doest thou these things?*504 inasmuch as all *saw the miracles* and wonders *which* he did,505 and because *where the Spirit of the Lord is, there is liberty.*506

[365] That is, while Malachy was in Iveragh.

[366] Cellach is here mentioned by name for the first time. See p. 14, n. 2.

[367] Harris (*Ware's Works*, ii., "Writers," p. 69) identifies this testament with the *Testamentum ad ecclesias*, a tract attributed to Cellach, which is apparently no longer extant. But it may be doubted whether the testament mentioned in the text was committed to writing.

[368] The designation by a coarb of his successor seems to have been unusual. But in 1124 Malachy had in this way been appointed abbot of Bangor (§ 12); and in 1134 Murtough designated Niall as his successor in the abbacy of Armagh (§ 22).

[369] Conor O'Brien, king of Thomond, and Cormac Mac Carthy, king of Desmond. See § 9, and p. 21, notes 1-3. Murtough O'Brien, king of Munster, fell into ill-health in 1114, and his brother Dermot attempted, evidently with some success, to seize the throne. Dermot died in 1118 and Murtough early in the following year. Turlough O'Conor, the powerful king of Connaught, promptly invaded Munster, and divided it into two vassal kingdoms, Thomond and Desmond. The former he gave to the sons of Dermot, of whom Conor was one, the latter to Teague Mac Carthy. Apparently Conor O'Brien soon established himself as sole king of Thomond, and Cormac Mac Carthy became king of Desmond on the death of his father, Teague, in 1124. We have seen that both of them were deposed in 1127, and quickly restored (§ 9 f.: see p. 21, n. 3; p. 23, n. 2). From that time Conor and Cormac were allies. Cormac married Conor's niece (*A.T.* 1138). Together in 1133 they invaded Connaught (*A.F.M.*), and the next year they made another successful expedition through Connaught into Ulster (then ruled by Conor O'Loughlin; see p. 40, n. 2), in the course of which they burned the church of Rathluraigh, now Maghera, co. Derry, near the border of the diocese of Armagh (*D.A.I.*). This expedition must be referred to hereafter (p. 51, n. 2). But Conor evidently aspired to be *ardrí* of Ireland, and he found it desirable to remove a possible rival. Accordingly Cormac was murdered by his father-in-law, Conor's brother, in 1138, and Conor became king of all Munster. He was now the most powerful prince in Ireland; but he died, after a lingering illness (Tundale, p. 42), in 1142, without attaining his ambition.

It is clear from the present passage that Conor O'Brien followed in the footsteps of his predecessors in the same family as a supporter of the new movement in the Irish Church. Cormac, as we know, was the friend and disciple of Malachy: his devotion to the Church is witnessed to by the beautiful edifice built by him at Cashel, still known as "Cormac's Chapel," which was consecrated in 1134; and by his title of "Bishop-King," which has been the subject of so much discussion. See Petrie, pp. 283-307; and for the crozier found in Cormac's supposed tomb, G. Coffey, *Guide to the Celtic Antiquities of the Christian Period in the National Museum, Dublin*, p. 64. But it must be added that the contemporary Vision of Tundale, which apparently emanated from Cormac's kingdom of Desmond, while bearing emphatic testimony to his generosity to "Christ's poor and pilgrims," charges him with heinous crimes strangely inconsistent with St. Bernard's sketch of his character (Tundale, p. 44 f.).

[370] It seems that the successor (coarb) of the founder of a church was supposed to speak with his authority. Cp. the Epistle of Cummian in Ussher, p. 442.

[371] Cp. § 65. It is generally believed that St. Patrick was buried at Downpatrick (see Reeves, p. 223 ff.); but Olden contended (not convincingly) that the statement made here by St. Bernard is correct (*R.I.A.* xviii, 655 ff.), while Bury (*Life of St. Patrick*, p.

211) has "little hesitation in deciding that the obscure grave was at Saul."

[372] This word cannot have been in St. Bernard's document, for it is unknown in early Irish ecclesiastical terminology, and in Irish hierarchical arrangements it would have no meaning. The context proves that the persons to whom it is here applied are the abbots of Armagh, of whom Cellach was one. It probably represents a Latin rendering of "coarb (successor) of Patrick," a title commonly given to the abbots of this period. The document portrayed the coarbs as rulers of the church of Armagh. St. Bernard would naturally infer that they were bishops. When he found that their authority extended beyond Armagh he would no less naturally style them archbishops or metropolitans. Cp. Serm. i, § 6, where the story of §§ 19-31 is briefly summarized.

[373] Armagh.

[374] *Quasi generationibus quindecim.* The "quasi-generations" are apparently the periods of office of successive coarbs. St. Bernard seems to have written "fifteen" in mistake for "twelve." See Additional Note B, p. 165.

[375] Adulterous, because it took possession of the church, which should have been married to true bishops. Cp. § 20, "the adultery of the church," Malachy "being joined to another spouse;" § 21, Malachy's "former spouse," and the vision of Cellach's wife.

[376] Matt. xii. 39; xvi. 4.

[377] On the statements in these sentences, see Additional Note B.

[378] That bishops were numerous in Ireland at this period is indubitable. Fifty attended the Synod of Fiadh meic Oengusa (*A.U.* 1111), and probably all of them came from the provinces of Ulster and Munster (above, p. xxxviii). But this cannot have been due to the irregularities at Armagh of which St. Bernard complains. There were many bishops in Ireland in its earliest Christian period. See Reeves, 123-136; Todd, 27 ff.

[379] Malachy was not of the Clann Sinaich, to which at this period the coarbs of Patrick belonged. See p. 6, n. 5, and Additional Note B, p. 165.

[380] 1 Sam. iii. 19, etc.

[381] Cellach died on April 1, 1129, and was buried at Lismore on April 4. On April 5, the day after his funeral, Murtough was appointed coarb (*A.U.*).

[382] He was probably supported by Conor O'Loughlin, who was king of Oriel, the district in which Armagh was situated (*A.F.M.* 1136). On him see p. 40, n. 2. The "five years" are the period from Murtough's election to his death, September 17, 1134 (*A.F.M.*)—nearly five years and a half.

[383] Geoffrey, St. Bernard's secretary, recalls a saying of his about "one of the saints," which actually appears in the first antiphon at Mattins in the office of St. Malachy, and which Geoffrey applies to St. Bernard himself: "Blessed is he who loved the law, but did not desire the chair [of dignity]." (*V.P.* iii. 8).

[384] On Malchus see p. 18, n. 6. He was now about eighty-five years of age.

[385] Gillebertus (as St. Bernard writes the name) is a latinized form of the Irish *Gilla espuig* (servant of the bishop), which is anglicized Gillespie. With that Irish name he subscribed the Acts of the Synod of Rathbreasail (Keating, iii. 306); and we may therefore affirm with confidence that he was an Irishman. Gilbert was a friend of the famous thinker and ecclesiastical statesman, Anselm, who was archbishop of Canterbury from 1093 to 1109. The two men met each other for the first time at Rouen, probably in 1087, when Anselm was called thither to the deathbed of William the Conqueror. Twenty

years later, Gilbert, then bishop of Limerick, wrote a letter of congratulation to Anselm on his victory over Henry I. in the controversy concerning investiture (August 1107). In his reply Anselm intimates that the long interval had not blurred his recollection of their former companionship, from which we may infer that Gilbert's personality had made a considerable impression upon him. Anselm also states that he had learned (probably from the superscription of his friend's letter) that he was now a bishop. It would seem, therefore, that Gilbert had been consecrated recently, and not, like the contemporary bishops of Danish sees in Ireland, by the English Primate (see the letters in Ussher, 511, 512). He probably became bishop of Limerick about 1105. Shortly after his correspondence with Anselm, and perhaps by his influence, he was appointed papal legate for Ireland, the first, as St. Bernard tells us, who had held that office. He was legate when in 1108 or 1109 he wrote his tract *De Statu Ecclesiæ* (see above, p. xxx. ff.); and in 1110, as legate, he presided over the Synod of Rathbreasail. In 1139 or 1140, being old and infirm, he resigned his legatine commission and his see (§ 38 and p. 73, note 1). He died in 1145. Gilbert was evidently a strong man, who had much influence on the affairs of the Irish Church. It is therefore surprising that the only reference to him in the native Annals is the notice of his death in the *Chronicon Scotorum*.

[386] *Senior.* This is almost a technical word for the head of a religious community. Malchus is called *ard senóir Gaoidheal* (high senior of the Irish) in *A.F.M.* 1135.

[387] His dissimulation was his disregard of the divine call in the vision described in § 21.

[388] Cp. *A.F.M.* 1132: "Mael Maedoc Ua Morgair sat in the coarbate of Patrick *by the request of the clerics of Ireland*."

[389] Ps. lxxxiii. 12 (vg.).—See Additional Note B, p. 165.

[390] Gen. ix. 6.

[391] The diocese of Connor.

[392] Matt. xix. 2; Mark x. 2.

[393] Ezek. xxxiii. 30.

[394] Jer. l. 11.

[395] The church of Armagh.

[396] The "spouse" is primarily the diocese of Connor. His voluntary poverty is especially associated with his episcopate there in Serm. i. § 6.

[397] It can hardly be doubted that this means the diocese of Armagh (cp. p. 45, n. 4). Both § 19 and the title "son of purity" (*A.U.* 1129) imply that Cellach was not married.

[398] Rom. ix. 19.

[399] That Malachy was in 1132 recognized by many as coarb of Patrick is confirmed by the Annals (see p. 48, n. 3). But that he exercised his episcopal office "throughout the entire province" is inconsistent with the fact that in 1133 Murtough "made a visitation of Tír Eoghain [counties of Derry and Tyrone] and received his tribute of cows and imparted his blessing" (*A.F.M.*).

[400] September 17, 1134 (*A.F.M.*). Sudden death is not suggested by the Annals.

[401] St. Bernard puns on the Latin name by which he represents Niall. It is a diminutive of *niger*, black.

[402] Josh. ix. 24 (vg.).

[403] The meaning of this somewhat difficult sentence is made clear by the reference to the Gibeonites (Josh. ix). By their stratagem they "made provision for their lives," that is, that they should continue to live instead of being exterminated with the rest of the Canaanites. In like manner Murtough provided that he should, as it were, live on and pursue his evil course, in the person of Niall.

[404] He was Murtough's cousin, and Cellach's brother. See the table, Additional Note B, p. 164.

[405] That the king was either Conor O'Brien or Cormac Mac Carthy is highly probable. To them Cellach had confided the duty of seeing that Malachy should be his successor (§ 19), and in this very year they reached the border of the diocese of Armagh (p. 43, n. 5). See p. 53, n. 5.

[406] Ps. xxii. 16.

[407] The narrative of this and the next section is illustrated by the Annals under the year 1134. *A.F.M.*, after recording the obit of Murtough, proceed: "Niall, son of Aedh, was installed in the coarbate of Patrick. A change of abbots in Armagh, *i.e.* Mael Maedoc Ua Morgair in place of Niall." In *A.T.* we have the statement, "Mael Maedog o Mongair ascended Patrick's chair. The Cinel Eoghain of Tulach Óg conspired against Mael Maedoc, and a flash of lightning consumed twelve men of them on the spot where they conspired against him." Thus it seems that the conspirators came from the place now known as Tullaghoge, in the county of Tyrone, then, as now, in the diocese of Armagh. It was the district inhabited by the sept of the O'Hagans, and in it was the *lía na rígh*, the inauguration chair of the O'Neills, kings of Ulster. The confirmation which St. Bernard's story receives from *A.T.* is the more important, because the two narratives are so far different that they must have come from independent sources.

[408] Ps. lii. 1 (vg.).

[409] Cp. John xviii. 2 (vg.).

[410] Ps. x. 8.

[411] Matt. xxiii. 35, combined with Rev. vi. 10; xix. 2.

[412] Ps. xcvii. 2.

[413] Ps. xviii. 11.

[414] Amos v. 8 (vg.).

[415] Rev. iv. 5.

[416] Ps. xi. 6, *horribilis spiritus procellarum*: apparently a conflation of the vg. with another rendering. A.V. has *an horrible tempest*.

[417] Virg., *Aen.* i. 91.

[418] Exod. iv. 19; Matt. ii. 20, etc.

[419] Job iii. 6 (vg.).

[420] Rom. xiii. 12.

[421] *Spiritus.* Cp. the "spirit of tempests" in § 22 (end).

[422] Ps. cii. 10.

[423] *Song of Three Children*, 27.

[424] Ecclus. xxxv. 16 (inexact quotation).

[425] Exod. x. 23 (inexact quotation).

[426] 2 Kings xviii. 41 ff.; Jas. v. 18.

[427] 2 Kings i. 9-12.

[428] John xiii. 31.

[429] This date is incorrect. The entry into the city of Armagh cannot have taken place before October 1134, when Malachy was in his fortieth (possibly thirty-ninth) year. His entry into the province (§ 21) was probably made in his thirty-eighth year. This was no doubt the cause of St. Bernard's error; for one of his documents may, like *A.F.M.* (p. 48, n. 3), have used words which seemed to imply that he entered Armagh on that earlier occasion.

[430] If "the king" was Cormac Mac Carthy (p. 51, n. 2), the statement that he returned home shortly after Malachy obtained possession of the see, is confirmed by *A.F.M.* For they record, under 1134, the consecration of Cormac's Chapel on the rock of Cashel.

[431] Wisd. iii. 1.

[432] 2 Cor. vii. 5.

[433] Ps. ii. 2; Acts iv. 26.

[434] The flight of Niall seems clearly to imply that he was in the city of Armagh. The natural inference is that "having been driven out" he was afterwards reinstated. This may have happened while Malachy was absent on a visitation of Munster, mentioned in *A.F.M.*, but apparently unknown to St. Bernard. The statement of the latter, that Malachy "remained" in Armagh, ignores it. See further, Additional Note C, p. 168 f.

[435] The *Book of Armagh*, now in the Library of Trinity College, Dublin. The manuscript was written at Armagh early in the ninth century by a scribe named Ferdomnach; but at an early date it came to be supposed that it was the work of St. Patrick himself. From this belief, perhaps, arose the name by which it was known for many centuries, and which can be traced back to the year 936—the Canon of Patrick. It is strange that it should be called here a "copy of the Gospels"; for in addition to the complete text of the New Testament it contains two lives of St. Patrick, his *Confession* and other historical documents. But the word *Gospel* was very loosely used in Ireland (see *R.I.A.* xxxiii. 327 f.). Misled by this description, de Backer (n. *ad loc.*) identifies the book mentioned by St. Bernard with the so-called "Gospels of St. Patrick," found in the shrine known as the Domnach Airgid, about 1830, which have no connexion with Armagh or St. Patrick (*R.I.A. Trans.* xviii., "Antiquities," pp. 14 ff.; xxx. 303 ff.; *R.I.A.* xxxiv. 108 ff.). For further information about the *Book of Armagh* the reader may consult Gwynn, especially pp. ci.-cxvi.

[436] The staff of Jesus was a wooden crozier (Giraldus, *Top.* iii. 34), richly adorned. The story of its presentation by Christ to St. Patrick is found in the tenth-century *Trip.* (p. 30), no doubt taken from an earlier source. The staff was much older than the *Book of Armagh*; for we find that it was "profaned" in 789, and it was then apparently regarded as the principal relic of St. Patrick (*A.U.* 788). It seems that there was a still more ancient tradition, that St. Patrick gave it to St. Mac Cairthinn (*R.I.A.* xxxiv. 114), from which it may be inferred that it once belonged to the church of Clogher. It was removed from Armagh to Dublin in 1180, and deposited in Christ Church. It was burnt in 1538 (*A.L.C.*). Apparently St. Bernard is the only authority for the statement that it was "fashioned" by Christ. It appears that the staff of Jesus, in the twelfth century, was regarded as a much more important relic than the *Book of Armagh*, and was more closely associated with the person and office of the coarb of Patrick. It is frequently mentioned in such a way as to suggest that it was one of the insignia of his authority (*A.U.* 1015, 1073, 1101, 1113, 1157, 1166, 1167; *A.F.M.* 1135, 1139, 1143, 1148, 1152). Similar references

to the *Book of Armagh* do not occur till near the close of the twelfth century, immediately after the removal of the staff from Armagh (*A.U.* 1179, 1196; Gwynn, p. civ.). A very full account of the later history of the staff may be read in *O.C.C.* pp. viii-xx.

[437] Deut. xxxii. 6.

[438] *Gyrovagus.* The word is commonly used of a monk who leaves his proper monastery, and wanders about from one cell to another (see, *e.g.*, St. Bernard, *Ep.* 68, § 4), or to a priest who deserts his parish (Du Cange, *s.v.*).

[439] Job i. 6, 7; ii. 2.

[440] King (*Primacy of Armagh*, p. 97) thought that this was Conor O'Loughlin. But he could hardly be described as "of the unrighteous race," or as a "prince," which would indicate a petty chieftain. Probably the conspirator was a local magnate.

[441] Matt. xxvi. 4, combined with Luke xxii. 2.

[442] Cp. Acts xxiii. 12 f.

[443] Matt. xxvi. 48.

[444] 1 Macc. i. 30.

[445] Cp. 1 Cor. xi. 1.

[446] Matt. x. 38, etc.

[447] Acts xxv. 11.

[448] 1 Pet. v. 3 (vg., inexact quotation).

[449] *Formam.* The word occurs in the verse just quoted, and in the context of that which follows (Phil. ii. 7).

[450] Phil. ii. 8.

[451] Ps. lxxviii. 7.

[452] Acts xxi. 13; John xi. 16.

[453] Cp. Apuleius, *Metamorph.* xi. 23.

[454] Eph. vi. 16.

[455] Gen. iv. 6.

[456] Exod. xv. 16.

[457] Ps. xxvii. 2 (vg.).

[458] John iv. 37.

[459] While accepting the facts here narrated, so far as they were capable of being observed, one cannot ignore the probability that they were misinterpreted. It is quite possible that the offer of peace was made in good faith, and that Malachy and his friends were unduly suspicious when they "foresaw guile." The prince may have surrounded himself with armed men as a mere matter of prudence.

[460] Susanna, 62.

[461] Luke xvi. 8.

[462] § 23.

[463] *Mulctatum in corpore.*

[464] *Mutatum in corde.*

[465] Ps. x. 2.

[466] Jer. xvii. 7, etc.

[467] *Plebes.*

[468] That is, the church of Armagh.

[469] Hos. ii. 6.

[470] Rom. xii. 3; xv. 15, etc.

[471] This statement can hardly be regarded as accurate. Flann Ua Sinaich, keeper of the staff of Jesus, having died, Malachy purchased it on July 7, 1135; or, in other words, as we may suppose, bribed the new keeper to hand it over to him (*A.F.M.*). Niall himself may have subsequently surrendered the *Book of Armagh.*

[472] 1 Tim. ii. 11.

[473] Rom. xv. 13 (vg.).—The success of Malachy in establishing peace in the latter years of his rule at Armagh may be attributed in part to the influence of a prince who is not mentioned in the text. Donough O'Carroll first appears in the Annals as chieftain of the men of Fearnmaigh (now represented by the barony of Farney, co. Monaghan), whom he led in an expedition against Fingal (the district north of Dublin) in 1133. He seems to have succeeded to the kingdom or lordship of Oriel (which included the present counties of Armagh, Monaghan and Louth) on the death of Conor O'Loughlin (May 1136); for in 1138, "with the Oirgialla," he took part in an invasion of Meath. His career was prosperous till 1152, when he assaulted the coarb of Patrick (Gelasius). In consequence he was attacked by the Cenél Eoghain, and expelled from Oriel. In 1155 he was imprisoned by Tighernan O'Rorke in Lough Sheelan, for six weeks; but he escaped and recovered his kingdom, and was present at the consecration of the Church of Mellifont Abbey in 1157. He was murdered in 1168. For his support of Malachy see Additional Note C, p. 170.

[474] This is obviously not the king mentioned in §§ 22, 24, 25. The reference may be to Conor O'Loughlin, who was king of Oriel till he was murdered in May 1136 (p. 40, note 2), or his successor, Donough O'Carroll.

[475] Ecclus. xxi. 7.

[476] Gal. ii. 11.

[477] Exod. xvi. 20 (vg., inexact quotation).

[478] Acts vi. 10 (vg.).

[479] Isa. ii. 22; cf. Job xxvii. 3; Wisd. ii. 2.—The words might be rendered "a spirit (*spiritus*) in her nostrils." The meaning is not clear. In the biblical passages in which the phrase occurs it indicates mortality. On the other hand, by the previous sentence St. Bernard suggests that, in contrast to Malachy, the woman spoke under the influence of an evil spirit.

[480] Mark xiv. 61.

[481] 2 Kings ii. 23.

[482] *Memoria sanctorum.* Probably a reliquary. A reliquary preserved at Clogher in 1300 was known as the *membra*, which, according to one explanation, was the equivalent of *memoriale scrinium*, memorial shrine. See *L.A.J.* iv. 245. Cp. Oengus, p. 345 (*s.v.* Memrae); Lightfoot, *Clement of Rome*, vol. i. p. 91.

[483] Susanna, 56.

[484] Exod. xiv. 25.

[485] Deut. vii. 2 (vg.).

[486] Ps. ix. 6 (vg.).

[487] Ps. lxxiii. 19.

[488] See Additional Note B, p. 166.

[489] John xx. 30.

[490] This date is vague. But the period of three years must be reckoned from the death of Murtough (September 17, 1134), or from the subsequent ejection of Niall. Since

stress is laid on the shortness, rather than the length of the period, we may therefore conclude that peace was established not long before October 1137, or, at any rate, after the beginning of that year. And as St. Bernard believed that the inauguration of Gelasius "immediately" followed the resignation of Malachy, we may gather that both these events took place in 1137. *A.F.M.* date Malachy's resignation in 1136; but the chronology of St. Bernard is to be preferred. See Additional Note C, pp. 168, 169.

[491] Ps. xciv. 2.

[492] Gelasius—in Irish Gilla meic Liag, the servant of the son of the poet—was born about 1087. His father was apparently the poet of a Tyrone sept, named Dermot (O'Hanlon, *Saints*, iii. 965). About 1121 he was appointed abbot of Derry, and held that office till he became archbishop of Armagh in 1137. He had a long episcopate and seems to have been a vigorous prelate. His age and infirmity (says Giraldus) prevented him from attending the Synod of Cashel in 1172. But he subsequently visited Henry II. in Dublin. Thither he brought the white cow, whose milk was his only food (Giraldus, *Expug.* i. 35). He died March 27, 1174, in his eighty-seventh year. For a Life of Gelasius, see Colgan, *A.S.H.* p. 772.

[493] See § 21.

[494] *I.e.* diocese.

[495] The two episcopal sees are evidently Connor and Down. But in early time there were many more sees than two in that district (see Reeves, p. 138), and there is no evidence that any one of them was the seat of a diocesan bishop. But, even if it were so, St. Bernard's statement that the two supposed dioceses were "welded into one" by some ambitious prelate prior to Malachy is unhistorical. A bishop of Connor and a bishop of Down both died in 1117, just seven years before Malachy became bishop of the diocese which included these two places; and there is no trace of a bishop in either of them in the interval. The fact seems to be that the diocese of Connor or Down was constituted for the first time at the Synod of Rathbreasail in 1110. It remained on paper until Malachy was appointed its first bishop. For the probable reason of Malachy's division of the diocese, see p. lvii. f.

[496] This cannot be the true reason for Malachy's choice of Down rather than Connor. If he had wished to go to Connor on his retirement from Armagh he could have consecrated a bishop for Down. It is more probable that his preference was due to his love for Bangor, where he resided during his first episcopate, and where he probably resided also when he was bishop of Down. But, however that may be, Bangor was necessarily under his jurisdiction as bishop of Down; his connexion with it would have been severed if he had assumed the oversight of the new diocese of Connor.

[497] Isa. li. 9; Amos ix. 11.

[498] Cp. Cant. i. 15; iv. i.; v. 12.—St. Bernard himself is said to have had "dove-like eyes" (*V.P.* v. 12); and the meaning of the phrase is explained thus: "In his eyes there shone a certain angelic *purity* and a dove-like *simplicity* (single-mindedness)" (*ibid.* iii. 1).

[499] Amos i. 13.

[500] Cp. § 44, p. 83.

[501] It has been commonly assumed that the house of this convent—which obviously consisted of Augustinian canons (the only order of regular clerics recognized at this period by the Roman Church: see Conc. Lat. 1139, can. 9, Mansi xxi. 528)—was in

Downpatrick. It has accordingly been identified with a monastery which in the Terrier of 1615 is described as "the monastery of the Irish, hard by the Cathedral," and called "the church of the channons" (Reeves, 43, 231). But it is not stated in the text to have been in Down. It seems more likely to have been the monastery of Bangor, which was destroyed in 1127 (§ 18), and must have been reconstituted about this time. There is no indication in the *Life* that Malachy resided in Down, while there are several hints that Bangor was his headquarters and that he was abbot of the community there as long as he lived. (See p. 33, n. 1.) In other words Bangor was, in fact if not in name, the see of the diocese of Ulaid, or Down. For this curious anomaly we have a parallel in the diocese of Tír Eoghain, the see of which for a long period was at Maghera, the bishop, the while, being often styled bishop of Derry (*Irish Church Quarterly*, x. 225 ff.); and for the bishop of a diocese serving as abbot of his cathedral chapter of regular canons we may point to Carlisle (*Trans. of Scottish Ecclesiological Society*, iii. 267 ff.), Louth (*L.A.J.* iv. 143 ff.) and Christ Church, Dublin (*ibid.* 145). That the canons of Bangor were at an early period the bishop's chapter we have independent evidence. For in 1244 the Pope gave judgement in a cause which had been pending for some time between the prior and monks of Down and the abbot and canons of Bangor, each of whom claimed that their church was cathedral (Theiner, p. 42). This claim on behalf of Bangor is easily explained if it was reckoned as the bishop's see in the time of Malachy.

[502] 2 Cor. x. 4.

[503] Luke viii. 5.

[504] Matt. xxi. 23; Mark xi. 28.

[505] Acts viii. 6; John ii. 23.

[506] 2 Cor. iii. 17.

CHAPTER V

The Roman Pilgrimage: the Miracles which were wrought in it.

1139   33. (20). It seemed to him, however, that one could not go on doing these things with sufficient security without the authority of the Apostolic See; and for that reason he determined to set out for Rome, and most of all because the metropolitan see still lacked, and from the beginning had lacked, the use of the pall, which is the fullness of honour.507 And it *seemed good in his eyes*508 that the church for which he had laboured so much509 should acquire, by his zeal and labour, that privilege which hitherto it had not had. There was also another metropolitan see, which Cellach had constituted anew, though subject to the first see and to its archbishop as primate.510 For it also Malachy no less desired the pall, and that the prerogative which it had attained by the gift of Cellach should be confirmed by the authority of the Apostolic See. When his purpose became known it displeased both the brothers and the magnates and people of the country; because all judged that they could not endure so long an absence of the loving father of them all, and because they feared he might die.

1139, June 12   34. It happened meanwhile that his brother, Christian by name, died,511 *a good man, full of grace and* power.512 He was a bishop second to Malachy in reputation, but in holiness of life and zeal for righteousness perhaps his equal. His departure made all the more afraid, and rendered a parting from Malachy more grievous. They said, in fact, that they would in no wise assent to the pilgrimage of their only protector, since *the whole land* would *be made desolate*513 if in one moment it was bereaved of two such *pillars*.514 Therefore all, with one voice, opposed him, and would have used force but that he threatened them with divine vengeance. They refused to desist, however, till the will of God on this matter should be asked by the casting of a lot. He forbade it: nevertheless they cast the lot, but thrice it was found to give an answer in favour of Malachy. For they were not content with one trial, so eager were they to retain him. Yielding at length they let him go, but not without *lamentation and weeping and great mourning*.515 But that he should leave nothing imperfect he began to take measures by which he might *raise up the seed of his* dead *brother*.516 And three of his disciples having been summoned to him he deliberated anxiously which should seem more worthy, or, in other words, more useful, for this work. 1140, JanuaryAnd when he had scrutinized them one by one, he said, "Do you, Edan" (that was the name of one of them), "undertake the burden."517 And when he hesitated and wept, he proceeded, "Do not fear; for you have been designated to me by the Lord; for just now I saw in anticipation the gold ring with which you are to be espoused on your finger."518 He assented, and when he had been consecrated Malachy set out on his journey.

35. And when he had left Scotland519 and reached York, a priest, named Sycarus,520 *steadfastly beholding him*521 recognized him. For though he had not seen his face before, because he *had the spirit of prophecy*522 he had received a revelation concerning him long ago. And now without hesitation he pointed him out with his finger to those who stood round him, saying, "*This is he of whom I had said* that from Ireland *there shall come*523 a holy bishop who *knoweth the thoughts of man*."524 So the *lamp* could not be hid *under a bushel*, for the Holy Spirit who *lighted* it525 brought it forth by the mouth of Sycarus. For also many secret things concerning the affairs of him and his companions were told him by Sycarus, all of which he acknowledged to be or to have been. But when the companions of Malachy went on to inquire about their return, Sycarus immediately replied—and *the event afterwards proved the truth of the saying*526 —that evidently very few of their number would return with the bishop. When they heard

that they imagined that he apprehended death: but God fulfilled it in another way; for on his way back from the City he left some with us, and some in other places, to learn the rule of life;527 and so, *according to the word* of Sycarus,528 he returned to his own country with very few companions. So much concerning Sycarus.

36. In the same city of York he was visited by a man of noble rank according to the standard of the world, Waltheof529 by name, then prior of the regular brothers at Kirkham,530 but now a monk, and father of the monks at Melrose, a monastery of our Order,531 who devoutly commended himself with humility to Malachy's prayers. And when he noticed that the bishop had many companions and few horses—for besides ministers532 and other clerks he had with him five presbyters, and only three horses—he offered him his own, on which he rode, saying that he regretted only one thing, that it was a pack-horse533 and a rough animal to ride. And he added, "I would have given it more willingly if it had been better; but, if you think it worth while, take it with you, such as it is." "And I," replied the bishop, "accept it the more willingly the more valueless you proclaim it, because nothing can be of no value to me which so precious a will offers;" and, turning to his companions, "Saddle this horse for me, for it is suitable for me, and will suffice for a long time." This done, he mounts. And at first he considered it rough, as it was, but afterwards, by a wonderful change, he found that it suited him well and ambled pleasantly. And that there might not *fall* on *the ground* any part of the word which he had spoken,534 till the ninth year, the year in which he died,535 it did not fail him, and became an excellent and very valuable palfrey. And—that which made the miracle more evident to those that saw—from being nearly black it began to grow white, and after no long time536 there was scarcely a whiter horse to be found than it.

1140, March   37. (21). To me also it was granted to see the man on that journey,537 and by the sight of him and by his word I was refreshed, and *I rejoiced as in all riches*;538 and I, in turn, though a sinner, *found grace in his sight*539 then, and from that time up to his death, as I said in the Preface.540 He also, deigning to turn aside to Clairvaux,541 when he saw the brothers was deeply moved; and they were not a little edified by his presence and his speech. So accepting the place and us, and gathering us into his inmost heart, he bade us farewell and departed. And crossing the Alps he came to Ivrea,542 a city of Italy, where he immediately healed the little son of his host who *was sick and ready to die*.543

1140, May   38. Pope Innocent II., of happy memory, was then in the Apostolic See.544 He received him courteously, and displayed kindly pity for him on account of his long pilgrimage. And Malachy in the first place asked with many tears for that which he had fixed most deeply in his heart, that he might be allowed to live and die at Clairvaux, with the permission and blessing of the chief Pontiff. He sought this, not forgetful of the purpose for which he had come, but influenced by the longing for Clairvaux which he had brought with him.545 But he did not obtain his request, because the apostolic man decided that he should be employed to more profitable advantage. He was not, however, wholly disappointed of *his heart's desire*,546 since it was granted him if not to live, at least to die there. He spent a whole month in the City, visiting the holy places and resorting to them for prayer. During that time the chief Pontiff made frequent and careful inquiry of him and those who were with him concerning the affairs of their country, the morals of the people, the state of the churches, and the great things that God had wrought by him in the land. And when he was already preparing to return home the Pope committed his own authority to him, appointing him legate throughout the whole of Ireland. For Bishop Gilbert, who, as we have mentioned above, was then legate, had intimated to him that by reason of age and infirmity of body *he could no longer discharge the duties of the office*.547 After this Malachy prayed that the constitution of the new metropolis548 should be confirmed, and that palls should be given him for both sees. The privilege of confirmation he soon received; "but regarding the palls," said the chief Pontiff, "more formal action must be taken. You must call together the bishops and clerks and the magnates of the land and hold a general council; and so with the assent and common desire of all ye shall demand the pall by persons of honest repute, and it shall be given you." Then he took his mitre from his own head, and placed it on Malachy's head,549 and more, he gave him the stole and maniple which he was accustomed to use in the offering; and saluting him with the kiss of peace he dismissed him, strengthened with the apostolic blessing and authority.

1140, July-August   39. And returning by Clairvaux he bestowed on us *a second* benediction.550 And sighing deeply that it was not allowed him to remain as he longed to do, he said, "Meanwhile I pray you to keep these men for me, that they may learn from you what they may afterwards teach us." And he added, "They will be to us for a seed, *and in* this *seed shall the nations be blessed,*551 even those nations which from ancient days have heard the name of monk, but have not seen a monk."552 And leaving four of his most intimate companions553 he departed: and they, when they were proved and found worthy, were made monks. After a time, when the saint was now in his own country, he sent others,554 and they were dealt with in like manner. And when they had been instructed for some time *and had applied their hearts unto1142 wisdom,*555 the holy brother Christian,556 who was one of themselves, was given to them to be their father, and we sent them out, adding from our own a sufficient number for an abbey.557 And this abbey *conceived and bare* five *daughters,*558 and the seed being thus multiplied559 the number of monks increases from day to day according to the desire and prophecy of Malachy. Now let us return to the order of the narrative.

40. (22). Malachy having set out from us had a prosperous journey through Scotland. And he found King David,560 who is still alive to-day, in one of his castles;561 and his son *was sick nigh unto death.*562 And when Malachy entered the king's house he was honourably received by him and prevailed upon by humble entreaty *that he would heal his son.*563 He sprinkled the youth with water which he had blessed, and *fastening his eyes upon him* said,564 "Trust me, my son; you shall not die this time." He said this, and on the next day, according to his word, there followed the cure, and after the cure the joy of the father and the shouting and noise of the whole exulting family. The *rumour went forth*565 to all, for what happened in the royal house and to the king's son *could not be hid.*566 And lo, everywhere there resounded *thanksgiving and the voice of praise,*567 both for the salvation of their lord, and for the novelty of the miracle. This is Henry;568 for he still lives, the only son of his father, a brave and prudent knight, taking after his father as they say, in *following after righteousness*569 and love of the truth. And both loved Malachy, as long as he lived, because he had recalled him from death. They asked him to remain some days; but he, shunning renown, was impatient of delay, and in the morning went on his way.

As he passed, therefore, through the village called Cruggleton,570 a dumb girl met him. While he prayed *the string of her tongue was loosed and she spake plain.*571

Then he entered the village which they call St. Michael's Church,572 and before all the people cured a woman who was brought to him, mad and bound with cords; and when he had sent her away restored he went on.

But when he came to Portus Lapasperi,573 he waited there for a passage some days; but the time of delay did not pass idly. In the interval an oratory is constructed of twigs woven into a hedge, he both giving directions and himself working. When it was finished he surrounded it with a wall, and blessed the enclosed space for a cemetery. The merits of him who blessed, the miracles, which are said to be wrought there frequently to this day, sufficiently declare.

41. Hence it came that they were in the habit of carrying thither from the neighbouring places those *that were* infirm and *diseased*, and *many* were healed.574 A woman paralysed in all her limbs, brought thither on a waggon, returned home on foot, having waited only one night in the holy place, not in vain, for the mercy of the Lord.575

Let these incidents—a few out of many—suffice with reference to that place; for now we must proceed with what remains.

[507] The pall is a sort of collar, made of lamb's wool, which every metropolitan is required to obtain from the Pope, and without which he cannot exercise his functions. From the end of the eleventh century it has been described in papal bulls as the symbol of "the fullness of the pontifical office" (*Catholic Encyclopedia*, xi. 428). For the date of Malachy's decision to go to Rome, see p. 72, n. 3.

[508] 1 Sam. xiv. 36, 40 (vg.).

[509] Armagh.

[510] Cashel, the seat of the kings of Munster. It was certainly the see of an archbishop in 1110, when Malchus subscribed the Acts of Rathbreasail as archbishop of Cashel. For the date of its foundation see p. xxxv. f.

[511] Christian, bishop of Clogher, was probably appointed bishop of that diocese in succession to Cinaeth Ua Baigill, who died in 1135 (*A.T.*). He seems to have transferred the see of the diocese to Louth, a large part of the diocese of Armagh (in which Louth was situated) being placed under his jurisdiction. This arrangement was no doubt made by Malachy with the support of Donough O'Carroll. See the document quoted in Additional Note C, p. 170, *L.A.J.* iv. 133 ff. and above, p. lix. Christian is commemorated in the contemporary Martyrology of Gorman on June 12. The year of his death is stated (*A.F.M.*) to have been 1138. St. Bernard obviously supposed it to have taken place in 1139 (p. 70, n. 2), and he appears to be right. For the work described in § 32 demands a longer period than can be allowed for it on the supposition that he divulged his scheme of visiting Rome before June 12, 1138. Moreover by that time he cannot have known that the papal schism had come to an end; for the Anti-pope did not submit till May 29. Cp. p. 72, n. 3, and *R.I.A.* xxxv. 245 ff. For another notice of Christian, see p. 89, n. 1.

[512] Acts vi. 8 (vg.), combined with Acts xi. 24.

[513] Jer. xii. 11.

[514] Gal. ii. 9.

[515] Matt. ii. 18.

[516] Deut. xxv. 5 (vg.).

[517] Edan O'Kelly was bishop of Louth till his death in 1182 (*A.L.C.*). He organized the diocese of Oriel, with its see at Louth—corresponding to the present

diocese of Clogher—by the help of Donough O'Carroll. In conjunction with him he founded the monastery of SS. Peter and Paul for Augustinian canons at Knock, by Louth, consecrated by Malachy in 1148 (*A.F.M.*; *L.A.J.* iv. 239, and document quoted, p. 170). Close to it he also founded the Augustinian monastery of St. Mary, the church of which was the cathedral church of the diocese. On the early history of this diocese see *L.A.J.* iv. 129 ff.

[518] This simple story was much developed in later times. Thus in a medieval register of Clogher we read that when Edan had anointed Christian on his deathbed "Malachy saw the ring which Christian wore leap to Edan's finger, and therefore he consecrated him bishop" (*L.A.J.* iv. 239).

[519] No particulars are given of the passage through Scotland. But Malachy probably sailed from Bangor to Cairngarroch (§ 40, p. 78, n. 4), and travelled thence by the shortest route through Carlisle to York. The kingdom of Scotland then extended southwards to the river Ribble at Gisburn (§ 69) and eastwards to the Tees (William of Newburgh, in *Chron. of Stephen* (R.S.), i. 70). For a full discussion of his journeys, the results of which are here assumed, see *R.I.A.* xxxv. 238-243.

[520] This probably represents the Saxon name Sighere. Jocelin, who tells this story (*Vita S. Waltheni* in *AA.SS.*, Aug., i. 255), says that Sycarus (or as the MSS. of his tract call him, Figarus) was a priest *de Neubato* (v.l. *Neuvelt*). *i.e.*, I suppose, of Newbald, a parish near Market Weighton, and about twenty-three miles from York.

[521] Acts xiv. 9.

[522] Rev. xix. 10.

[523] John i. 30.

[524] Ps. xciv. 11.

[525] Matt. v. 15; Mark iv. 21; Luke xi. 33.

[526] Gen. xli. 13 (vg.).

[527] Cp. § 39.

[528] 2 Kings vi. 18, etc.

[529] Printed text, *Wallenus*, obviously an error for *Walleuus* (*Wallevus*), which is the reading of A. The name occurs also in the form Waldeve. St. Waltheof was the younger son of Simon de St. Liz, earl of Northampton, by his wife Matilda, daughter of Waltheof, earl of Northumberland. After Simon's death Matilda married David, afterwards (1124) king of Scots. That Waltheof was the stepson of David I. is a fact not unimportant for readers of the *Life of St. Malachy*. After living for some time in Scotland Waltheof retired to the Augustinian priory of St. Oswald, Nostal. Subsequently, but at what date seems to be unknown, he was appointed prior of Kirkham. But, desirous of a more austere life, he resigned the priory, and entered a Cistercian house at Wardon, Bedfordshire. From it he soon migrated to Rievaulx in Yorkshire, and took the vows of the Order. On the deposition of Richard, first abbot of Melrose, he was elected as his successor in 1148. He died August 3, 1159. (Life by Jocelin in *AA.SS.*, Aug, i. 248). His visit to Malachy proves that the fame of the latter had come to his ears—probably through the Scots who knew him at Lismore (§ 8). It indicates also that Malachy stayed at York long enough to allow the news of his arrival to be sent to Kirkham.

[530] The ruins of Kirkham Abbey remain in the parish of Weston, about sixteen miles north-east of York. This house of Augustinian canons was founded in 1121 by Walter Espec and his wife Adeline. The first prior was William, rector of Garton, uncle

of Espec. Dugdale (vol. vi. 1. pp. 207-209), overlooking Waltheof, mentions no other before 1190.

[531] The first Cistercian monastery in Scotland, founded in 1136 by David I. It was a daughter of Rievaulx, from which, as we have seen, Waltheof was called to be its abbot. Its church of St. Mary was consecrated July 28, 1146. It is on the bank of the Tweed, not far from Old Melrose, the site of a community founded in the seventh century, of which St. Cuthbert was a member. See James A. Wade, *History of Melrose*.

[532] Deacons.

[533] *Runcinus*, the Old English *rouncy* (Chaucer, *Prol.* 390). From this incident the inference is clear that during the whole journey to Rome and back most of Malachy's companions were always on foot, and that the party went at a walking pace.

[534] 1 Sam. iii. 19. Cp. Matt. x. 29.

[535] An important date. Since Malachy died on November 2, 1148, he must have reached York not earlier than November 1139. For reasons for putting the visit somewhat later see *R.I.A.*, xxxv. 247 f.

[536] "Within a few days," says Jocelin in his version of the story! See *AA.SS.* l.c.

[537] After leaving York Malachy no doubt followed approximately the line of the Roman road known as Erming Street to London and Canterbury. Thanks to the preservation of the Itinerary of Archbishop Sigeric on his journey from Rome to Canterbury in 990 (Stubbs, *Memorials of St. Dunstan* (R.S.), pp. 391-395), to our knowledge of the routes of travellers contemporary with Malachy, and to the rare mention in the *Life* of places through which he passed, we can follow him almost step by step from Canterbury to Rome and back. He probably sailed from Dover, and landed on the French coast at or near Wissant. Thence he went by Arras, Rheims, Châlons-sur-Marne, Bar-sur-Aube, Lausanne, Martigny, and over the Great St. Bernard to Ivrea. Then he followed the beaten tract through Vercelli, Pavia, Piacenza, Pontremoli, Lucca and Viterbo to Rome. On the whole journey, from Bangor to Rome and back, the company traversed about 3000 miles on land, besides crossing the sea four times. Allowing for stoppages at Rome, Clairvaux and elsewhere, and for a weekly rest on Sunday, Malachy must have been absent from Ireland about nine months. For details see *R.I.A.* xxxv. 238 ff. The marginal dates are based on that investigation, and are to be regarded merely as approximations.

[538] Ps. cxix. 14.

[539] Gen. xxxiii. 10, etc.

[540] Pref. § 2.

[541] Malachy probably "turned aside" from the main road at Bar-sur-Aube, from which Clairvaux is distant eight miles. A few words may be said about this famous monastery and its first abbot. Bernard, the son of a nobleman named Tescelin and his saintly wife Aleth, whose memory exercised a powerful influence on the lives of her children, was born at Fontaines, a mile or two from Dijon, in 1090. In Oct. 1111 he persuaded his brothers and many of his friends to embrace the religious life. Early in the following year the whole band, thirty in number, entered the austere and now declining community which had been established in 1098 at Citeaux, twelve miles from Dijon. Their arrival was the beginning of the prosperity of the great Cistercian Order. In 1115 Bernard was sent out, with some brothers, by the abbot, Stephen Harding, to found a daughter house on the river Aube, in a valley which had once been known, from its

desolation, as the Valley of Wormwood. After incredible hardships a monastery was built, and the place was so transformed by the labours of the monks that henceforth it deserved its newer name of Clara Vallis, or Clairvaux. The community rapidly increased in numbers; and in 1133, in spite of the opposition of the abbot when the proposal was first made, the building of a large monastery on a different site was begun. It was probably far advanced when Malachy arrived in 1140 (Vacandard, i. 413, 423). It was just completed when he came again in 1148 (see p. 143, n. 5). St. Bernard died on August 20, 1153. At this time he was the most powerful ecclesiastic in Europe, not excepting his nominee Pope Innocent II. (see p. 72, n. 3). Doubtless the main purpose of Malachy's visit to Clairvaux was to secure St. Bernard's support of the petition which he was about to present to the Pope. For further information about St. Bernard the reader may consult *V.P.*, Vacandard, J. Cotter Morison, *The Life and Times of St. Bernard, Abbot of Clairvaux* (1868), and Richard S. Storrs, *Bernard of Clairvaux, the Times, the Man, and his Work* (1892).

[542] *Yporia.* Its ancient name was Eporedia. From it there are two routes across the Alps, by the Great St. Bernard and the Little St. Bernard respectively.

[543] Luke vii. 2.

[544] On the death of Pope Honorius II. (February 14, 1130) two Popes were elected by different groups of cardinals, Innocent II. and Anacletus II. St. Bernard espoused the cause of the former, and by his untiring efforts almost all the sovereigns of Europe were enlisted on his side (see Vacandard, chaps. x.-xiii., xviii.; Storrs, pp. 523-540; Morison, pp. 149-165, 209-213). But the schism lasted for eight years. At length Anacletus died (January 7, 1138), and the surrender of his successor, Victor IV., on May 29, 1138 (*Ep.* 317), left Innocent in undisputed occupation of the papal chair. The news of the pacification was not announced in Scotland till the end of September (Richard of Hexham, 170). It probably reached Ireland a little later. It must have been after he was assured of the end of the schism that Malachy proposed his journey to Rome, *i.e.* at the end of 1138 or in 1139.

[545] *Quo uenerat.*

[546] Ps. xxi. 2.

[547] Luke xvi. 2 (vg.).—For Gilbert see p. 47, n. 3. Patrick, successor of Gilbert in the see of Limerick, was consecrated by Theobald, archbishop of Canterbury, who was himself consecrated on January 8, 1139 (W. Stubbs, *Reg. Sac. Angl.*, p. 45). His profession of obedience (Ussher, p. 565) appears in the roll of professions at Canterbury immediately before that of Uhtred of Llandaff, who was consecrated in 1140 (Stubbs, *l.c.*). If we assume that Gilbert resigned his see and his legatine commission at the same time, this gives 1139-40 as the date of Malachy's journey, in agreement with the hint of St. Bernard in § 36. It is possible that Gilbert's resignation of his office as legate was sent to Rome by Malachy.

[548] Cashel. See p. 65, note 4.

[549] Fleming in 1623 saw a mitre of Malachy at Clairvaux, which was supposed to have been the one placed on his head by Innocent at Orbiers, ten leagues away, his wooden drinking cup was preserved: it was in a leathern case, adorned with Irish interlacings (*Irish Ecclesiastical Record*, vii. 63).

[550] Cp. 2 Cor. i. 15.

[551] Gen. xxii. 18; xxvi. 4.

[552] Compare the passage concerning a brother who had been sent from Clairvaux to Sweden in 1143, and had founded a daughter monastery there: "The lord [St. Bernard] sent to his faithful servant learned and discreet persons from the parts of Germany and England, by whom the discipline of monastic religion founded in that kingdom increased and bore worthy fruit among peoples who had indeed heard the name of monk, but had never before seen a monk" (*V.P.* vii. 54). It was literally true that no monastic communities had previously existed in Sweden (C. H. Robinson, *Conversion of Europe*, p. 482 f. Cp. Vacandard, ii. 416). But the passage before us cannot be construed as an assertion that Ireland was in like case; for in § 12 mention is made of the "monks" of Bangor in the time of Congall. St. Bernard (or Malachy, if the words are really his) must be taken to mean simply that the so-called monks of the decadent contemporary Church of Ireland were not monks in the true sense of the word. (Cp. Lett. iii. § 2). There is nothing to be said for the explanation suggested by Lanigan (iv. 114) that the "nations" are nations other than the Irish, who had no monks. For where were those nations to whom the Irish might send colonies of monks? The fact is that the Latin word for "nations" (*gentes*) may quite well mean here what it certainly means in § 42, the Irish tribes.

[553] He left others in other Cistercian houses (§ 35).

[554] Cp. Letter i. § 1.

[555] Ps. xc. 12.

[556] Gilla Críst Ua Condoirche was probably a native of the district of Bangor (§ 14). He seems to have been one of the four who were left by Malachy at Clairvaux; and, as is here stated, he was the first abbot of Mellifont. He seems, however, to have proved not well suited for the office, for he was sent back to Clairvaux for further instruction (Letter iii. § 3). Some of the Clairvaux brothers (if not all of them) refused to remain in Ireland, and it is perhaps hinted that the cause of their return was dissatisfaction with his administration (*ib.* § 2). About 1150 he was promoted to the bishopric of Lismore, and at the Synod of Kells in 1152 he appeared as papal legate (Keating, iii. 317). He was present at the consecration of the church of Mellifont Abbey in 1157 (*A.U.*) As legate he also presided at the Synod of Cashel in 1172 (Giraldus, *Expug.* i. 34). He died in 1186 (*A.L.C.*). Felix, bishop of Lismore, attended the Lateran Council of 1179 (Mansi, xxii. 217). Christian must therefore have resigned his see before that date.

[557] Mellifont Abbey, the ruins of which still remain in a secluded valley, beside the stream known as the Mattock, about two miles from the Boyne, and five miles west of Drogheda. Some time after Malachy returned to Ireland he wrote to St. Bernard, asking him to send two of the four brothers who had been left at Clairvaux to select a site for the abbey. This request was declined (Lett. i. § 1), and the site—doubtless the gift of Donough O'Carroll (see the document quoted p. 170)—was apparently chosen by Malachy himself. In 1142 (*C.M.A.* ii. 262, *Clyn's Annals*, *Annals of Boyle*), the four brothers, together with a contingent of monks from Clairvaux, arrived, and the monastery was founded, with Christian as its first abbot (Lett. ii.). Considerable progress was made with the buildings, and endowments poured in. But after a while it became necessary to send Christian back to France for further instruction, and the Clairvaux monks went with him, never to return. In due time Christian resumed his office as abbot, and with him came one Robert, to assist him in the work of building and organization (Lett. iii). The Abbey Church was not consecrated till 1157, nine years after Malachy's death (*A.U.*).

Mellifont remained the principal Cistercian house in Ireland up to the Reformation. After the dissolution (1539) it was granted, with its possessions, to Sir Edward Moore, ancestor of the earls of Drogheda. The only portions of the monastery which remain in a fair state of preservation are the Chapter House and the Lavabo. The latter belongs to the original building. Excavations made about twenty years ago revealed the ground plan of the entire monastery, most of which was of later date than Malachy. Traces were discovered of the foundation of the eastern portion of the original church, about forty feet west of the east wall of the structure which later took its place. It had six chapels at the east end, four of which were apsidal (*71st Report of Commissioners of Public Works, Ireland*, p. 11).

[558] 1 Sam. ii. 21.—The five daughters were apparently Bective (de Beatitudine) founded in 1147, Boyle, 1147-8, Monasternenagh, 1148, Baltinglas (de Valle Salutis), 1148, and Inislounaght (Janauschek, *Origines Cistercienses*, Vindoboniæ, 1877, pp. 70, 92, 113). The last-named seems to have been in existence in 1148 (see § 64), and it may have been an off-shoot of Mellifont, though at an early date it was subject to Monasternenagh (*ibid.* 131). Gougaud (*Les Chrétientés Celtiques*, 1911, p. 364) gives Shrule (de Benedictione Dei) the fifth place; but it appears to have been founded (1150?) after the *Life* was written (Janauschek, p. 114).

[559] Cp. Gen. xxii. 17; xxvi. 4.

[560] David I. of Scotland, son of Malcolm Canmore and St. Margaret, the sister of Edgar the Atheling. He was born in 1084. His sister Matilda was the wife of Henry I. of England; and thus he was uncle of Matilda, the empress, for whom he fought against Stephen, though Stephen's wife, Queen Matilda, was also his niece. In 1113 David married Matilda, the widow of Simon de St. Liz, earl of Northampton (cp. p. 69, n. 1). He succeeded Alexander I. in 1124 and died in 1153. As the founder of several Scottish dioceses and as having introduced the Cistercian Order into his kingdom he had much in common with St. Malachy.

[561] This is probably an error. There is no record that David I. had any castles in Galloway; and the chronicles seem to show that at this period his principal residences were at Roxburgh and Carlisle. The narrative suggests that the castle referred to was in the immediate neighbourhood of Cruggleton (p. 78, n. 1), and it was probably the predecessor of that of which the scanty ruins—believed to be of thirteenth-century date—remain on the coast not far from the village. They are on a peninsula of such natural strength that we may suppose it was in very early times the site of a fortress (*Fourth Report of Commission on Ancient Monuments in Scotland*, vol. i. p. 144). Possibly, as has been suggested, David was there as the guest of Fergus, lord of Galloway (1124-1161), to whom, subsequently to the Battle of the Standard (August 22, 1138), and probably not long before this visit of Malachy, he had been reconciled after a long estrangement (Agnew, *Hereditary Sheriffs of Galloway*, 1893. vol. i. p. 58).

[562] Phil. ii. 27 (inexact quotation).

[563] 2 John iv. 47.

[564] Acts iii. 4.

[565] Luke vii. 17.

[566] Mark vii. 24.

[567] Isa. li. 3 (vg.).

[568] The only son of David: "a man gentle and pious, a man of sweet nature and of pure heart, and worthy in all things to be born of such a father" (Ailred of Rievaulx, in

A. O. Anderson, *Scottish Annals from English Chroniclers*, p. 156). He died before his father, in May or June 1152 (John of Hexham). Two of his sons became kings of Scots, Malcolm IV. and William I.

[569] Rom. ix. 30, etc.

[570] *Crugeldum.* Cruggleton is on the west coast of Wigtown Bay, in the parish of Sorby, Wigtownshire. In passing through this village Malachy made a détour, probably in order to visit King David, which considerably lengthened his journey.

[571] Mark vii. 35.

[572] The parish church of Mochrum, Wigtownshire, as Sir Herbert Maxwell informs me, was anciently dedicated to St. Michael. Thus the village called St. Michael's Church is undoubtedly Kirk Mochrum, which clusters round the church, and through which every traveller from Cruggleton to Cairngarroch (see next note) must pass. It is twelve miles from Cruggleton.

[573] *Lapasperi* is obviously the gen. of *Lapasper*, a corruption of *Lapis asper* (rough stone). This seems to be a Latin rendering of Cairngarroch (= *Carn garbh*), a name which occurs three times on the shores of Wigtownshire. One of the places so called, on the west coast of Luce Bay, may be set aside. The other two are seven or eight miles apart, within sight of the Bangor coast, and nearly equidistant from it; one in the parish of Stoneykirk, the other (now known as Rough Cairn) in the parish of Geswalt. The late Sir Andrew Agnew (*op. cit.* p. 59) regarded the latter as the place referred to in the text on grounds which do not seem conclusive. Cairngarroch in Stoneykirk is to be preferred for two reasons: it is more easily approached from inland than its rival; and it has impressed its name on the actual coast-line, which the other has not done; "Cairngarroch Bay" is equivalent to *Port Cairn garbh*, and that to the *Portus Lapasperi* of the text. This identification was first proposed by O'Hanlon (p. 81); and its probability is increased now that the position of St. Michael's Church has been fixed (see preceding note). But one of his arguments in favour of it, based on the name of the parish, is fallacious; for "Stoneykirk" has nothing to do with stones: it is a late corruption of Steiniekirk = St. Stephen's Church.

[574] Mark i. 32, 34.

[575] For the passage here omitted see Appendix, p. 171.

CHAPTER VI

St. Malachy's Apostolic Labours, Praises and Miracles.

1140, October 42. (23). Malachy embarked in a ship, and after a prosperous voyage landed at his monastery of Bangor,576 so that his first sons might receive the first *benefit*.577 In what state of mind do you suppose they were when they received their father—and such a father—in good health from so long a journey? No wonder if their whole heart gave itself over to joy at his return, when swift rumour soon brought incredible gladness even to the tribes578 outside round about them. In fine, from the cities and castles and hamlets they ran to meet him, and wherever he turned he was received with *the joy of the whole land*.579 But honour is not to his taste. He exercises his office as legate; many assemblies are held in many places, so that no region, or part of a region, may be defrauded of the fruit and advantage of his legation. He *sows beside all waters*;580 there is not one who can escape from his sedulous care. Neither sex, nor age, nor condition, nor [religious] profession is held in account.581 Everywhere the saving seed is scattered, everywhere the heavenly trumpet sounds. He scours every place, everywhere he breaks in, with *the sword* of his tongue unsheathed *to execute vengeance upon the nations and punishments upon the peoples*.582 The terror of him is *on them that do evil*.583 He cries *unto the unrighteous, deal not unrighteously, and to the wicked, lift not up the horn*.584 Religion is planted everywhere, is propagated, is tended. His *eyes are upon* them,585 his care is for their necessities. In councils, which are everywhere held, the ancient traditions are revived, which, though their excellence was undisputed, had fallen into disuse by the negligence of the priests. And not only are the old restored, new customs are also devised; and whatsoever things he promulgated are accepted as though issued from heaven, are held fast, are committed to writing for a memorial to posterity. Why should we not believe those things were sent from heaven which so many heavenly miracles confirm? And that I may make what has been said credible, let me touch on some of these miracles in a few words. For who can enumerate all? Though I confess I had rather dwell on those things which can be imitated than on those which can only excite wonder.

43. (24). And in my judgement the first and greatest miracle that he exhibited was himself.586 For to say nothing of his *inner man*,587 the beauty and strength and purity of which his habits and life sufficiently attested, he so bore himself even outwardly in a uniform and consistent manner, and that the most modest and becoming, that absolutely nothing appeared in him which could offend the beholders. And, indeed, *he who offends not in word, the same is a perfect man*.588 But yet in Malachy, who, though he observed with unusual care, ever detected, I will not say an *idle word*,589 but an idle nod? Who ever knew his hand or his foot to move without purpose? Yea, what was there that was not edifying in his gait, his mien, his bearing, his countenance? In fine, neither did sadness darken nor laughter turn to levity the joyousness of his countenance.590 Everything in him was under *discipline*, everything a mark *of virtue*, *a rule*591 of perfection. Always he was grave, but not austere. Relaxing at times, but never careless; neglecting nothing, though for a time ignoring many things. Quiet often, but by no means at any time idle.592 From the first day of his conversion to the last of his life, he lived without personal possessions.593 He had neither *menservants* nor *maidservants*,594 nor villages nor hamlets, nor in fact any revenues, ecclesiastical or secular, even when he was a bishop. There was nothing whatever ordained or assigned for his episcopal mensa, by which the bishop might live; for he had not even a house of his own. But he was almost always going about all the parishes595 serving the Gospel,596 and *living of the*

Gospel,597 as the Lord appointed for him when he said, *The labourer is worthy of his hire.*598 Except that more frequently, *making the Gospel* itself *without charge*,599 as a result of the labours of himself and his companions, he brought with him that by which he might sustain himself and *those who laboured with him in the work of the ministry.*600 Further, if at times he had to rest he did so in the holy places which he himself had scattered through the whole of Ireland; but he conformed to the customs and observances of those with whom it pleased him to tarry, content with the common life and the common table. There was nought in his food, nought in his clothing, by which Malachy could be distinguished from the rest of the brethren; to such a degree, though he was *greatest*, did he *humble himself in all things.*601

44. Then, when he went out to preach, he was accompanied by others on foot, and on foot went he himself, the bishop and legate. That was the apostolic rule; and it is the more to be admired in Malachy because it is too rare in others. The true successor of the Apostles assuredly is he who does such things. But it is to be observed how he *divides the inheritance with his brothers*,602 equally descendants of the Apostles. They *lord it among the clergy*;603 he, *though he was free from all men, made himself the servant of all.*604 They either do not preach the Gospel and yet eat, or preach the Gospel in order that they may eat; Malachy, imitating Paul, eats that he may preach the Gospel.605 They *suppose that* arrogance and *gain are godliness*;606 Malachy claims for himself by inheritance labour and a load.607 They believe themselves happy if they *enlarge their borders*;608 Malachy glories in enlarging charity.609 They *gather into barns*610 and fill the wine-jars, that they may load their tables; Malachy collects [men] into deserts and solitudes that he may fill the heavens. They, though they receive tithes and first-fruits and oblations, besides customs and tributes by the gift of Cæsar and countless other revenues, nevertheless *take thought what they shall eat or what they shall drink*;611 Malachy *having nothing* of such things, yet *makes many rich*612 out of the store-house of faith. Of their desire and anxiety there is no end; Malachy, desiring nothing, knows not how to think about the morrow.613 They exact from the poor that which they may give to the rich; Malachy implores the rich to provide for the poor. They empty the purses of their subjects; he for their sins *heaps altars*614 with vows and *peace-offerings.*615 They build lofty palaces, raise up towers and ramparts to the heavens.616 Malachy, *not having where to lay his head,617 does the work of an evangelist.*618 They *ride on horses*619 with a crowd of men, who *eat bread for nought*, and that not *their own*;620 Malachy, hedged round with a college of holy brothers, goes about on foot, bearing *the bread of angels*,621 with which to *satisfy the hungry souls.*622 They do not even know the congregations;623 he instructs them. They honour powerful men and tyrants; he punishes them. O, apostolic man, whom so many and so striking *signs of his apostleship*624 ennoble! What wonder, then, if he has wrought wondrous things when he himself is so wonderful? Yet truly not he but God in him.625 Moreover, it is said, *Thou art the God that doest wonders.*626

45. (25). There was a woman in the city of Coleraine627 who had a demon. Malachy was called; he prayed for the possessed; he commanded the invader and he went out. But his iniquity was not yet fully satisfied, and he entered into an unhappy woman who happened to be standing by. And Malachy said, "I did not release that woman from your grasp in order that you might enter this one; go out of her also." He obeyed, but went back to the former woman; and driven forth from her once more, he again went into

the second. So for some time he vexed them alternately, fleeing to and fro. Then the saint, indignant that he was mocked by a demon, summoned up his spirit, and shouted; and when he had made an attack on the adversary with all the forces of faith, he drove the demon away from both, no less vexed than those whom he had vexed. But do not suppose, reader, that the delay which he caused the saint was due to his own strength: it was permitted by the divine dispensation, evidently in order that by this as well the power of the evil one as the victory of Malachy might be made more manifest.

Hear now what he did elsewhere, but not by reason of his presence. Assuredly what he had power to accomplish when absent, he could do also when present.

46. In a district of the northern part of Ireland a sick man lay in his house. His sickness was beyond doubt due to the evil influence of demons. For one night he heard them talking; and one said to another, "See that this wretched man does not touch the bed or bedding of that hypocrite, and so escape from our hands." The man perceived that they were speaking of Malachy, who, as he remembered, had not long before passed a night in that house. And the bedding was still in its place; and taking courage, with his utmost effort he began to crawl, weak in body but strong in faith. And lo, in the air there was clamour and shouting: "Stop him, stop him, hold him, hold him; we are losing our prey." But, carried on by faith and the desire to escape, the more they shouted the more he hastened to the remedy, straining with knees and hands. And when he reached the couch, and went up on it, he rolled himself in the bed-clothes, and heard the wailing of them that lamented, "Alas, alas, we have betrayed ourselves, we have been deceived, he has escaped."628 And quicker than a word, there left him the terror of the demons and the horror which he suffered, and with them all his sickness.

In the city of Lismore a man vexed by a demon was delivered by Malachy.

Also once, when he was passing through Leinster, an infant was brought to him who had a demon, and he was brought back whole.

In the same region he ordered a mad woman,629 bound with cords, to be loosed and to be bathed in water which he blessed. She washed and was healed.

Another woman also in Saul,630 a region of Ulaid,631 who was tearing her own limbs with her teeth, he cured by praying and touching her.

There was a madman, who predicted many things to come. His friends and neighbours brought him to the man of God, bound strongly with cords, because his very madness had made him strong to do hurt and exceeding terrible. Malachy prayed, and immediately the sick man was healed and released. This was done in a certain place, the name of which we omit because it has a very barbarous sound, as also have many others.632

At another time in the above-mentioned city of Lismore,633 the parents of a dumb girl634 brought her to him in the midst of the street as he passed, asking him with much entreaty that he would deign to help her. Malachy stood and prayed; and he *touched her tongue* with his finger and *spat*635 upon her mouth, and sent her away speaking.

47. (26). Going out of a certain church he met a man with his wife, and she could not speak. And when he was asked to have mercy on her, he stood in the gate, the people surrounding him; and he gave a blessing upon her, and bade her say the Lord's Prayer. She said it, and the people blessed the Lord.

In a city called Antrim636 a certain man lying on a bed, now deprived for twelve days of the use of his tongue, at the bidding of the saint, who visited him, recovered his speech and received the Eucharist; and so fortified he breathed his last breath in *a good confession*.637 O, *fruitful olive tree in the house of God*!638 O, *oil* of gladness,639 giving both anointing and light! By the splendour of the miracle he gave light to those who were whole, by the graciousness of the favour he anointed the sick man, and obtained for him, soon about to die, the saving power of confession and communion.640

One of the nobles came in to him, *having somewhat to say to him*;641 and while they were speaking, *full of faith*642 piously stole three rushes from the couch on which Malachy sat, and took them with him: and God wrought many things as a result of the pious theft, by that man's faith and the sanctity of the prelate.

By chance he had come to a city called Cloyne.643 And when he was sitting at table a nobleman of that city came in and humbly prayed him for his wife, who was pregnant, and had passed the appointed time of parturition, so that all wondered, and there was none who did not believe that her life was in danger. With him also Nehemiah,644 the bishop of that city, who was sitting next to him, made request to Malachy, and others also as many as were present reclining together. Then he said, "I pity her, for she is a good and modest woman." And offering the man a cup which he had blessed, he said, "Go, give her to drink, and know that when she has taken the draught of blessing645 she will bring forth without delay, and without danger." It was done as he commanded, and that very night there followed that which he promised.

He was sitting in a plain with the count of Ulaid, dealing with certain matters, *and a great multitude*646 was about them. There came a woman who had long been with child. She declared that contrary to all the laws of nature she had already been pregnant for fifteen months and twenty days. Malachy having pity for this new and unheard-of trouble, prayed, and the woman was delivered. Those who were present rejoiced and wondered. For all saw with what ease and rapidity she brought forth in the same place, and the sad portent of birth denied was changed to a happier marvel.

48. (27). There happened in the same place an event with a similar miracle but a different issue. He saw a man who was reported to be consorting publicly with his brother's concubine; and he was a knight, a servant of the count. And publicly accosting the incestuous man he displayed himself to him as another John, saying, *It is not lawful for thee to have thy brother's* concubine.647 But he, nevertheless, in his turn displaying himself to Malachy as another Herod, not only did not hearken to him, but even answered him haughtily, and before them all swore that he would never put her away. Then Malachy, much agitated, for he was vehemently zealous for righteousness, said, "Then God shall separate you from her against your will." Paying little heed the man went away at once in a rage. And meeting the woman not far from the crowd which was in the place, he treated her evilly and with violence, as though he wholly belonged to *Satan* to whom he had a little before been *delivered*.648 Nor was the crime hidden. The damsel who accompanied the lady ran back to the house (for it was not far from the place), and, breathless, announced the wickedness that had taken place. At the word her brothers, who were at home, enraged at the dishonour done to their sister, rushed thither with all haste and slew the enemy of virtue, *taken in the very* place and *act*649 of crime, piercing him with many wounds. The assembly was not yet dismissed when, lo! his armour-bearer proclaimed what had happened. And all wondered that the sentence of Malachy had taken such speedy effect. When this word was heard all evil-doers (for there were many in the

land) feared and, being terrified, purified themselves, *washing their hands in the blood of the ungodly*.650

49. (28). Dermot the count,651 who had now for a long time lain on his bed, he sprinkled with blessed water, and caused him to rise up without delay, and so strong that he mounted his horse on the spot, surpassing assuredly the hope of himself and of his friends—rebuking him severely at the same time because he was a bad man *serving his belly*652 and his appetite immoderately.

In the town of Cashel a man came before him with his paralysed son, asking that he should be healed.653 And Malachy, praying briefly, said, "*Go thy way; thy son* shall be made whole."654 He went, and on the morrow he returned with his son, who was nevertheless by no means whole. Then Malachy rose and standing over him prayed at greater length, and he was made whole. And turning to the father he said, "Offer him to God." The man assented, but did not keep his promise; and after some years his son, now a young man, relapsed into the same state, no doubt because of his father's disobedience and his violation of the pledge.

Another man came from a long distance, when Malachy was in the borders of Munster, bringing to him his son, who was entirely deprived of the use of his feet. When he inquired how this had happened to him, he said, "As I suspect, by the malignity of demons"; adding, "It was they, if I mistake not, who, when he was playing in a field, *caused a sleep to fall* upon him,655 and when the child awoke he found himself so." Saying this, he poured forth his petition with tears, and earnestly sought help. Malachy pitying him prayed, bidding the sick boy in the meantime to sleep there upon the ground. He slept, and he arose whole. Because he had *come from far*656 he kept him some time in his company, and he used to walk with him.

50. In the monastery of Bangor a certain poor man was maintained by the alms of the brothers; and he received a small sum every day, for performing some office in the mill. He had been lame for twelve years, creeping on the ground with his hands, and dragging his dead feet after him. Him Malachy found one day before his cell, sad and sorrowful, and asked him the cause. And he said, "You see how for a long time I am miserably troubled and *the hand of the Lord is upon me*;657 and lo, to increase my distress, men who ought to have had pity, rather laugh at me and cast my wretchedness in my teeth." And when he heard him, moved with compassion, he *looked up to heaven*,658 at the same time raising his hands. Having said a short prayer he entered his cell, and the other rose up. And standing upon his feet he wondered if it was true, suspecting that he was in a dream.659 But he began to move with slow steps, for he did not altogether believe that he could walk. At length, *as it were waking out of a deep sleep*,660 he recognized the mercy of the Lord upon him; he walked firmly, and returned to the mill *leaping* and exulting *and praising God*. When those saw him who had before seen and *known him* they *were filled with wonder and amazement*,661 *supposing it to be a spirit*.662

Malachy likewise healed a dropsical man by praying, who remained there in the monastery and was appointed shepherd.

51. A city of Ireland called Cork was without a bishop. They proceeded to an election; but the various parties did not agree, each, as is usual, wishing to appoint their own bishop, not God's.663 Malachy came to the place when he heard of the disagreement. Calling together the clergy and people he took pains to unite the hearts and

89

desires of the opposing parties. And when they had been persuaded that the whole business ought to be entrusted to him, on whom in a very special manner lay *the care of* that as also of the other *churches*664 throughout Ireland,665 immediately he named to them, not any of the nobles of the land,666 but rather a certain poor man whom he knew to be holy and learned; *and he was a stranger*.667 He was sought; and it was announced that he was lying in bed, and so weak that he could in no wise go out unless carried in the hands of those who ministered to him. "Let him rise," said Malachy; "in the name of the Lord I command it; obedience will save him." What was he to do? He wished to obey, but he thought himself unfitted; for though it should be possible for him to go, he dreaded to be a bishop. So with the will to be obedient twin enemies were contending, the load of weakness and the fear of the burden. But the first conquered, the hope of salvation being given him as an aid. Therefore he made the attempt, he moved, tested his power, discovered that he was stronger than usual. Faith increased along with power, and again faith made stronger gave in its turn increase of power. Now he was able to rise unassisted, now to walk somewhat better, now not even to perceive weariness in walking; at length, to come to Malachy without difficulty and quickly, unaided by man. He promoted him, and put him into the chair, with the applause of clergy and people. This was done without question, because neither did they dare to oppose the will of Malachy in any way, seeing the sign which he had wrought; nor did he hesitate to obey, being made surer, by so evident a proof, of the will of God.

52. (29). A certain *woman was diseased with an issue of blood*;668 and she was of noble birth and very dear to Malachy, though by reason of the nobility rather of her character than of her descent. When she was entirely failing, her strength no doubt being exhausted with her blood, and was now near the end, she sent to the man of God, in order that—the only thing that remained to be done—he might help her soul who should see her no more in the body. When Malachy heard it he was troubled, because she was a woman of virtue, and her life fruitful in work and example. And perceiving that he could not reach her in time he called Malchus, for he was young and active (he is that brother of Abbot Christian whom we mentioned above),669 and said, "Haste, take her these three apples on which I have invoked the name of the Lord; I am assured of this, that when she tastes these she *shall not taste of death* before *she sees* us,670 though we shall follow somewhat more slowly." Malchus hastened as he was commanded, and when he came he went in to the dying woman, showing himself another servant of Elisha, except that his work was more efficacious.671 He bade her take that which Malachy had blessed and sent to her, and to taste it if by any means she could. But she was so refreshed when she heard Malachy's name, that she was able to obey, and indicated by a nod (for she could not speak) that she wished to be raised up for a little while. She was raised up, she tasted; she was strengthened by what she tasted, she spoke, and gave thanks. *And the Lord caused a deep sleep to fall upon* her,672 and she rested most sweetly in it, having long ceased to enjoy the benefit of sleep, or to partake of food. Meanwhile *her blood was staunched*673 and awaking after a while she found herself whole,674 but she was still weak from long fasting and loss of blood. If in any degree the cure was not complete,675 on the following day the wished-for presence and appearance of Malachy made it perfect.

53. (30). A nobleman lived in the neighbourhood of the monastery of Bangor, whose wife was *sick nigh unto death*.676 Malachy, being asked to *come down ere she died*,677 to *anoint the sick* woman *with oil*,678 came down and went in to her; and when

she saw him she rejoiced greatly, animated by the hope of salvation. And when he was preparing to anoint her, it seemed to all that it ought rather to be postponed to the morning; for it was evening. Malachy assented, and when he had given a blessing over the sick woman, he went out with those who were with him. But shortly afterwards, suddenly *there was a cry made*,679 lamentation and great wailing through the whole house, for it was reported that she had died. Malachy ran up when he heard the tumult, and his disciples followed him. And coming to the bed, when he had assured himself that she had breathed her last, he was greatly troubled in mind, blaming himself that she had died without the grace of the sacrament. And lifting up his hands to heaven he said, "*I beseech thee*, Lord, *I have done very foolishly*. I, even *I, have sinned*,680 who postponed, not she who desired it." Saying this he protested in the hearing of all that *he* would not *be comforted*,681 that he would give *no rest to his spirit*,682 unless he should be allowed to restore the grace which he had taken away. And standing over her, all night *he laboured in his groaning*; and, instead of the holy oil, flooding the dead woman with a great rain of *tears*,683 he bestowed on her such a substitute for the unction as he could. Thus did he; but to his companions he said, "*Watch and pray.*"684 So they in psalms, he in tears, passed a night of vigil. And when the morning came the Lord heard His saint, for the *Spirit* of the Lord was *making intercession for him*, who *maketh intercession for* the saints *with groanings that cannot be uttered.*685 Why more? She who had been dead *opened her eyes*,686 and, as those do who wake from a deep sleep, rubbing her forehead and temples with her hands, she rose upon the bed, and recognizing Malachy, devoutly saluted him with bowed head. And mourning being *turned into joy*,687 amazement took hold of all, both those who saw and those who heard. And Malachy also gave thanks and blessed the Lord. And he anointed her, nevertheless, knowing that in that sacrament *sins are forgiven*, and that *the prayer of faith saves the sick.*688 After this he went away, and she recovered, and after living for some time in good health, *that the* glory *of God should be made manifest in her*,689 she accomplished the penance which Malachy had enjoined upon her, and again *fell asleep*690 in a *good confession*,691 and passed to the Lord.

54. (3). There was also a woman whom *a spirit of* anger and *fury*692 dominated to such an extent that not only her neighbours and relatives fled from her society, but even her own sons could scarcely endure to live with her. Shouting, rancour and *a mighty tempest*693 wherever she was. Violent, fiery, hasty, terrible with tongue and hand, intolerable to all, and hated. Her sons, grieving both for her and for themselves, dragged her into the presence of Malachy, setting forth their lamentable complaint with tears. But the holy man, pitying both the sickness of the mother and the trouble of her sons, called her aside, and made urgent inquiry whether she had ever confessed her sins. She replied, "Never." "Confess," said he. She obeyed; and he enjoined penance on her when she made confession, and prayed over her that Almighty God might give her *the spirit of meekness*,694 and in the name of the Lord Jesus bade her to be angry no more. Such meekness followed that it was plain to all that it was nothing else than a marvellous *change effected by the right hand of the Most High.*695 It is said that she is still living to-day, and is so patient and gentle that, though she used to exasperate all, now she cannot be exasperated by any injuries or insults or afflictions. If it be allowed me, as the Apostle says, *to be fully persuaded in my own mind*,696 let each accept it as he will; for me, I give it as my opinion that this miracle should be regarded as superior to that of raising the dead woman, mentioned above, inasmuch as there the outward, but here the *inner*

*man*697 was restored to life. And now let us hasten to what remains.

55. A man who as regards the world was honourable, as regards God devout, came to Malachy and complained to him concerning *the barrenness of his soul*,698 praying that he would obtain for him from Almighty God the grace of tears. And Malachy, smiling because he was pleased that there should be spiritual desire from a man of the world, laid his cheek on the cheek of the other as though caressing him, and said, "*Be it done unto you as you have asked.*"699 From that time *rivers of waters ran down his eyes*700 so great and so nearly incessant that the phrase of Scripture might seem applicable to him: "*A fountain of gardens, a well of living waters.*"701

There is an island of the sea in Ireland, from of old fruitful of fishes;702 and the sea there abounds in fish. By the sins of the inhabitants, as it is believed, the wonted supply was taken away, and *she that had many children was waxed feeble*,703 and her own great usefulness utterly dwindled away. While the natives were grieving, and the peoples taking ill the great loss, it was revealed to a certain woman that a remedy might be effected by the prayers of Malachy; and that became known to all, for she herself proclaimed it. By the will of God it happened that Malachy arrived. For while he was going round and filling the region with the Gospel, he turned aside thither that to them also he might impart the same grace.704 But *the barbarous people*,705 who cared more for the fishes,706 demanded with all vehemence that he would deign to regard rather the sterility of their island. And when he answered that it was not for that he had come, but that he desired to catch men rather than fish,707 yet seeing their faith708 he *kneeled down on the shore and prayed*709 to the Lord that, though they were unworthy of it, he would not deny them the benefit granted long before, since they sought it again with so great faith. *The prayer went up*,710 there came up also *a multitude of fishes*,711 and perhaps more fruitful than in ancient days; and the people of the land continue to enjoy that abundance to this day. What wonder if *the prayer of a righteous man* which *penetrates the heavens*,712 penetrated *the abysses*,713 and called forth from the depth of the sea so great supplies of fish?

56. There came, on one occasion, three bishops into the village of Faughart,714 which they say was the birthplace of Brigit the virgin;715 and Malachy was a fourth. And the presbyter who had received them with hospitality, said to him, "What shall I do, for I have no fish?" And when he answered that he should seek them from the fishermen, he said, "For the last two years no fish have been found in the river;716 and for that reason the fishermen also are all scattered and have even abandoned their art." And Malachy replied "Command them to *let down the nets*717 in the name of the Lord." It was done, and twelve salmon were caught. They lowered them a second time, and catching as many more they brought to the tables both an unlooked-for dish and an unlooked-for miracle. And that it might be clear that this was granted to the merits of Malachy, the same sterility nevertheless continued also for the following two years.

[576] Of which, it appears from this and other passages (see p. 33, n. 1), he was still abbot.

[577] 2 Cor. i. 15.

[578] *Gentibus.*

[579] Ps. xlviii. 2.

[580] Isa. xxxii. 20.

[581] Cp. Serm. ii. § 3. Perhaps here, as in that passage, we should read *person* (*persona*) for *profession* (*professio*).

[582] Ps. cxlix. 6, 7.

[583] Ps. xxxiv. 16; 1 Pet. iii. 12.

[584] Ps. lxxv. 4 (vg.).

[585] Ps. xxxiv. 15; 1 Pet. iii. 12.

[586] St. Bernard's secretary, Geoffrey, recalls this sentence (*V.P.* iii. 1). He mentions the saint's many miracles and then proceeds, "But, as he himself says, in commendation of St. Malachy, the first and greatest miracle that he displayed was himself." About half of the present section is embodied by Gerlatus in his description of the character of Godscalcus (*M.G.H.*, Scr. xvii. 700).

[587] Eph. iii. 16.

[588] Jas. iii. 2.

[589] Matt. xii. 36.

[590] Cp. Serm. ii. § 4.

[591] Cp. Consecratio in Ordering of Deacons (Gregorian Sacramentary).

[592] Cp. Serm. ii. § 4.

[593] This statement must be accepted with some reserve. Malachy must have had personal property while he was coarb of Patrick. And accordingly Serm. i. § 6, connects his voluntary poverty with his episcopate in Down, and above (§ 21) his departure from Armagh is represented as a return to poverty. The context shows that St. Bernard is here thinking of the period when he was legate.

[594] Gen. xxxii. 5, etc.

[595] *I.e.* dioceses.

[596] Cp. Rom. i. 9.

[597] 1 Cor. ix. 14.

[598] Luke x. 7.

[599] 1 Cor. ix. 18; cp. Serm. ii. § 1.

[600] Phil. iv. 3 combined with Eph. iv 12; cp. Acts xx. 34.

[601] Matt. xviii. 4, combined with Ecclus. iii. 20.

[602] Luke xii. 13.

[603] 1 Pet. v. 3 (vg.).

[604] 1 Cor. ix. 19.

[605] Cp. *De Dil.* 17: "Paul did not preach the Gospel that he might eat, but ate that he might preach the Gospel; for he loved not food but the Gospel." The reference is of course to 1 Cor. ix.

[606] 1 Tim. vi. 5.

[607] *Opus et onus.*

[608] Amos i. 13.

[609] Cp. 2 Cor. vi. 11.

[610] Matt. vi. 26.

[611] Matt. vi. 25, 31.

[612] 2 Cor. vi. 10.

[613] Cp. Matt. vi. 34.

[614] Secret of Mass for Nativity of St. John Baptist, etc.

[615] Exod. xxxii. 6, etc.

[616] Cp. Gen. xi. 4.

[617] Matt. viii. 20; Luke ix. 58.

[618] 2 Tim. iv. 5.

[619] Jer. vi. 23, etc.

[620] 2 Thess. iii. 8, 12.

[621] Ps. lxxviii. 25.

[622] Ps. cvii. 9.

[623] *Plebes.*

[624] 2 Cor. xii. 12 (vg.).

[625] Cp. 1 Cor. xv. 10.

[626] Ps. lxxvii. 14.—The following narratives of Malachy's miracles are not in chronological order. They are arranged according to their character. Thus the first four (§§ 45, 46) are instances of his power over demons.

[627] Coleraine is said to have been founded by St. Patrick; and it was certainly a religious establishment at least as early as the sixth century (Adamnan, i. 50). One of its erenachs died in 1122 (*A.F.M.*). The word "city" implies that the community was still in existence.

[628] Compare the story of St. Gall listening to the conversation of the demon of the mountain and the demon of the waters, told in Stokes's *Celtic Church in Ireland*, p. 145, from the Life of St. Gall in *M.G.H.*, Scr. i. 7.

[629] The first of three miracles of healing the insane.

[630] In Lecale, co. Down, near Downpatrick. There St. Patrick made his first convert, and there he died. It is not easy to explain why St. Bernard calls it a "region." See further, p. 113, n. 3.

[631] Ulaid was a district which included the greater part of the present county of Down, and the southern part of Antrim.

[632] For a similar avowal by Jocelin, who wrote in the same century as St. Bernard, and other illustrative passages, see Adamnan, p. 4.

[633] See § 8, and above in this section.

[634] The first of three healings of dumb persons.

[635] Mark vii. 33.

[636] The word "city" implies that there was a religious community at Antrim. That this was the case is proved by the round tower which still remains, and other evidence (Reeves, p. 63). But apparently the *Annals* do not refer to any monastery or church at that place. See, however, *U.A.* and *A.F.M.* at 1096 for a possible exception.

[637] 1 Tim. vi. 13.

[638] Ps. lii. 8 (vg.).

[639] Ps. xlv. 7.

[640] Cp. Serm. ii. § 8.

[641] Luke vii. 40.

[642] Acts vi. 5.

[643] Printed text, *Conuama*, no MS. variants being recorded in the margin: perhaps a misprint for *Clonuama*. Mabillon has *Duevania* and K *Duenuania*. A seems to read *Clueuuania*. All these variants point to *Cluain uama* (the meadow of the cave), the Irish name for Cloyne, which is undoubtedly the place referred to (see next note). The next two miracles are concerned with childbirth. The first of them may have been related to St. Bernard by Marcus, the author of Tundale's Vision (see Friedel and Meyer, *La Vision de Tondale*, p. iv., and above p. lxv. n. 3).

[644] Nehemiah Moriarty, who died in 1149 (*A.F.M.*), being then, it is said, 95 years old (Tundale, p. 5). In Tundale (p. 53 f.) he is one of four bishops who were with St. Patrick in Paradise, the others being Cellach, Malachy and Christian O'Morgair. He is there (pp. 5, 54) called bishop of Cloyne (*Cluanensis*).

[645] Cp. 1 Cor. x. 16.

[646] Luke vi. 17.

[647] Mark vi. 18.

[648] 1 Cor. v. 5; 1 Tim. i. 20.

[649] John viii. 4.

[650] Ps. lviii. 10 (vg.).

[651] Probably Dermot MacMurrough, who became king of Leinster in 1126, and died in 1171. He was driven out of his kingdom in 1166, and then invited the Anglo-Normans to come to his aid. The result was the conquest of Ireland. His character merits the description which St. Bernard gives of it.

[652] Rom. xvi. 18.

[653] The first of three healings of paralysis.

[654] John iv. 50.

[655] Gen. ii. 21.

[656] Mark viii. 3.

[657] Acts xiii. 11, etc.

[658] Mark vii. 34.

[659] Cp. Acts xii. 9.

[660] Gen. xlv. 26 (vg.).

[661] Acts iii. 8-10.

[662] Mark vi. 49.

[663] This implies that the diocese of Cork had already been founded. But we cannot be sure that St. Bernard is correct when he says that the clergy and people met to elect a bishop, in view of his inability elsewhere (§ 19) to distinguish bishops from abbots. It is at least possible that there was strife between different septs concerning the appointment of a coarb of Barre, founder of the church of Cork. Malachy may have taken advantage of the strife to nominate a ruler who belonged to no sept in the district and who would allow himself to be consecrated bishop. The vacancy may have been made by the death of Donnell Shalvey, erenach of Cork, in 1140 (*A.F.M.*). The word *erenach* is sometimes used at this period where we might have expected to find *abbot* (cp. *A.F.M.* 1137, quoted in Additional Note C, p. 167).

[664] 2 Cor. xi. 28.

[665] Evidently Malachy was now papal legate. The date of the incident is therefore not earlier than 1140.

[666] It would seem that it was taken for granted that one of the leading men of a sept would be appointed, according to prevalent custom, exemplified in the case of Armagh. This suggests that the vacant office was that of abbot. There would be nothing surprising in the selection of a "poor man," who was not a local magnate, as diocesan bishop.

[667] Luke xvii. 16, 18.—This was probably Gilla Aedha Ua Muidhin, who attended the Synod of Kells in 1152 as bishop of Cork (Keating, iii. 317), and died in 1172 (*A.U.*). Since he attained "a good old age" there is no reason why he should not have been consecrated as early as 1140 or 1141. He had been a monk of Errew in Lough Con, co. Mayo (*A.T.* 1172), and was therefore "a stranger," *i.e.* not a native of Munster. He is called a "poor man," no doubt, for the same reason as Malachy himself (§ 24), because he had embraced the life of voluntary poverty. He had a reputation for piety and learning, for the Annals describe him as "full of the grace of God" (*A.U.*), and "the tower of devotion and wisdom and virginity of Ireland" (*A.T.*). And if the tradition is trustworthy that he was abbot of St. John the Evangelist at Cork, founded by Cormac Mac Carthy "for pilgrims from Connaught" (see the charter of Dermot Mac Carthy printed in Gibson's *History of Cork*, ii. 348), and that it received its later name of Gill Abbey from him, we can explain how he came to be near at hand when the election was taking place.

[668] Matt. ix. 20.—In this and the next two sections we have three miracles wrought on women; one at the point of death, another dead, and the third spiritually dead.

[669] See § 14.

[670] Matt. xvi. 28; Mark ix. 1; Luke ix. 27.

[671] See 2 Kings iv. 29 ff.

[672] Gen. ii. 21.

[673] Luke viii. 44.

[674] Cp. Mark v. 29.

[675] *Si quominus.* The text seems to be corrupt. A friend suggests the emendation *sed quominus deficeret.*

[676] Phil. ii. 27 (inexact quotation).—The story told in this section was a favourite of St. Charles Borromeo (Alban Butler, *Lives of Saints*, ed. Husenbeth, ii. 607).

[677] John iv. 49.

[678] Cp. Mark vi. 13; Jas. v. 14.

[679] Matt. xxv. 6.

[680] 1 Chron. xxi. 8, 17.

[681] Gen. xxxvii. 35.

[682] 2 Cor. ii. 13; cp. Jer. xlv. 3.

[683] Ps. vi. 6 (vg.); Jer. xlv. 3.

[684] Matt. xxvi. 41, etc.

[685] Rom. viii. 26.

[686] Acts ix. 40.

[687] John xvi. 20.

[688] Jas. v. 15.

[689] John ix. 3.

[690] Acts vii. 60.

[691] 1 Tim. vi. 13.

[692] Exod. xv. 8 (vg.).

[693] Ps. l. 3 (vg.).

[694] 1 Cor. iv. 21.

[695] Ps. lxxvii. 10 (vg.).

[696] Rom. xiv. 5.

[697] Eph. iii. 16; cp. 2 Cor. iv. 16.

[698] Ps. xxxv. 12 (vg.).

[699] Matt. viii. 13, combined with John xv. 7.

[700] Ps. cxix. 136.

[701] Cant. iv. 15.

[702] Here and in § 56 we have two miraculous draughts of fish.

[703] 1 Sam. ii. 5.

[704] Cp. Rom. i. 11.

[705] Acts xxviii. 2.

[706] Cp. 1 Cor. ix. 9.

[707] Cp. Luke v. 10.

[708] Cp. Mark ii. 5; Luke v. 20.

[709] Acts xxi. 5.

[710] Acts x. 4.

[711] Luke v. 6; John xxi. 6.

[712] Ecclus. xxxv. 21 (inexact quotation).

[713] Cp. Ps. cvii. 26 (vg.).

[714] Faughart is a parish north of Dundalk.

[715] Apparently the only authority earlier than St. Bernard which makes Faughart the birthplace of St. Brigit is her fourth *Life* (i. 6, *Trias*, 547).

[716] The Kilcurry River.

[717] Luke v. 4.

CHAPTER VII

He does battle for the faith; he restores peace among those who were at variance; he takes in hand to build a stone church.

57. (32). There was a certain clerk in Lismore whose life, as it is said, was good, but his faith not so. He was a man of some knowledge in his own eyes, and dared to say that in the Eucharist there is only a sacrament and not the fact718 of the sacrament, that is, mere sanctification and not the truth of the Body. On this subject he was often addressed by Malachy in secret, but in vain; and finally he was called before a public assembly, the laity however being excluded, in order that if it were possible, he should be healed and not put to confusion.719 So in a gathering of clerics the man was given opportunity to answer for his opinion. And when with all his powers of ingenuity, in which he had no slight skill, he attempted to assert and defend his error, Malachy disputing against him and convicting him, in the judgement of all, he was worsted; and he retired, put to confusion by the unanimity though not sentenced to punishment.720 But he

said that he was not overcome by reason, but crushed by the authority of the bishop. "And you, Malachy," said he, "have put me to confusion this day without good reason, speaking assuredly against the truth and contrary to your own conscience." Malachy, sad for a man so hardened, but grieving more for the injury that was done to the faith, and fearing dangerous developments, called the church together,721 publicly censured the erring one, publicly admonished him to repent, the bishops and the whole clergy urging him to the same effect. When he did not submit, they pronounced an anathema upon him as contumacious and proclaimed him a heretic. But not aroused from sleep by this he said, "You all favour the man, not the truth; I do not accept persons so that I should *forsake the truth*."722 To this word the saint made answer with some heat, "The Lord make you confess the truth even of necessity;" and when he replied "Amen" the assembly was dissolved. Burnt with such a branding-iron he meditated flight, for he could not bear to be of ill repute and dishonoured. And forthwith he departed, carrying his belongings; when lo, seized with sudden weakness, he stood still, and his strength failing he threw himself on the ground in the same spot, panting and weary. A vagabond madman, arriving by chance at that place, came upon the man and asked him what he did there. He replied that he was suffering from great weakness and unable either to advance or to go back. And the other said, "This weakness is nothing else than death itself." *But this he spake not of himself, but*723 God fitly rebuked by means of a madman him who would not submit to the sane counsels of men of understanding. And he said, "Return home, I will help you." Finally with his guidance he went back into the city: he returned to his right mind and to the mercy of the Lord. In the same hour the bishop was summoned, the truth was acknowledged, error was renounced. He confessed his guilt and was absolved. He asked for the viaticum, and reconciliation was granted; and almost in the same moment his perfidy was renounced by his mouth and dissolved by his death. So, to the wonder of all, with all speed was fulfilled the word of Malachy, and with it that of the Scripture which says, "*Trouble gives understanding to the hearing.*"724

58. (33). Between the peoples of certain regions there once arose grievous discord.725 Malachy was importuned to make peace between them, and because he was hindered by other business he committed this matter to one of the bishops. He made excuse and refused, saying that Malachy, not he, had been sought for, that he would be despised, that he was unwilling to take trouble to no purpose. "*Go,*" said Malachy, "*and the Lord be with you.*"726 He replied, "I assent, but if they will not hear me, know that I will appeal to your Fatherhood." Smiling, Malachy said, "Be it so." Then the bishop, having called the parties together, dictated terms of peace; they assented and were reconciled to one another, security was given on both sides, and peace was established; and so he dismissed them. But one party, seeing that their enemies had become careless and were unprepared, because peace having been made they suspected no harm, *said* among themselves, each man *to his neighbour*,727 "What are we minded to do? Victory and vengeance on our foes is in our grasp"; and they began to attack them. What was happening became known to the bishop, and hastening up he charged their chief with wickedness and guile, but he treated him with contempt. He invoked the name of Malachy against him, and he paid no attention to it. Laughing at the bishop he said, "Do you suppose that for you we ought to let those go who did evil to us, whom *God hath delivered into our hands*?"728 And the bishop, remembering the conversation which he had had with Malachy, *weeping and wailing*,729 turned his face towards Malachy's

monastery730 and said, "Where art thou, man of God, where art thou? Is not this, my father, what I told thee of? Alas, alas, I came here that I might do good and not evil; and behold, through me all are perishing, these in the body, those in the soul." Many things in this manner said he as he *mourned* and *lamented*,731 and he urged and addressed Malachy, as though he were present, against the wicked. But meanwhile the impious men did not cease to attack those with whom they had made peace, so as to destroy them; and behold there was *a lying spirit in the mouth of* certain men to *deceive* them.732 And these men met them in the way announcing that a raid had been made into their lands by their adversaries, that all things were being consumed *with the edge of the sword*,733 and that their goods were being laid waste, and their wives and children taken and led away. When they heard this they returned in haste. The hindmost followed the first, *not knowing whither they went*734 or what had happened; for they had not all heard the men who spoke. And when they came and found none of those things which had been told them they were confounded, taken in their own wickedness;735 and they *knew* that they had been given up to *the spirit of error*,736 on account of the messenger of Malachy whom they deceived and his *name* which *they despised.*737 Further, the bishop, when he heard that the traitors were foiled in the iniquity which they had devised, returned with joy to Malachy and told him all things in order which had happened to him.

59. Malachy, knowing that by such an event the peace was disturbed, taking suitable opportunity was at pains in his own person to restore peace once more between them, and to confirm it when restored by the giving and receiving of security and an oath on both sides. But those who before had suffered from the violation of peace, mindful of the injury, and ignoring the agreement and the command of Malachy, took in hand to make reprisals. And all coming together, they set out to take their enemies unprepared and to return upon their own head the evil which they had thought to do to them.738 And when they had very easily forded a great river which lay between them, they were stopped by a rivulet to which they came, not far from it. For indeed now it was not a rivulet, but appeared clearly to be a huge river, denying passage in every part of it to those who desired to cross it. All wondered that it was now so great, knowing how small it had been before, and they said among themselves, "What has caused this inundation? The air is clear, there are no rains, and we do not remember that there have been any lately; and even if there had been much rain, which of us remembers that, to however great a flood it swelled, it ever before covered the land, spreading over sown ground and meadow? *This is the finger of God*,739 and the Lord *is hedging up our ways*,740 on account of Malachy, His saint, whose *covenant we have transgressed*741 and disobeyed his commandment."742 So these also, without accomplishing their purpose, returned to their own territory, likewise confounded. The report was spread *throughout all the region*;743 and they blessed God, who *took the wise in their own craftiness*,744 *and cutting off the horns of the wicked*,745 *exalted the horn of His anointed.*746

60. One of the nobles hostile to the king747 was reconciled by means of Malachy. For he did not trust the king sufficiently to make peace with him except by the mediation of Malachy, or of one for whom the king had equal reverence. His distrust was not unfounded, as afterwards appeared. For when he had become careless, and was no longer taking precautions, the king captured him and put him in bonds, more truly himself captured by ancient hate. His own friends demanded him by *the hand of the mediator*;748 for neither did they expect anything but his death. What should Malachy do? There was

nothing to be done except to recur to that one accustomed refuge of his. Gathering an exceeding mighty army, a great crowd of his own disciples, he went to the king, and demanded him who was bound; he was refused. But Malachy said, "You act unrighteously against the Lord, and against me, and against yourself, *transgressing the covenant*,749 if you disregard it, yet shall not I. A man has entrusted himself to my guarantee; if he should die, I have betrayed him. I am guilty of his blood. Why has it seemed good to you to make me a traitor, yourself a transgressor? Know that *I will eat nothing until*750 he is liberated; no, nor these either."751 Having said this he entered the church. He called upon Almighty God with anxious groanings, his own and those of his disciples, that He would deign to *deliver out of the hand of the transgressor and cruel man*752 him who was unjustly sentenced. And that day and the following night they persisted in fasting and prayer. Word was brought to the king of that which was being done; and his *heart was* the more *hardened*753 by that by which it ought to have been softened. The carnal man took to flight, fearing lest if he remained near at hand he might not be able to withstand the power of prayer; as though, forsooth, if he was hidden it could not find him, nor would penetrate to a remote place. Do you put bounds, wretched man, to *the prayers of saints*?754 Is prayer an arrow that has been shot, that you may *flee from the face of the bow*?755 *Whither wilt thou go from the Spirit of God*, who carries it, *or whither wilt thou flee from His presence*?756 At last Malachy pursues the fugitive, he finds him who lies hidden. "*You shall be blind and not seeing*,757 that you may see better, and may understand that *it is hard for you to kick against the pricks.*758 Nay, perceive even now that *sharp arrows of the mighty*759 have come to you, which, although they have rebounded from your heart, because it is of stone, have not rebounded from your eyes. Would that even through the windows of the eyes they might reach to the heart, and *trouble give understanding*760 to blindness." It could be seen that *Saul* again was *led by the hand*761 and brought to Ananias, a wolf to a sheep, that he might disgorge his prey. He disgorged it and *received sight*,762 for to such a degree was Malachy like a sheep, if, for example, it were to take pity even on the wolf. Note carefully from this, reader, with whom Malachy had his dwelling, what sort of princes they were, what sort of peoples. How is it that he also was not *a brother to dragons, and a companion to owls*? 763 And therefore the Lord *gave him power to tread upon serpents and scorpions*,764 *to bind their kings with chains and their nobles with fetters of iron.*765 Hear now what follows.

61. (34). He to whom Malachy had yielded the possessions of the monastery of Bangor,766 ungrateful for the benefit, from that time forward behaved himself always most arrogantly against him and his followers, hostile to them in all things, plotting everywhere, and disparaging his deeds. But not without punishment. He had an only son, who, imitating his father and daring himself to act in opposition to Malachy, died the same year. And thus he died. It seemed good to Malachy that a stone oratory should be erected at Bangor like those which he had seen constructed in other regions.767 And when he began to lay the foundations the natives wondered, because in that land no such buildings were yet to be found.768 But that worthless fellow, presumptuous and arrogant as he was, not only wondered but was indignant. And from that indignation *he conceived grief and brought forth iniquity*.769 And he became a *talebearer among the peoples*,770 now *disparaging secretly*,771 now speaking evil openly; drawing attention to Malachy's frivolity, shuddering at the novelty, exaggerating the expense. With such poisonous

words as these he was urging and inducing many to put a stop to it: "Follow me, and what ought not to be done by any but ourselves let us not permit to be done against our will." Then with many whom he was able to persuade—*himself the* first *leader in speech*772 as well as the origin of the evil—he went down to the place, and finding the man of God accosted him: "Good sir, why have you thought good to introduce this novelty into our regions? We are Scots, not Gauls. What is this frivolity? What need was there for a work so superfluous, so proud? Where will you, *a poor and needy man,*773 find *the means to finish it*?774 Who will see it finished? What sort of presumption is this, to begin, I say not what you cannot finish, but what you cannot even see finished? Though indeed it is the act of a maniac rather than of a presumptuous man to attempt what is beyond his measure, what exceeds his strength, what baffles his abilities. Cease, cease, desist from this madness. If not, we shall not permit it, we shall not tolerate it." This he said, proclaiming what he would do, but not considering what it was within his power to do. For some of those on whom he counted and whom he had brought with him, when they saw the man775 changed their minds and went no more with him.776

62. And to him the holy man spoke quite freely: "Wretched man, the work which you see begun, and on which you look askance, shall undoubtedly be finished: many shall see it finished. But you, because you do not wish it, will not see it;777 and that which you wish not shall be yours—to die: take heed that you do not *die in your sins.*"778 So it happened: he died, and the work was finished; but he saw it not, for, as we have said already, he died the same year. Meanwhile the father, who soon heard what the holy man had foretold concerning his son, and knew that his word was *quick and powerful,*779 said, "He *has slain my son.*"780 And by the instigation of the devil he burned with such rage against him that he was not afraid, before the duke and magnates of Ulaid, to accuse of falsehood and lying him who was most truthful and a disciple and lover of the Truth; and he used violent language against him, calling him an ape.781 And Malachy, who had been taught not to *render railing for railing,782 was dumb, and opened not his mouth783 while the wicked was before him.*784 But the Lord was not forgetful of His word which He had spoken, *Vengeance is mine, I will repay.*785 The same day when the man returned home he expiated the rashness of his unbridled tongue, the avenger being the very one at whose instigation he had let it loose. The demon seized him and cast him into the fire, but he was soon pulled out by those that stood by; yet with his body partly burnt, and deprived of reason. And while he was raving Malachy was called, and when he came he found the accursed man, his foaming mouth contorted, terrifying all things with horrible sounds and movements, his whole body writhing, and scarcely to be kept in restraint by many men. And when he prayed for his enemy the man of all perfection was heard, but only in part. For in a moment, while the saint was praying, he opened his eyes, and recovered his understanding. But *an evil spirit of the Lord*786 was left to him *to buffet him,787 that he might learn not to blaspheme.*788 We believe that he still lives, and up to this time is expiating the great sin which he sinned against the saint; but they say that at certain times he is a lunatic. Further, the aforesaid possessions, since he could no longer hold them by reason of his helplessness and uselessness, returned in peace to the place to which they had belonged. Nor did Malachy refuse them, when the prospect of peace was held out at length after so much trouble.

63. But now our narrative must return to the work of the building which Malachy

had undertaken. And though Malachy had not the means, I do not say to finish it, but to do any part of it, yet *his heart trusted in the Lord*.789 The Lord, in fact, provided that, though he *set not his hope on treasures of money*,790 money should not be lacking. For who else caused a treasure to be stored in that place, and being stored, not to be found till the time and work of Malachy? The servant of God found in God's purse what was not in his own. Deservedly, indeed. For what more just than that he who for God's sake possessed nothing should enter into partnership with God, and that they should both *have one purse*.791 For the man who believes, the whole world is a treasury of riches; and what is it but a kind of purse of God? Indeed He says, *The world is mine, and the fulness thereof*.792 Hence it was that when many pieces of silver were found Malachy did not put them back in their place, but took them out of their place; for he bade the whole gift of God to be spent on the work of God.793 He considered not his own necessities nor those of his companions, but *cast his* thought upon *the Lord*,794 to whom he did not doubt that he ought to resort as often as need required. And there is no doubt that that was the work of God, because Malachy had foreseen it by God's revelation. He had first consulted with the brothers concerning that work; and many on account of their lack of means were unwilling to assent to it. Anxious therefore and doubtful what he should do, he began to inquire earnestly in prayer what was the will of God. And one day coming back from a journey,795 when he drew near to the place he viewed it some way off; and lo, there appeared a great oratory, of stone and very beautiful. And paying careful attention to its position, form and construction, he took up the work with confidence, having first however related the vision to a few of the elder brothers. Indeed so carefully did he adhere to all his attentive observations regarding place and manner and quality that when the work was finished that which was made appeared closely similar to that which he had seen, as if he also as well as Moses had heard the saying, *Look* that *thou make all things according to the pattern shewed to thee in the mount*.796 By the same kind of vision there was shown to him before it was built, not only the oratory, but also the whole monastery, which is situated at Saul.797

64. (35). As he was passing through a certain city and a great multitude was running together to him, by chance he saw a young man among the rest eager *to see* him.798 He had *climbed up* on a stone, and standing on tip-toes, with outstretched neck, contemplating him with eyes and mind, showed himself to him as a kind of new Zacchaeus.799 And it was not hid from Malachy (for the Holy Spirit revealed it) that he had truly come *in the spirit and power of* Zacchaeus.800 He took no notice, however, at the time, and passed on in silence. But in the hospice that night he told the brothers how he had seen him and what he had foreseen concerning him. But on the third day behold he came with a certain nobleman, his lord, who disclosed the wish and desire of the young man, and asked that he would deign to receive him on his commendation, and have him henceforth among his companions. And Malachy recognizing him said, "There is no need that man should commend him *whom* already *God has commended.*"801 And taking him by the hand he delivered him over to our abbot Congan802 and he to the brothers. But that young man—still living if I mistake not—the first lay conversus of the monastery of the Suir,803 has testimony from all that he lives a holy life among the brothers, according to the Cistercian Order. And the disciples recognized also in this incident that Malachy had *the spirit of prophecy,*804 and not in this only, but in that which we shall add.

65. When he was offering the sacraments,805 and the deacon had approached him to do something belonging to his office, the priest beholding him groaned because he had perceived that something was hidden in him that was not meet. When the sacrifice was over, having been probed privately concerning his conscience *he confessed and denied not*806 that he had been *mocked*807 in a dream that night. And Malachy enjoined penance upon him and said, "It was your duty not to have ministered to-day, but reverently to withdraw from sacred things and to show respect to so great and divine mysteries, that purified by this humiliation you might in future minister more worthily."

Likewise on another occasion,808 when he was sacrificing and praying at the hour of sacrifice with his accustomed sanctity and purity of heart, the deacon standing by him, a dove was seen to enter through the window in great glory. And with that glory the priest was completely flooded, and the whole of the gloomy basilica became suffused with light. But the dove, after flitting about for a while, at length settled down on the cross before the face of the priest. The deacon was amazed; and trembling on account of the novelty both of the light and of the bird, for that is a rare bird in the land, fell upon his face, and palpitating, scarcely dared to rise even when the necessity of his office required it. After Mass Malachy spoke to him privately and bade him, as he valued his life, on no account to divulge the mystery which he had seen, as long as he himself was alive.

Once, when he was at Armagh with one of his fellow-bishops, he rose in the night and began to go round the memorials of the saints, of which there are many in the cemetery of St. Patrick,809 with prayer. And lo, they saw one of the altars suddenly take fire. For both saw this great vision, and both wondered. And Malachy, understanding that it was a sign of the great merit of him, or those, whose bodies rested under that altar, ran and plunged into the midst of the flames with outstretched arms and embraced the sacred altar. What he did there, or what he perceived, none knows; but that from that fire he went forth ablaze more than his wont with heavenly fire, I suppose there is none of the brothers who were with him then that does not know.

66. These things have been mentioned, a few out of many, but many for this time.

For these are not times of signs, as it is written, *We see not signs; there is no more any prophet.*810 Whence it appears sufficiently how great in merits was my Malachy, who was so rich in signs, rare as they now are. For in what kind of *ancient miracles*811 was not Malachy conspicuous? If we consider well those few that have been mentioned, he lacked not prophecy,812 nor revelation,813 nor vengeance upon the impious,814 nor *the grace of healings*,815 nor transformation of minds,816 nor lastly raising the dead.817 By all these things God was blessed who so loved and adorned him, who also magnified him *before kings*,818 and gave him *the crown of glory*.819 That he was loved is proved in his merits, that he was adorned, in his signs, that he was magnified, in his vengeance on enemies, that he had glory, in recompense of rewards. You have in Malachy, diligent reader, something to wonder at, you have also something to imitate. Now carefully note what you may hope for as the result of these things. For *the end of these things is a precious death.*820

[718] *Rem.* This may have been a follower of Berengarius, who in his recantation in 1059 anathematized the heresy that the bread and wine "after consecration are merely a sacrament and not the true Body and Blood of our Lord Jesus Christ" (Mansi, xix. 900).

[719] Compare St. Bernard's method with Abélard, *V.P.* iii. 13; and for his dealing with a brother who did not believe in transubstantiation, *ibid.* vii. 8, 9.

[720] I follow the printed text: *de consensu confusus quidem exiit, sed non correptus*. But Mabillon, supported by A, has "he retired from the assembly confounded, but not brought to the right opinion" (*de conuentu ... non correctus*). K reads *de conuentu ... non correptus*.

[721] It would seem from this that Malachy was acting as legate. The date is therefore after 1140.

[722] Prov. xxviii. 21 (vg.).

[723] John xi. 51.

[724] Isa. xxviii. 19 (vg.).

[725] In §§ 58-62 we have three stories in which Malachy appears as a peacemaker.

[726] 1 Sam. xvii. 37, combined with 1 Chron. xxii. 16.

[727] Gen. xi. 3 (vg.).

[728] Judg. xvi. 24.

[729] Mark v. 38.

[730] This expression indicates that Malachy had a special relation to one monastery. It can hardly have been any other than Bangor.

[731] Matt. xi. 17.

[732] 1 Kings xxii. 22; 2 Chron. xviii. 21.

[733] Josh. vi. 21; Judg. iv. 15, etc.

[734] Heb. xi. 8.

[735] Cp. Ps. x. 2.

[736] 1 John iv. 6.

[737] Cp. Mal. i. 6.

[738] Cp. Ps. vii. 16.

[739] Exod. viii. 19.

[740] Hos. ii. 6.

[741] Josh. vii. 15, etc.

[742] In Serm. ii. § 2, where this story is again briefly told, the miracle is more directly ascribed to Malachy, and the stream is said to have swelled suddenly.

[743] Cp. Luke iv. 14, etc.

[744] Job v. 13, combined with 1 Cor. iii. 19.

[745] Ps. lxxv. 10.

[746] 1 Sam. ii. 10.

[747] Probably Turlough O'Conor, who is said by the annalists to have imprisoned illegally several persons of high position, viz. (1) his own son Rory O'Conor, together with Donnell O'Flaherty and Cathal O'Conor, in 1143, (2) Murrough Ua Maelsechlainn, king of Meath, in 1143, and (3) Teague O'Brien, in 1148. Release was obtained, in the first instance, in 1144 by the clergy of Ireland and the "coarb of Patrick," who fasted at Rathbrennan. The coarb may have been Malachy. In the second instance, it was secured through the influence of certain "sureties"; and in the third, "at the intercession of the bishops of Ireland with the coarb of Patrick, Mael Maedoc Ua Morgair" (*A.F.M.*, *A.T.*). The Annals, however, know nothing of the blinding of O'Conor. The incident in the text is mentioned in Serm. ii. § 2.

[748] Gal iii. 19.

[749] Josh. vii. 15, etc.

[750] Acts xxiii. 14.

[751] An example of the well-known Irish custom of "fasting on" a person with a view to his discomfiture (cp. p. 106, n. 9).

[752] Ps. lxxi. 4 (inexact quotation).

[753] Exod. viii. 19.

[754] Rev. v. 8.

[755] Isa. xxi. 15 (vg.).

[756] Ps. cxxxix. 7.

[757] Acts xiii. 11.

[758] Acts xxvi. 14.

[759] Ps. cxx. 4.

[760] Isa. xxviii. 19.

[761] Acts ix. 8.

[762] Acts ix. 18.

[763] Job xxx. 29.

[764] Luke x. 19 (quotation not exact).

[765] Ps. cxlix.

[766] See § 13.

[767] This remark proves that the building of the oratory was begun after Malachy's return from France. The same conclusion follows from the words "We are Scots, *not Gauls*," lower down.

[768] St. Bernard is speaking, not of stone churches in general, as has sometimes been assumed, but of stone oratories, which may have been unknown in "that land," *i.e.* the district about Bangor (see p. 32, n. 3). The innovation would naturally cause dissatisfaction among a conservative people. Indignation may also have been excited by the unusual size of the building; for it was "a great oratory" (§ 63). But on the other hand, its ornate style cannot have contributed to the opposition which the project aroused; for it commenced when the foundations were being laid. Indeed, however "beautiful" it may

have been (§ 63), it was probably, like the churches of the Cistercians, of simple design and devoid of ornament. See St. Bernard's *Apologia ad Guillelmum*, § 28 ff. (*P.L.* clxxxii. 914 f.). The only relic of the medieval monastery of Bangor is a rudely built wall, once pierced by a door and a window, now built up. It seems to be later than the twelfth century. About 120 yards to the south-west of it is "The Abbey Church," still used for worship. The main part of this structure dates from the seventeenth century. But the core of the tower appears to be much earlier, and may be on the site of St. Malachy's oratory.

[769] Job xv. 35 (vg.); Ps. vii. 14 (vg.).

[770] Lev. xix. 16.

[771] Ps. ci. 5.

[772] Acts xiv. 12.

[773] Ps. lxxiv. 21.

[774] Luke xiv. 28.

[775] *Viro, i.e.* Malachy.

[776] Cp. John vi. 66.

[777] *Quia non uis non uidebis.*

[778] John viii. 21.

[779] Heb. iv. 12.

[780] 1 Kings xvii. 18.

[781] Perhaps because he imitated the customs of the Gauls.

[782] 1 Pet. iii. 9.

[783] Isa. liii. 7.

[784] Ps. xxxix. 1.

[785] Rom. xii. 19.

[786] 1 Sam. xvi. 14; xix. 9 (vg.).

[787] 2 Cor. xii. 7

[788] 1 Tim. i. 20.

[789] Susanna, 35.

[790] Ecclus. xxxi. 8 (vg.: with variant).

[791] Prov. i. 14.

[792] Ps. l. 12.

[793] Malachy disposed of the treasure according to his will. That fact, together with his relation to the brothers, revealed by the next few sentences, makes it exceedingly probable that he was still their abbot.

[794] Ps. lv. 23 (vg.).

[795] Bangor was apparently his headquarters.

[796] Heb. viii. 5.

[797] Jocelin, writing towards the end of the twelfth century, declares that St. Patrick founded a monastery at Saul (*Vita S. Patricii*, cap. 32). But, apparently, neither in the Annals nor in any other authority earlier than Jocelin, is mention made of a monastery there before St. Malachy's time. The text seems to imply that there were no monastic buildings on the site when he founded (or re-founded) it. Malachy placed in his new monastery a convent of regular canons of St. Augustine (*A.U.* 1170); but it never became an important establishment, though it was still in existence in the sixteenth century. See Reeves, pp. 40, 220 ff.

[798] This and the next story (§ 65) illustrate Malachy's power of reading the

hearts of men.

[799] Luke xix. 1-4.

[800] Luke i. 17.

[801] 2 Cor. x. 18.

[802] See p. 4, n. 7.

[803] *Suriensis monasterii.* The monastery of Inislounaght, close to the River Suir, a mile or two to the west of Clonmel, co. Tipperary, is commonly known as *De Surio.* The present passage seems to show that it was founded before 1148. For information about it see an article by the late Dr. Bagwell, in *J.R.S.A.I.* xxxix. 267 f. and Janauschek, *Orig. Cist.* p. 131. This incident must have been considerably later than the foundation of Mellifont (see p. 75, n. 4). It may therefore be dated between 1143 and 1147.

[804] Rev. xix. 10.

[805] This word is constantly used in the plural of the Eucharist, each of the elements being regarded as a "sacrament."

[806] John i. 20.

[807] Gen. xxxix. 17.

[808] This story is suggested by the last because the incident occurred during the celebration of Mass.

[809] Evidently the cemetery in which, according to local tradition, St. Patrick was buried (see § 19). It was probably the *Ferta Martair*, the site of St. Patrick's earlier settlement at Armagh (Reeves, *Churches*, p. 5; *R.I.A.* xviii. 660). It seems to be hinted that St. Malachy received a revelation of the position of his grave.

[810] Ps. lxxiv. 9.

[811] Secret of Mass for Kings, etc.

[812] A fresh classification of Malachy's miracles. For prophecy see §§ 36, 48, 52, 57, 62, 64 f.

[813] §§ 11, 63, 64, 65.

[814] §§ 22 f., 48, 57, 60, 62.

[815] 1 Cor. xii. 9 (vg.).—§§ 14, 15, 40, 45-47, 49-52, 60, 62.

[816] §§ 26, 54, 57, 61.

[817] § 53.

[818] Ps. cxix. 46.—§§ 10, 40, 60.

[819] 1 Pet. v. 4.

[820] Rom. vi. 21, combined with Ps. cxvi. 15.

CHAPTER VIII

Departure from Ireland. Death and Burial at Clairvaux.

1148, May (?)   67. (30). Being asked once, in what place, if a choice were given him, he would prefer to spend his last day—for on this subject the brothers used to ask one another what place each would select for himself—he hesitated, and made no reply. But when they insisted, he said, "If I take my departure hence821 I shall do so nowhere more gladly than whence I may rise together with our Apostle"822—he referred to St. Patrick; "but if it behoves me to make a pilgrimage, and if God so permits, I have selected Clairvaux." When asked also about the time, [he named in reply] the festival of all the dead.823 If it is regarded as a mere wish, it was fulfilled, if as a prophecy, not *a jot passed* from it.824 *As we have heard so have we seen*825 alike concerning place and day. Let us relate briefly in what order and by what occasion it came to pass. Malachy took it amiss that Ireland was still without a pall; for he was zealous for the sacraments, and would not that his nation should be wholly deprived of any one of them.826 And remembering that it had been promised to him by Pope Innocent,827 he was the more sad that while he was still alive it had not been sent for. And taking advantage of the fact that Pope Eugenius828 held the chief rule and was reported to have gone at that time to France,829 he rejoiced that he had found opportunity for claiming it. He took for granted that, the Pope being such a man as he was, and having been promoted from such a religious profession—and the more because he had been a special son of his own Clairvaux—he need not fear that he should have any difficulty with him. Therefore the bishops were summoned; a council assembled.830 Matters which were of immediate importance at the time were discussed for three days, and on the fourth the scheme of obtaining the pall was broached. Assent was given, but on condition that it should be obtained by another. However, since the journey was a comparatively short one, and on that account the pilgrimage seemed more easy to be endured, none presumed to oppose his counsel and will. And when the council was dissolved Malachy started on his way.831 Such brothers as had come together followed him to the shore; but not many, for he doubtless restrained them. One of them, Catholicus by name, with tearful voice and face, said to him, "Alas! you are going away; and in how great, almost daily, trouble you leave me you are not ignorant, and yet you do not, of your pity, give me help. If I deserve to suffer, what sin have the brothers committed that they are scarcely allowed to have any day or night free from the labour of caring for and guarding me?" By these words and tears of his son (for he wept) the father's *heart was* troubled,832 and he embraced him with caresses, and making the sign of the cross on his breast said, "Be assured that you will have no such suffering till I return." Now he was an epileptic, and fell often; insomuch that at times he suffered not once but many times a day. He had been a victim to this horrible disease for six years; but at the word of Malachy he made a perfect recovery. From that hour he has suffered no such thing; no such thing, as we believe, will he suffer henceforth, for henceforth Malachy will not return.

68. When he was just about to embark there *came unto him* two of those who *clave unto him*833 more closely, boldly *desiring a certain thing of him*. And he said to them, *"What would ye?"*834 And they answered, "We will not say, except you promise that you will give it." He pledged himself. And they said, "We would have you certainly promise of your condescension, that you will return in good health to Ireland." All the others also insisted upon it. Then he deliberated for a while, repenting at first that he had bound himself, and not finding any way of escape. He was *straitened on every side*,835 while no way of safety presented itself from both dangers—of forfeiting his wish and of breaking his promise. It seemed at length that he should rather choose that which influenced him more strongly at the moment, and leave the rest to higher guidance. He assented, sadly it is true; but he was more unwilling that they should be made sad; and pledging himself as they wished, he went on board the ship. And when they had

completed nearly half the voyage suddenly a contrary wind drove the ship back and brought it to the land of Ireland again. Leaving the ship he passed the night in the port itself in one of his churches. And he joyfully gave thanks for the resourcefulness of the divine providence, by which it came about that he had now satisfied his promise. But in the morning, he went on board, and the same day, after a prosperous crossing, came into Scotland. On the third day836 he reached a place which is called Viride Stagnum;837 which he had caused to be prepared that he might found an abbey there. And leaving there some of his sons, our brothers, as a convent of monks and abbot838 (for he had brought them with him for that purpose) he bade them farewell and set out.

69. And as he passed on, King David met him, by whom he was received with joy and was detained as his guest for some days.839 And having done many things pleasing to God he resumed the journey that he had begun. And passing through Scotland, at the very border of England he went aside to the Church of Gisburn, where there dwell religious men leading a canonical life,840 familiar to him of old for their religious conversation and honourable character. At that place a woman was brought to him, suffering from a disease horrible to see, which is commonly called cancer; and he healed her. For when water which he blessed was sprinkled on the sores she ceased to feel pain. On the next day scarcely a sore was to be seen.

Departing thence he came to the sea, but was refused passage. The reason, if I am not mistaken, was that some difference had arisen between the chief pontiff and the king of England: for the king suspected in that good man I know not what evil, if he should cross the sea;841 for neither did he allow other bishops to cross.842 That obstacle, though contrary to the will of Malachy, was not contrary to the object of his wish. He grieved that the attainment of his desire should be postponed, not knowing that by this it would be the rather fulfilled. For if he had immediately passed over the sea he would have been obliged to pass by Clairvaux in order to follow the chief Pontiff. For by that time he had left it and was at or near Rome.843 But now through this delay it was brought about that he crossed later, and so, as was fitting, he came to the place of his most holy death, and at the hour of its approach.

1148, Oct. 13 or 14   70. (37). And he was received by us, though he came from the west, as the true *day-spring844 from on high visiting us.*845 O, how greatly did that radiant sun fill our Clairvaux with added glory! How pleasant was the festal day that dawned upon us at his coming! *This was the day which the Lord had made, we rejoiced and were glad in it.*846 As for me, with what rapid and bounding step, though trembling and weak,847 did I soon *run* to meet him! With what joy I *kissed him*! With what joyful arms I *embraced*848 this grace sent to me from heaven! With what eager face and mind, my father, *I brought thee into my mother's house and into the chamber of her that conceived me*!849 What festive days I spent with thee then, though few! But how did he in his turn greet us? In truth our pilgrim showed himself cheerful and kindly to all, to all incredibly gracious. *How good and how pleasant*850 a part he played among us as our guest, whom, forsooth, *he had come from the uttermost parts of the earth* to see, not that he should *hear*, but that he should show us, a *Solomon*! In fact we *heard* his *wisdom*,851 we had his presence, and we have it still. 1148, Oct. 18Already four or five days of this our festival had passed, when lo, on the feast day of Blessed Luke the Evangelist,852 when he had celebrated Mass in the convent853 with that holy devotion of his, he was taken with a fever and lay down in his bed: and all of us were [sick] with him. *The end of our mirth is sorrow*,854 but moderate sorrow, because for a time the fever seemed to be slight. You should see the brothers running about, eager to give, or to receive. To whom was it not sweet to see him? To whom was it not sweeter to minister to him? Both were pleasant and both salutary. It was an act of kindness to do him service, and it was repaid also to each one of them, by the gift of grace. All assisted, all were busied *with much serving*,855 searching for medicines, applying poultices, urging him often to eat. But he said to them, "These things are without avail, yet for love of you I do whatever you bid me." For he knew that *the time* of his departure was at hand.856

71. And when the brothers who had come with him857 urged him more boldly, saying that it behoved him not to despair of life, for that no signs of death appeared in him,858 he said, "It behoves Malachy to leave the body this year."859 And he added, "See, the day is drawing near which, as you very well know, I have always desired to be the day of *my dissolution.*860 *I know whom I have believed and am persuaded*;861 I shall *not be disappointed of* the rest of *my desire*,862 since I already have part of it. He who by his mercy has led me to the place which I sought, will not deny me the time for which I wished no less. As regards this mean body, *here is my rest*;863 as regards my soul, the Lord will provide, *who saveth them that put their trust in Him*.864 And *there is* no small hope *laid up for me at that day*865 in which so great benefits are bestowed by the living on the dead."866 Not far away was that day when he spoke thus. Meanwhile he ordered that he should be anointed with the sacred oil. When the convent of brothers was going out that it might be done solemnly,867 he would not permit them to come up to him; he went down to them. For he was lying in the balcony868 of the upper house. He was anointed; and when he had received the viaticum, he commended himself to the prayers of the brothers, and the brothers to God,869 and went back to bed. He went down from the high balcony870 on his feet, and again, as if that were not enough, he went up on his feet; yet he said that death *was at the doors.*871 Who should believe that this man was dying? Himself alone and God could know it. His face did not seem to have become pallid or wasted. His brow was not wrinkled, his eyes were not sunken, his nostrils were not thin, his lips were not contracted, his teeth were not brown, his neck was not gaunt

and lean, his shoulders were not bowed, the flesh on the rest of his body had not failed. Such was the grace of his body, and such the *glory of his countenance which was* not *to be done away*,872 even in death. As he appeared in life so was he also in death, more like to one alive.

72. (38). Hitherto our story has run a rapid course; but now it stays because Malachy *has finished his course*.873 He is still, and with him we are still. Moreover, who would willingly hasten to [tell of] death? Especially thy death, holy father, who could describe it? Who would wish to hear the story? Yet we loved *in life, in death we shall not be divided*.874 Brothers, let us not forsake in death him with whom we companied in life. From further Scotland875 he ran hither to death; *let us also go and die with him*.876 I must, I must tell that which of necessity I saw. The celebration, everywhere renowned, of All Saints877 comes, and according to the ancient saying, *Music in mourning is an unseasonable discourse*.878 We come, we sing, even against our will. We weep while we sing and we sing while we weep. Malachy, though he sings not, yet does not lament. For why should he lament, who is drawing near to joy? For *us who remain*,879 mourning remains. Malachy alone keeps festival. For what he cannot do with his body he does with his mind, as it is written, *The thought of man shall confess to thee, and the residue of thought shall keep the day of festival to thee.*880 When the instrument of the body fails him, and the organ of the mouth is silent, and the office of the voice ceases, it remains that with songs in his heart he keeps festival. Why should not the saint keep festival, who is being brought to the festival of the saints?881 He presents to them what will soon be due to himself. *Yet a little while*882 and he will be one of them.

73. Towards the dusk of night, when now somehow the celebration of the day had been finished by us, Malachy had drawn near, not to dusk but to dawn. Was it not dawn to him883 for whom *the night is far spent and the day is at hand*?884 So, the fever increasing, a burning sweat from within him began to break out over his whole body, that, as it were *going through fire and through water, he might be brought into a wealthy place*.885 Now his life was despaired of, now each one condemned his own judgement, now none doubted that Malachy's word886 was prevailing. We were called; we came. And lifting up his eyes on those who stood round him, he said, "*With desire I have desired to eat this passover* with *you*;887 I give thanks to the divine compassion, I have *not been disappointed of my desire*."888 Do you see the man free from care in death, and, not yet dead, already certain of life? No wonder. Seeing that the night was come to which he had looked forward, and that in it the day was dawning for him, so to speak triumphing over the night, he seemed to scoff at the darkness and as it were to cry, "*I shall* not *say, surely the darkness shall cover me*, because this *night shall be light about me in my pleasure*."889 And tenderly consoling us he said, "Take care of me; if it be allowed me I shall not forget you. And it shall be allowed. *I have believed in God*,890 and *all things are possible to him that believeth*.891 I have loved God; I have loved you, and *charity never faileth*."892 *And looking up to heaven*893 he said, "O God, *keep them in Thy name*;894 *and not these* only *but* all them *also who through* my *word*895 and ministry have given themselves to thy service." Then, laying his hands on each one severally and blessing all,896 he bade them go to rest, *because his hour was not yet come*.897

1148, November 2   74. We went. We returned about midnight, for at that hour it was announced that *the light shineth in darkness*.898 The house filled, the whole community was present, many abbots also who had assembled. *With psalms and hymns and spiritual songs*899 we followed our friend as he returned to his own country.900 In the fifty-fourth year of his age,901 at the place and time which he had chosen beforehand and predicted, Malachy, the bishop and legate of the holy Apostolic See, taken up *by the angels*,902 as it were from our hands, happily *fell asleep in the Lord*.903 And indeed he slept. His placid face was the sign of a placid departure. And verily *the eyes of all were* fixed *upon him*;904 but none could perceive when he departed. When dead he was thought to be alive, when alive, dead; so true was it that there was no difference which might distinguish death from life. The same vivacity of face, the same serenity, as commonly appears in one who sleeps. You might say that death robbed him of none of these things, but rather very greatly increased them. He was not changed; but he changed us all. In wondrous fashion the sorrow and groaning of all suddenly sank to rest, *sadness* was changed *into joy*,905 singing banished lamentation.906 He is borne forth, voices are borne to heaven, he is borne into the oratory on the shoulders of the abbots. *Faith has conquered*,907 affection triumphs, things assume their normal course. All things are carried out in order, all proceed in the way of reason.

75. And in truth what reason is there to lament Malachy immoderately, as though his *death* was not *precious*,908 as though it was not rather sleep than death, as though it was not the port of death and the portal of life?909 *Our friend* Malachy *sleepeth*;910 and I, must I mourn? such mourning is based on custom, not on reason. If the Lord *hath given His beloved one sleep*, and such sleep, in which there is *an heritage of the Lord*, even *children, and the reward, the fruit of the womb*,911 which of these things seems to call for weeping? Must I weep for him who has escaped from weeping? He rejoices, he triumphs, he has been brought *into the joy of his Lord*,912 and I, must I lament for him? I desire these things for myself, I do not grudge them to him. Meanwhile the obsequies are prepared, the sacrifice is offered for him,913 all is performed according to custom with the greatest devotion. There stood some way off a boy whose arm hung by his side dead, rather burdensome to him than useful. When I discovered him I signed to him to come near, and taking his withered hand I laid it on the hand of the bishop, and it restored it to life. For in truth *the grace of healings*914 lived in the dead; and his hand was to the dead hand what Elisha was to the dead man.915 The boy *had come from far*916 and the hand which he brought hanging down, he carried back whole to his own country. Now, all things having been duly accomplished in the very oratory of Saint Mary, Mother of God, *in which he was well pleased*,917 Malachy is carried to his burial918 in the eleven hundred and forty-eighth year from the Incarnation of the Lord, on the fourth of the Nones of November.919 Thine, good Jesus, is *the deposit* which has been committed to us,920 Thine is the treasure which is laid up with us.921 We *keep* it922 to be given back at the time when Thou shalt see fit to recall it; only that he may not go forth without his comrades, but that him whom we have had as our guest we may have also as our leader, when we *shall reign* with Thee, and with him also, *for ever and ever*.923 Amen.

[821] *I.e.* "If I die in Ireland."

[822] In Armagh. See §§ 19, 65.

[823] All Souls' Day, November 2.

[824] Matt. v. 18.

[825] Ps. xlviii. 8.

[826] Note that the pall is called a sacrament.

[827] See § 38.

[828] Bernard Paganelli, a monk of Clairvaux, was sent to Rome by St. Bernard at the request of Innocent II. and was appointed abbot of the monastery of St. Anastasius. On the death of Lucius II. he was elected Pope, February 15, 1144, and assumed the title of Eugenius III. (H. K. Mann, *Lives of the Popes*, ix. 131 ff.)

[829] Eugenius left Viterbo at the beginning of 1147. He was at Lyons in March, and at Troyes on April 10 (Jaffé, p. 624 ff.; Mann, ix. 185).

[830] In accordance with the instructions of Innocent II. (§ 38): "A Synod was convened at Inis Patraic by Mael Maedoc, coarb of Patrick, at which were present fifteen bishops and two hundred priests, to establish rules and morals for all, both laity and clergy; and Mael Maedoc Ua Morgair, by the advice of the Synod, went a second time to Rome (*sic*) to confer with the comarb of Peter" (*A.F.M.* 1148). Inispatrick is a small island off Skerries, co. Dublin. For the date see *R.A.I.* xxxv. 249 f. In the same year Malachy had consecrated the monastery of Knock (*A.F.M.* See p. 67, n. 3).

[831] St. Bernard seems to have thought that St. Malachy set sail immediately after the Synod, and from a port not far from the place where it met. But this is impossible, for one day's sail brought him to Scotland (§ 68). He seems to have embarked at Bangor, which is about a hundred miles north of Inispatrick.

[832] Cp. Lam. ii. 11.

[833] Ruth i. 14.

[834] Matt. xx. 20, combined with Mark x. 35, 36.

[835] Susanna, 22.

[836] That is, the first day after his landing in Scotland.

[837] The Green Lake. It is now Soulseat, about eight miles from Cairngarroch. At this place Fergus, lord of Galloway (p. 76, n. 4), founded a famous monastery of Premonstratensian canons (Grub, *Eccl. Hist. of Scotland*, i. 269), which must not be confused with Malachy's more humble community.

[838] The abbot was Michael, who had belonged to the community at Bangor (§ 15). As this new community is called "a convent of monks" we may infer that it was of the Cistercian Order.

[839] Note the leisureliness of the journey in its earlier stages. Later on Malachy encountered difficulties, which no doubt involved further delay (Serm. i. § 1).

[840] Gisburn is a village in the West Riding of Yorkshire on the river Ribble, not far from the border of Lancashire. It is clear that on this occasion Malachy followed the line of Watling Street, which ran through Ribchester, on the Ribble, about fourteen miles from Gisburn. His road probably passed within three miles of that place between Settle and Chetburn. He seems to have avoided entering England as long as possible— supposing no doubt, and with good reason, that he was safer in the dominions of David than in those of Stephen. For details of the journey see *R.I.A.* xxxv. 239 ff., 249. The monastery of Gisburn, of which the ruins remain to the south of the parish church, was founded for Augustinian canons, in 1129, by Robert de Brus (Dugdale, vi. 1, 265 ff.).

[841] Malachy was probably suspected (not without cause) of being an emissary of the supporters of the Empress Matilda. He had just spent some days with David I., and with him and his stepson Waltheof he was on terms of intimate friendship (§§ 36, 40). King David invaded England in the following year.

[842] The reference is apparently to King Stephen's attempt to prevent Theobald

of Canterbury and other bishops from attending the Council of Rheims in March 1148. But Malachy does not seem to have been summoned to the Council, and he did not reach the Channel till long after it was over (see next note).

[843] Eugenius left Clairvaux on April 27, and Lausanne on May 20 (Jaffé, p. 634). At this rate he might have been expected to reach Rome by the end of July. About that time, therefore, we may conjecture that Malachy was on the coast of Kent. Actually, the Pope was not near Rome till he reached Viterbo on November 30 (*ibid.* 636). St. Bernard, therefore, when he wrote this passage, was ignorant of his movements for a considerable time before Malachy's death.

[844] *Oriens*: literally, "east."

[845] Luke i. 78.

[846] Ps. cxviii. 24.

[847] St. Bernard's life-long and ever-increasing frailty is constantly alluded to by his biographers. It was largely due to his extreme austerity. In this incident we have an example of the way in which, on many occasions, the strength of his mind conquered the weakness of his body (*V. P.* v. 4).

[848] Gen. xxix. 13.

[849] Cant. iii. 4.

[850] Ps. cxxxiii. 1.

[851] Matt. xii. 42; Luke xi. 31.

[852] October 18. Malachy had therefore reached Clairvaux on October 13 or 14. In the interval he met St. Gilbert of Sempringham and presented him with a pastoral staff (Dugdale, vi. 2, p. xii.). In France Malachy travelled alone—having been parted from his companions in England—and probably on horseback (§ 36). He may, therefore, have left England about September 30, and traversed the 270 miles from Wissant to Clairvaux by October 14. He apparently intended to start for Rome on St. Luke's Day (Serm. i. § 1).

[853] That is, in the presence of the community.

[854] Prov. xiv. 13 (inexact quotation).

[855] Luke x. 40.

[856] Cp. 2 Tim. iv. 6, in which the phraseology of the vg. differs entirely from that of the text.

[857] Not strictly accurate. Malachy reached Clairvaux before his companions. See p. 123, n. 3.

[858] The physicians said the same (Serm. i. § 2).

[859] This saying is quoted in a slightly different form in Serm. i. § 2.

[860] 2 Tim. iv. 6.

[861] 2 Tim. i. 12.

[862] Ps. lxxviii. 30 (vg.).

[863] Ps. cxxxii. 14 (inexact quotation).

[864] Ps. xvii. 7.

[865] 2 Tim. iv. 8.

[866] All Souls' Day.

[867] For the Cistercian method of administering unction see *Usus antiquiores ordinis Cisterciensis*, iii. 94 (*P.L.* clxvi. 1471).

[868] *Solario.*

[869] Cp. Letter iv. § 2, where it is added that he commended the Irish brothers to

the care of St. Bernard.

[870] *Solio.*

[871] Matt. xxiv. 33.

[872] 2 Cor. iii. 7.

[873] Tim. iv. 7.

[874] 2 Sam. i. 23 (inaccurate quotation).—Contrast St. Bernard's lament for his brother Gerard (*Cant.* xxvi. 4): "We loved in life, how have we been divided in death? Most bitter separation!"

[875] Ireland.

[876] John xi. 16.

[877] November 1. For the translation of relics which took place, apparently on that day, see Serm. i. § 2.

[878] Ecclus. xxii. 6.

[879] 1 Thess. iv. 17.

[880] Ps. lxxvi. 10 (vg.).

[881] *Sanctorum ... sollemnitatem.* Not the Festival of All Saints, for that had already come, but, as the next sentence shows, the festival assembly of the saints in heaven. Compare Ps. lxxiv. 4, where *congregations* represents *solemnitatis* in the Vulgate.

[882] John xiv. 19, etc.

[883] Cp. *Cant.* xxvi. 11, "For thee, brother, even at midnight the day dawned."

[884] Rom. xiii. 12.

[885] Ps. lxvi. 12.

[886] See § 71.

[887] Luke xxii. 51.—This saying is quoted in Serm. i. § 5.

[888] Ps. lxxviii. 30 (vg.).

[889] Ps. cxxxix. 11 (vg.).—Cp. *Cant.* xxvi. 11: "Already for thee, my brother, even at midnight the day was dawning, and *the night was shining as the day*; straightway *that night was light about thee in thy pleasure.* I was summoned to that miracle, to see a man exulting in death and mocking death."

[890] John xiv. 1.

[891] Mark ix. 23.

[892] 1 Cor. xiii. 8.

[893] Mark vii. 34.

[894] John xvii. 11.

[895] John xvii. 20.

[896] Cp. Praef. 2.

[897] John vii. 30.

[898] John i. 5.

[899] Eph. v. 19; Col. iii. 16.

[900] The meaning of the phrase is explained in *De Cons.* v. 2: "This will be a returning to our own country, when we leave the country of our bodies and reach the realm of spirits—I mean our God, the Mighty Spirit, the great abiding place of the spirits of the blest" (Lewis's translation, slightly altered). Cp. Serm. ii., § 6.

[901] *A.F.M.* say, "after the fifty-fourth year of his age." St. Bernard appears to be right. For Malachy was made bishop of Connor when he was just entering his thirtieth

year (§ 16), *i.e.* about his twenty-ninth birthday. *A.F.M.* give the date as 1124. But if he was over fifty-four on November 2, 1148 (§ 75), his twenty-ninth birthday would have been before November 1123. If he was under fifty-four on that day it may have been in 1124.

[902] Luke xvi. 22.

[903] Acts vii. 60 (vg.).

[904] Luke iv. 20.

[905] Esth. xiii. 17 (vg.); xvi. 21 (vg.); cp. John xvi. 20, etc.

[906] Cp. Amos viii. 10.

[907] 1 John v. 5.

[908] Ps. cxvi. 15.

[909] Cp. Serm. ii. § 8.

[910] John xi. 11.

[911] Ps. cxxvii. 2, 3 (vg.).

[912] Matt. xxv. 21, 23.

[913] St. Bernard himself celebrated Mass, and by divine inspiration, "when the sacrifice was finished, changed the order of the prayer and introduced the collect for the commemoration of saints who were bishops instead of that which was used for the commendation of the dead," anticipating, as we may suppose, Malachy's canonization. He then devoutly kissed his feet (*V.P.* iv. 21).

[914] 1 Cor. xii. 9 (vg.).

[915] 2 Kings xiii. 21.

[916] Mark viii. 3.

[917] Matt. iii. 17.

[918] Malachy was buried on the north side of the Oratory, vested in St. Bernard's habit. Five years later St. Bernard was buried before the Altar of Saint Mary, clad in the habit in which Malachy died, and which he had worn ever since his death when he celebrated Mass (*V.P.* v. 15, 23, 24). For further particulars of St. Malachy's burial and the disposal of his relics see *R.Q.H.* lii. 43 f.

[919] November 2. From this statement (see p. 128, n. 1) we may infer that Malachy was born in 1095, before November.

[920] 2 Tim. i. 12.

[921] The biographers of St. Bernard give no detailed account of any of Malachy's visits to Clairvaux. But one of them—Geoffrey, St. Bernard's secretary—wrote a prayer for the Bright Valley, in which he placed Malachy on a par with the great Cistercian, thereby revealing to us the extraordinary impression which he made on the community (*V.P.* v. 25). I owe the following translation of it to a friend: "Grant, O Lord, thy never-failing bounty to the spiritual harvest of the Valley, which thou didst deem worthy to illumine with two stars of such surpassing brightness, so making it brighter in very truth even than in name. Do thou guard the house wherein this twofold treasure is laid up and guarded for thee. Be it also unto us according to thy word, that as thy treasure is there so may thy heart be also; there too thy grace and mercy: and may the favour of thy compassion for ever rest on all who are gathered together in the self-same place in thy Name, which is above every name, even as thou art over all, God blessed for ever.— Amen."

[922] 2 Tim. i. 12.

LETTERS OF ST. BERNARD

I

To Malachy. 1141.924

(Epistle 341.)

To the venerable lord and most blessed father, Malachy, by the grace of God archbishop of the Irish, legate of the Apostolic See, Brother Bernard called to be abbot of Clairvaux, [desiring] to find grace with the Lord.

1. Amid the manifold *anxieties* and *cares* of my *heart*,925 by the multitude of which *my soul is sore vexed*,926 the brothers *coming from a far country*927 that they may serve the Lord,928 *thy* letter, *and thy staff, they comfort me*:929 the letter, as a proof of good will; the staff, to support my weak body; the brothers, because they serve the Lord *in a humble spirit*.930 We have received them all, we are pleased with all, *all* alike *work together for good*.931 But as to the wish that you have expressed that two of the brothers932 should be sent to look out a place for you beforehand, having taken counsel with the brothers, we have not thought it meet that they should be *separated one from another*933 *until Christ be more fully formed in them*,934 until they are wholly instructed in *the battles of the Lord*.935 When therefore they have been taught in the school of the Holy Spirit, when they have been *endued with power from on high*,936 then at length the sons shall return to their father that they may *sing the Lord's song*, not now *in a strange land*,937 but in their own.

2. But do you yourselves in the mean time, according to *the wisdom given you*938 by the Lord, look out beforehand and *prepare* beforehand *a place for them*,939 like the places which you have seen here, apart from the commotions of the world. *For the time is at hand*940 when, by the operation of the grace of God, we shall bring forth for you *new men* out of the *old*.941 *Blessed be the Name of the Lord for ever,*942 *of whose only gift it cometh that*943 I have sons in common with you, whom your preaching *planted* and our exhortation *watered*, but *God gave the increase*.944 We beseech your holiness to *preach the word of the Lord*945 so that you may *give knowledge of salvation unto His people*.946 *For* a double *necessity is laid upon you*,947 both from your office as legate and your duty as bishop. Finally, since *in many things we offend all*,948 and, being often thrown among the men of this age, we are much besmirched with the dust of the world, I commend myself to your prayers and to those of your companions, that in His fountain of mercy Jesus Christ, himself the fountain of pity, may deign to wash and cleanse us, who said to Peter, *If I wash thee not, thou shalt have no part with me.*949 And, indeed, I not only earnestly entreat this of you, but also require it as in some sense the payment of a debt, since I cry to the Lord for you, if the prayer of a sinner can do anything. Farewell in the Lord.

II

To Malachy. 1141 *or* 1142.950

(Epistle 356.)

To Malachy, by the grace of God bishop, legate of the Apostolic See, Brother Bernard, called to be abbot of Clairvaux, if the prayer of a sinner can do anything, and if the devotion of a poor man is of any advantage.

We have done what your holiness commanded, not perhaps as it was worthy to be done, yet as well as was possible considering the time in which we live. So great evil everywhere struts about among us that it was scarcely possible to do the little that has been done. We have sent only a few grains of seed,951 as you see, to sow at least a small part of that *field* into which the true *Isaac* once went out *to meditate*, when *Rebekah* was first brought to him by Abraham's *servant*, to be happily joined to him in everlasting marriage.952 And the seed is not to be despised concerning which we find that word fulfilled at this time in your regions,953 *Except the Lord of Sabaoth had left us a seed, we had been as Sodoma, and been made like unto Gomorrha.*954 *I*, therefore, have sown, do you *water*, and *God shall give the increase.*955 All the saints who are with you we salute through you, humbly commending ourselves to their holy prayers and yours. Farewell.

III

To Malachy. 1143 *or* 1144.956

(Epistle 357.)

To our most loving father and most revered lord, Malachy, by the grace of God bishop, legate of the Holy and Apostolic See, the servant of his holiness, Brother Bernard, called to be abbot of Clairvaux, health and our prayers, of whatever value they may be.

1. *How sweet are thy words unto my taste*,957 my lord and father. How pleasant is *the remembrance of thy holiness.*958 If there is any love, any devotedness, any good will in us, without doubt the charity of your belovedness claims it all as its due. There is no need for a multitude of words where affection blossoms abundantly. For I am confident that *the Spirit which* you have *from God*959 bears *witness with your spirit that*960 *what we are*,961 however small it be, *is yours.*962 You also, most loving and most longed-for father, *deliver not* to forgetfulness *the soul of the poor man*, which cleaves *to thee* with the bonds of charity, *and forget not the soul of thy poor man for ever.*963 For neither, as it were anew, *do we commend ourselves unto you*964 when now for a long time we *glory in the Lord*965 that our littleness has been worthy *to find grace in the sight of* your holiness;966 but we pray that our affection, no longer new, may advance with new accessions day by day. We commend to you our sons, yea also yours, and the more earnestly because they are so far removed from us. You know that, after God, all our trust

was in you, in sending them, because it seemed to us wrong not to fulfil the prayers of your holiness. See, as becomes you, that with your whole heart of love you embrace them and cherish them. In no wise for any cause let your earnest care for them grow cold, nor let that perish *which thy right hand hath planted*.967

2. We have now indeed learned both from your letter and from the report of our brothers968 that the house is making good progress, [and] is being enriched both in temporal and spiritual possessions.969 Wherefore we rejoice greatly with you and give thanks with our whole heart to God and to your fatherly care. And because there is still need of great watchfulness, because the place is new, and the land unaccustomed to the monastic life, yea, without any experience of it, *we beseech you in the Lord,970 that you slack not your hand*,971 but perfectly accomplish that which you have well begun. Concerning our brothers who have returned from that place,972 it had pleased us well if they had remained. But perhaps the brothers973 of your country, whose characters are less disciplined and who have lent a less ready ear to advice in those observances, which were new to them, have been in some measure the reason for their return.

3. We have sent back to you Christian, our very dear son, and yours. We have instructed him more fully, as far as we could, in the things which belong to the [Cistercian] Order, and henceforth, as we hope, he will be more careful concerning its obligations.974 Do not be surprised that we have not sent any other brothers with him; for we did not find competent brothers who were ready to assent to our wishes, and it was not our plan to compel the unwilling. Our much-loved brother, Robert,975 assented on this occasion also to our prayers, *as an obedient son*.976 It will be your part to assist him that your house may now be set forward, both in buildings and in other necessaries. This also we suggest to your fatherhood, that you persuade religious men and those who, you hope, will be useful to the monastery, to come into their Order, for this will be of the greatest advantage to the house, and to you they will pay the greater heed. May your holiness have good health, being always mindful of us in Christ.

IV

To the Brothers in Ireland. November 1148.977

(Epistle 374.)

To the religious brothers who are in Ireland, and especially to those communities which Malachy the bishop, of blessed memory, founded, Brother Bernard, called to be abbot of Clairvaux, [wishing them] *the consolation of the Comforter*.978

1. If *here we had a continuing city* we should rightly mourn with most abundant tears that we had lost such a fellow-citizen. But if *we* rather *seek one to come*,979 as befits us, it is nevertheless no small cause of grief that we are bereaved of a guide so indispensable. We ought, however, to regulate passion with knowledge and to mitigate grief with the *confidence of hope*.980 Nor does it become any one to wonder if love compels groaning, if desolation draws forth tears: yet we must set a limit to these things, nay in no small measure be consoled while we gaze *not at the things which are seen, but at the things which are not seen; for the things which are seen are temporal, but the*

*things which are not seen are eternal.*981 First, indeed, we ought to rejoice with the holy soul, lest he accuse us of want of charity, saying also himself what the Lord said to the apostles, "*If ye loved me ye would rejoice because I go unto the Father.*"982 The spirit of our father has gone before us to *the Father of spirits*,983 and we are convicted, not only as wanting in charity, but even as guilty of ingratitude for all the benefits which came to us through him, if we do not rejoice with him who has *departed* from labour to rest, from danger to safety, from *the world unto the Father.*984 Therefore, if it is an act of filial piety to weep for Malachy who is dead, yet more is it an act of piety to rejoice with Malachy who is alive. Is he not alive? Assuredly he is, and in bliss. *In the eyes of the foolish he seemed to have died; but he is in peace.*985

2. Hence even the thought of our own advantage provides us with another motive for great joy and gladness, because so powerful a patron, so faithful an advocate has gone before us to the heavenly court.986 For his most fervent charity cannot forget his sons, and his approved holiness must secure *favour with God.*987 For who would dare to suppose that this holy Malachy can now be less profitable [than before] or less loving to his own? Assuredly, if he was loved aforetime, now he receives from God surer proofs of His love, and *having loved his own, he loved them unto the end.*988 Far be it from us, holy soul, to esteem thy prayer now less effectual, for now thou canst make supplication with more vigour in the presence of *the Majesty*989 and thou no longer *walkest in faith*, but reignest *in the sight* of Him.990 Far be it from us to count that laborious charity of thine as diminished, not to say made void, now that thou prostratest thyself at the very fountain of eternal charity, quaffing full draughts of that for the very drops of which thou didst thirst before. Charity, *strong as death*,991 yea even stronger than death itself, could not yield to death. For even at the moment of his departure he was not unmindful of you, with exceptional affection commending you to God, and with his accustomed *meekness and lowliness*992 praying our insignificance also that we should not *forget you for ever.*993 Wherefore also we thought good to write to you that you may know that we are ready to bestow upon you all consolation with entire devotion, whether in spiritual things, if in them our insignificance can ever do anything by the merits of this our blessed father, or in temporal, if ever perchance opportunity should be given us.

3. And now also, dearly beloved, we are filled with heartfelt pity for this grievous bereavement of the Irish Church.994 And we unite ourselves the more with you in suffering because we know that by this very thing we have become the more your debtors. For the *Lord did great things for us*995 when He deigned to honour this place of ours by making it the scene of his blessed death, and to enrich it with the most costly treasure of his body.996 But do not take it ill that he is buried among us; for God so ordered, *according to the multitude of His mercies*,997 that you should possess him in life, and that it might be allowed to us to possess him, if only in death. And to us, indeed, in common with you, he was, and still is, father. *For* even *in* his *death* this *testament was confirmed* to us.998 Wherefore as, for the sake of so great a father, we embrace you all as our true brothers, with the unstinted yearning of charity, so also concerning yourselves, spiritual kinship persuades us that you are like-minded.

4. But we exhort you, brothers, that you be always careful to *walk in the steps of* this *our* blessed *father*,999 by so much the more zealously as by daily proofs his *holy conversation*1000 was more certainly known to you. For in this you shall prove yourselves to be his true sons, if you manfully maintain the father's ordinances, and if, as

you have seen in him, and heard *from him how you ought to walk, you so walk that you may abound more and more*:1001 for the glory of a father is the wisdom of his sons.1002 For even for us the example of so great perfection in our midst has begun in no slight degree both to expel our sloth and impel us to reverence. And would that he may in such wise *draw us after him* that he may draw us to the goal, *running* more eagerly and more quickly in *the fragrance* which his virtues have left so fresh behind them.1003 May Christ guard all of you *while you pray for us*.1004

[924] When this letter was written certain brothers, sent by Malachy after his return from Rome (October 1140), had arrived at Clairvaux, and had spent some time there (see notes 5, 7); and the brothers left there on his return journey had had a considerable amount of instruction (n. 7). The date is therefore not earlier than 1141. But it is evidently earlier than that of Letter ii.

[925] Cp. Hor., *Sat.* i. 2. 110.

[926] Ps. vi. 3.

[927] Josh. ix. 6.

[928] These were some of the brothers sent from Ireland (*Life*, § 39).

[929] Ps. xxiii. 4.

[930] Song of Three Children, 16.—They had evidently been a good while under St. Bernard's eye.

[931] Rom. viii. 28.

[932] No doubt the four brothers who had been left at Clairvaux (*Life*, § 39).

[933] Matt. xxv. 32.

[934] Gal. iv. 19.

[935] 1 Sam. xxv. 28.

[936] Luke xxiv. 49.

[937] Ps. cxxxvii. 4.

[938] 2 Pet. iii. 15.

[939] John xiv. 2.

[940] Rev. i. 3; xxii. 10.

[941] Cp. Rom. vi. 6; Eph. ii. 15; iv. 22, 24.

[942] Dan. ii. 20, etc.

[943] Coll. for 13th Sunday after Pentecost.

[944] 1 Cor. iii. 6.

[945] Acts xv. 36.

[946] Luke i. 77.

[947] 1 Cor. ix. 16.

[948] Jas. iii. 2.

[949] John xiii. 8 (inexact quotation).

[950] Mellifont was probably founded immediately after the brothers mentioned in the letter reached Ireland. The date is therefore in or before 1142. They would hardly have been sent till news had reached St. Bernard that the site had been chosen (Lett. i, § 2). Cp. p. 75, n. 4.

[951] The brothers sent from Clairvaux "sufficient in number for an abbey" (*Life*, § 39).

[952] Gen. xxiv. 63 ff.—Cp. *De Cons.* ii. 13, where the same passage of Genesis is referred to. It is there (§ 12) explained that the field is the world, which has been placed

in charge of the Pope.

[953] Printed text *patribus*. I read *partibus*.

[954] Rom. ix. 29 (inexact quotation).

[955] 1 Cor. iii. 6.

[956] Mellifont had been founded a good while before the letter was written. Christian had returned to Clairvaux; and now after further instruction he was sent back, apparently as the bearer of the letter. The house had made good progress, but the buildings were still far from complete (§§ 2, 3).

[957] Ps. cxix. 103.

[958] Ps. xxx. 4.

[959] 1 Cor. ii. 12.

[960] Rom. viii. 16.

[961] 1 Cor xv. 10.

[962] 1 Cor. iii. 22.

[963] Ps. lxxiv. 19 (vg.); Jer. xx. 13.

[964] 2 Cor. v. 12.

[965] 2 Cor. x. 17; 1 Cor. i. 31.

[966] 1 Sam. i. 18, etc.

[967] Ps. lxxx. 15.

[968] Apparently the returned brothers mentioned below.

[969] Cp. the passage quoted p. 170.

[970] 1 Thess. iv. 1.

[971] Josh. x. 6.

[972] The monks of Clairvaux seem to have been reluctant to undertake work elsewhere, when St. Bernard desired them to do so (*V.P.* vii. 52 f.); and we have one instance of an abbot of a daughter house—Humbert of Igny—who resigned his office and returned to Clairvaux against St. Bernard's will (*Ep.* 141).

[973] Printed text, *fratrum*. Read *fratres*.

[974] Evidently Christian did not prove a satisfactory abbot. This may in part account for the return of the monks who went with him to Ireland.

[975] Of this Robert, apparently the architect of Mellifont, we know nothing; for suggestions that he should be identified with one or other of the monks of Clairvaux who bore the same name are mere guesses.

[976] 1 Pet. i. 14 (vg., inexact quotation).

[977] Clearly this letter must have been penned a few days after Malachy's death.

[978] Acts ix. 31, combined with John xiv. 26, etc.

[979] Heb. xiii. 14.

[980] Cp. Heb. iii. 6.

[981] 2 Cor. iv. 18.

[982] John xiv. 28.

[983] Heb. xii. 9.

[984] John xiii. 1.—Cp. Serm. i. § 4 f., "It is the end of labours ... and the entrance to perfect safety. Let us rejoice therefore ... with our father"; § 8, "Threefold is the rejoicing of the man, since he is delivered from all sin and from labour and from danger"; and words ascribed to St. Bernard in *V.P.* vii. 49, "Believe, my son, for now thou art about to pass from death to life, from temporal labour to eternal rest."

[985] Communio for All Saints' Day (from Wisd. iii. 2, 3).—For the last four sentences of the section cp. Serm. i. § 5, where an identical passage immediately follows the first parallel quoted in n. 3.

[986] Serm. i. § 1 (end) is somewhat similar in expression, and § 8 (end) in thought. There is a closer, but not very striking, parallel in Serm. ii. § 5 (end).

[987] Luke ii. 52.

[988] John xiii. 1 (inexact quotation).

[989] Heb. i. 3.

[990] 2 Cor. v. 7 (inexact quotation).

[991] Cant. viii. 6.

[992] Cp. Eph. iv. 2.

[993] Ps. lxxiv, 19.

[994] Cp. Serm. i. § 3 (beginning).

[995] Ps. cxxvi. 3.

[996] Cp. Serm. i. § 2, "Therefore we render thanks," etc.

[997] Ps. cvi. 45.

[998] Heb. ix. 17 (vg., inexact quotation).

[999] Rom. iv. 12.

[1000] 2 Pet. iii. 11.

[1001] 1 Thess. iv. 1 (vg.).

[1002] Cp. Prov. x. 1.

[1003] Cant. i. 3, 4.—Cp. Serm. i. § 8 (end).

[1004] Col. iv. 3.

SERMONS OF ST. BERNARD ON THE PASSING OF MALACHY

Sermon I

(November 2, 1148.)1005

1. A certain abundant blessing, dearly beloved, has been sent by the counsel of heaven to you this day; and if it were not faithfully divided, you would suffer loss, and I, to whom of a surety this office seems to have been committed, would incur danger. I fear therefore your loss, I fear my own damnation,1006 if perchance it be said, *The young children ask bread, and no man offereth it unto them.*1007 For I know how necessary for you is the consolation which comes from heaven, since it is certain that you have manfully renounced carnal delights and worldly pleasures. None can reasonably doubt that it was by the good gift of heaven, and *determined by* divine *purpose,*1008 that Bishop Malachy should fall asleep among you to-day, and among you have his place of burial, as he desired. For if not even a leaf of a tree *falls* to *the ground without* the will of God,1009 who is so dull as not to see plainly in the coming of this blessed man, and his passing, a truly great purpose of the divine compassion?1010 *From the uttermost parts of*

*the earth he came*1011 to leave his earth here. He was hastening, it is true, on another errand; but we know that by reason of his special love for us he desired that most of all.1012 He suffered many hindrances in the journey itself, and he was refused permission to cross the sea till the time of his consummation was drawing near,1013 and the goal which could not be passed. And when, with many labours, he came to us *we received him as an angel of God*1014 out of reverence for his holiness; but he, out of his very deeply rooted *meekness and lowliness,*1015 far beyond our merits, received us with devoted love. Then he spent a few days with us in his usual health: for he was waiting for his companions, who had been scattered in England, when the baseless distrust of the king was hindering the man of God. And when they had all assembled to him, he was preparing to set out to the Roman Court, on his way to which he had come hither;1016 when suddenly he was overtaken by sickness, and he immediately perceived that he was being summoned rather to the heavenly palace, *God having provided some better thing for us*, lest going out from *us he should be made perfect* elsewhere.1017

2. There appeared to the physicians no sign in him, I say not of death, but even of serious illness; but he, gladdened in spirit, said that in every way it was befitting that this year Malachy should depart from this life.1018 We laboured to prevent it, both by earnest prayers to God, and by whatever other means we could; but his merits prevailed, that *his heart's desire should be given him and* that *the request of his lips* should *not be withholden.*1019 For so all things happened to him in accordance with his wishes; that by the inspiration of the divine goodness he had chosen this place above all others, and that he had long desired that he should have as the day of his burial this day on which the general memory of all the faithful is celebrated.1020 Moreover, these joys of ours were worthily increased by the circumstance that we had selected that same day, by God's will, for bringing hither from the former cemetery for their second burial the bones of our brothers.1021 And when we were bringing them, and singing psalms in the accustomed manner, the same holy man said that he was very greatly delighted with that chanting. And not long after, he himself also followed, having sunk into a most sweet and blessed sleep. Therefore we render thanks to God for all the things that He has disposed, because He willed to honour us, unworthy as we are, by his blessed death among us, to enrich His poor with the most costly treasure of his body, and to strengthen us, who are weak, by so great a *pillar*1022 of His church. For one or other of two *signs* proves that it was *wrought for us for good,*1023 either that this place is pleasing to God, or that it is His will to make it pleasing to Him, since He led to it *from the uttermost parts of the earth*1024 so holy a man to die and to be buried there.

3. But our very love for this blessed father compels us to sorrow with that people from our heart, and to shudder exceedingly at the cruelty of him, even Death, who has not spared to inflict this terrible wound on the Church, now so much to be pitied. Terrible and unpitying surely is death, which has punished so great a multitude of men by smiting one; blind and without foresight, which has tied the tongue of Malachy, arrested his steps, relaxed his hands, closed his eyes. Those devout eyes, I say, which were wont to restore divine grace to sinners, by most tender tears; those most holy *hands*, which had always loved to be occupied in laborious and humble deeds, which so often *offered for* sinners *the saving sacrifice*1025 of the Lord's body, and were *lifted up* to heaven in prayer *without wrath and doubting,*1026 which are known to have bestowed many benefits on the sick and to have been resplendent with manifold signs; those *beautiful* steps also of

him that preached the Gospel of peace and brought glad tidings of good things; those *feet*,1027 which were so often wearied with eagerness to show pity; those footprints which were always worthy to merit devout kisses;1028 finally, those holy *lips of the priest*, which *kept knowledge*,1029 *the mouth of the righteous*, which *spoke wisdom, and his tongue* which, *talking of judgement*,1030 yea *and of mercy*,1031 was wont to heal so great wounds of souls. And it is no wonder, brothers, that *death* is iniquitous, since iniquity *brought* it *forth*,1032 that it is heedless, since it is known to have been born of *seduction*.1033 It is nothing wonderful, I say, if it strikes without distinction, since it came from *the transgression*;1034 if it is cruel and mad, since it was produced by the subtlety of *the old serpent*1035 and the folly of the woman. But why do we charge against it that it dared to assail Malachy, a faithful *member*, it is true, *of Christ*,1036 when it also rushed madly upon the very *head* of1037 Malachy and of all the elect as well? It rushed, assuredly, upon One whom it could not hurt; but it did not rush away unhurt. Death hurled itself against life, and life shut up death within itself, and *death* was *swallowed up of life*.1038 Gulping down the hook to its hurt, it began to be held by Him whom it seemed to have held.1039

4. But perhaps some one may say, How does it appear that death has been overcome by the Head, if it still rages with so great liberty against the members? If death is dead, how did it kill Malachy? If it is conquered how has it still power over all, and *there is no man that liveth and shall not see death*?1040 Death is clearly conquered—*the work of the devil*1041 and the penalty of sin: sin is conquered, the cause of death; and *the wicked one* himself is *conquered*,1042 the author both of sin and death. And not only are these things conquered, they are, moreover, already judged and condemned. The sentence is determined, but not yet published. In fact, *the fire is prepared for the devil*,1043 though he is not yet cast into the fire, though still for *a short time*1044 he is allowed to work wickedness. He is become, as it were, the hammer of the Heavenly Workman, *the hammer of the whole earth*.1045 He crushes the elect *for* their *profit*,1046 he crushes to powder the reprobate for their damnation. As is the *master of the house*, so are *they of his household*,1047 that is, sin and death. For *sin*, though it is not to be doubted that it was *nailed* with Christ *to His cross*,1048 was yet allowed still for a time, *not* indeed to *reign*,1049 but to dwell even in the Apostle himself while he lived. I lie if he does not himself say, *It is no more I that do it, but sin dwelleth in me.*1050 So also death itself is by no means, indeed, yet compelled not to be present, but it is compelled not to be present to men's hurt. But there will come a time when it is said, *O death, where is thy victory?*1051 For death also is *the last enemy that shall be destroyed.*1052 But now, since He rules *who has the power* of life and *death*1053 and confines the very sea within the fixed limits of its shores, death itself to the beloved of the Lord is a sleep of refreshment. The prophet bears witness who says, *When he giveth his beloved sleep, behold the heritage of the Lord.*1054 *The death of the wicked is indeed most evil*,1055 since their birth is evil and their life more evil; but *precious is the death of the saints.*1056 Precious clearly, for it is the end of labours, the consummation of victory, the gate of life, and the entrance to perfect safety.

5. Let us rejoice therefore, brothers, let us rejoice as is meet, with our father, for if it is an act of filial piety to mourn for Malachy who is dead, yet more is it an act of piety to rejoice with Malachy who is alive. Is he not alive? He is, and in bliss. Certainly, *in the eyes of the foolish he seemed to have died; but he is in peace.*1057 In fine, *now a fellow-*

citizen with the saints, and of the household of God,1058 he at once sings and gives thanks, saying, *We went through fire and water; but thou broughtest us out into a wealthy place.*1059 He *went*, clearly, in manly fashion, and he *went through*1060 happily. The true Hebrew celebrated the Passover in spirit, and as he went, he said to us, "*With desire I have desired to eat this Passover with you.*"1061 *He went through fire and water*,1062 whom neither experiences of sadness could crush, nor pleasures hold back. For there is below us a place which fire wholly claims as its own, so that the wretched Dives could not have there even the least drop of *water* from the *finger* of *Lazarus.*1063 There is also above *the city of God* which *the streams of the river make glad*,1064 *a torrent of pleasure*,1065 *a cup which inebriates, how goodly!*1066 Here, *in the midst,* truly is found *the knowledge of good and evil*,1067 and in this place we may receive the *trial* of pleasure and *of affliction.*1068 Unhappy Eve brought us into these alternations. Here clearly is day and night; for in the lower world there is only night, and in heaven only day.1069 Blessed is the soul which passes through both, neither ensnared by pleasure nor *fainting at tribulation.*1070

6. I think it right to relate to you, briefly, a specimen of the many splendid deeds of this man, in which he is known to have *gone*, with no little vigour, *through fire and water.*1071 A tyrannous race laid claim to the metropolitan see of Patrick, the great apostle of the Irish, creating archbishops in regular succession, and *possessing the sanctuary of God by hereditary right.*1072 Our Malachy was therefore asked by the faithful to combat such great evils; and *putting his life in his hand*1073 he advanced to the attack with vigour, he undertook the archbishopric, exposing himself to evident danger, that he might put an end to so great a crime. Surrounded by perils he ruled the church; when the perils were passed, immediately he canonically ordained another as his successor. For he had undertaken the office on this condition, that when the fury of persecution had ceased and it thus became possible that another should safely be appointed, he should be allowed to return to his own see.1074 And there, without ecclesiastical or secular revenues he lived in the religious communities which he himself had formed, dwelling among them up to this time as one of themselves, and abjuring all personal property.1075 So the fire of *affliction tried*1076 the man of God, but did not consume1077 him; for he was gold. So neither did pleasure hold him captive or destroy him, nor did he stand a curious spectator on the way, forgetful of his own pilgrimage.

7. Which of you, brothers, would not earnestly desire to imitate his holiness, if he dared even to hope for such an attainment? I believe, therefore, you will gladly hear, if I perchance can tell it, what made Malachy holy. But lest our testimony should seem not easy to be received, hear what the Scripture says: *He made him holy in his faith and meekness.*1078 By faith he trampled on the world, as John bears witness when he says, *This is the victory that overcometh the world, even our faith.*1079 For *in the spirit of meekness*1080 he endured all things whatsoever that were hard and contrary with *good cheer.*1081 On the one hand, indeed, after the example of Christ, by faith he trampled on the seas,1082 lest he should be entangled in pleasures; on the other, *in his patience he possessed his soul*,1083 lest he should be crushed by troubles. For concerning these two things you have the saying in the Psalm, *A thousand shall fall at thy side, and ten thousand at thy right hand*;1084 for many more are cast down by the deceitfulness of prosperity than by the lashes of adversity. Therefore, dearly beloved, let none of us, allured by the level surface of the easier way, suppose that road of the sea to be more

convenient for himself. This plain1085 has great mountains, invisible indeed, but for that very reason more dangerous. That way perhaps seems more laborious which passes through the steeps of the hills and the ruggedness of rocks; but to them that have tried it, it is found far safer and more to be desired. But on both sides there is labour, on both sides danger, as he knew who said, *By the armour of righteousness on the right hand and on the left;*1086 so that we may rightly rejoice with those that *went through fire and water and have been brought into a wealthy place.*1087 Do you wish to hear something about the *wealthy place?* Would that another might speak to you of it. For as for me, that which I have not tasted I cannot indite.

8. But I seem to hear Malachy saying to me to-day about this *wealthy place, Return unto thy rest, O my soul; for the Lord hath dealt bountifully with thee: for he hath delivered my soul from death, [mine eyes from tears, and my feet from falling].*1088 And what I understand to be expressed in those words hear in a few sentences; *for the day is far spent,*1089 and I have spoken at greater length than I intended, because I am unwilling to tear myself away from the sweetness of the father's name, and my tongue, dreading to be silent about Malachy, fears to cease. The death of the soul,1090 my brothers, is sin; unless you have overlooked that which you have read in the prophet: *The soul that sinneth, it shall die.*1091 Threefold, then, is the rejoicing of the man, since he is delivered from all sin, and from labour, and from danger. For from this time neither is *sin* said to *dwell in him,*1092 nor is the sorrow of penitence enjoined, nor from henceforth is he warned to guard himself *from* any *falling.*1093 *Elijah*1094 has laid aside his *mantle;*1095 it was not that he feared, it was not that he was afraid that it should be touched, still less *retained,* by an adulteress.1096 He went up into the *chariot;*1097 he is not now in terror of falling; he mounts delightfully; he labours not to fly by his own power, but sits in a swift vehicle. To this *wealthy place,* dearly beloved, *let us run* with all eagerness of spirit, in *the fragrance of the ointments* of this our blessed father, who this day has been seen to have stirred up our torpor to most fervent desire. Let us run after him, I say, crying to him again and again, "*Draw us after thee*";1098 and, with earnest heart and advancing holiness of life, returning devout thanks to the Almighty Pity, that He has willed that His unworthy servants, who are without merits of their own, should at least not be without the prayers of another.

Sermon II

(November 2, 1149)1099

1. It is clear, dearly beloved, *that whilst we are* detained *in the body we are absent from the Lord.*1100 And throughout this wretched time of detention banishment and conscience of faults enjoins upon us sorrow rather than joy. But because by the mouth of the apostle we are exhorted to *rejoice with them that do rejoice,*1101 the time and the occasion require that we should be stirred up to all gladness. For if it is true, as the prophet perceived, that *the righteous rejoice before God,*1102 without doubt Malachy rejoices, who *in his days1103 pleased God*1104 and *was found righteous.*1105 Malachy ministered in *holiness and righteousness before Him:*1106 the ministry pleased Him; the

minister also pleased Him. Why should he not please Him? He *made the Gospel without charge*,1107 he filled the country with the Gospel, he tamed the deathly barbarism of his Irishmen, with the *sword of the spirit*1108 he subdued foreign nations to the *light yoke* of Christ,1109 *restoring His inheritance to Him1110 even unto the ends of the earth*.1111 O, fruitful ministry! O, faithful minister! Is not the promise of the Father to the Son fulfilled through him? Did not the Father behold him long ago when He said to the Son, *I shall give thee the heathen for thine inheritance, and the uttermost parts of the earth for thy possession.*1112 How willingly the Saviour received what He had *bought*,1113 and had *bought with the price*1114 of *His own blood*,1115 with the shame of the Cross, with the horror of the Passion. How willingly from the hands of Malachy, because he ministered *freely*.1116 So in the minister the freely executed office was acceptable,1117 and in the ministry the conversion of sinners was pleasing. Acceptable and pleasing, I say, in the minister was the *singleness of eye*,1118 but in the ministry *the salvation of the people*.1119

2. However, even though a less effective result of the ministry followed, He would nevertheless justly have had regard to Malachy and his works, He to whom purity is a friend and single-mindedness one of his household, to whose righteousness it belongs to weigh the work in accordance with its purpose, from the character of *the eye* to measure the state of *the whole body*.1120 But now *the works of the Lord are great, sought out according to all* the *desires*1121 and efforts of Malachy; they are great and many and *very good*,1122 though better in proportion to the good origin of the pure purpose. What work of piety escaped the attention of Malachy? He was poor as regards himself, but rich to the poor. He was a *father of the fatherless*, a husband *of the widows*,1123 a protector of the oppressed. *A cheerful giver*,1124 seldom making petitions, modest in receiving gifts. He was specially solicitous, and had much success, in restoring peace between those who were at variance. Who was as tender as he in sharing the sufferings of others? who as ready to help? who as free in rebuke? For he was zealous, and yet not wanting in knowledge, the restrainer of zeal. And, indeed, *to the weak* he was *weak*,1125 but none the less strong to the strong: he *resisted the proud*,1126 he lashed the tyrants, a teacher of kings and princes. It was he who by prayer deprived a king of sight when he worked wickedness, and restored it when he was humbled.1127 It was he, when certain men broke a peace which he had made, who gave them up to *the spirit of error*,1128 and foiled them in the evil which they devised to do; and who compelled them to accept peace a second time, confounded and stunned by that which had happened to them. It was he1129 to whom a river most opportunely lent its aid against the others, who were equally *transgressors of a covenant*.1130 In wonderful fashion, by throwing itself before them, it made void the efforts of the ungodly. There had been no rains, no floods of waters, no gathering of clouds, no melting of snows, when suddenly the mere rivulet was converted into a great river; and it rushed along1131 and swelling up overflowed the banks, and utterly denied passage to those who wished to do wickedly.1132

3. What things we have heard and known of the wrath of the man and his vengeance on his enemies, while yet he was *sweet and gentle and plenteous in mercy unto all*1133 that suffered need! For he lived for all as though he were the one parent of all.1134 *As a hen her chickens*,1135 so he cherished all and *protected them under the*

*covert of his wings.*1136 He made no distinction of sex or age, of condition or person;1137 he failed none, his loving heart embraced all. In whatsoever affliction men cried to him he counted it his own: even more than that, for in regard to his own afflictions he was patient, in regard to those of others he was compassionate, very often even passionate. For indeed sometimes, filled with wrath, he was stirred to take the part of one against another, that by *delivering the poor* and restraining the *strong*1138 he might take thought in equal measure for the salvation of all. Therefore he was angry; but it was in order that he might not sin by not being angry, according to the words of the Psalm, *Be ye angry and sin not.*1139 Anger did not rule him, but he himself *ruled his spirit.*1140 He had power over himself. Assuredly he who had the victory over himself could not be *mastered by anger.*1141 His anger was kept in hand. When it was summoned it came, going forth, not bursting forth; it was brought into action by his will, not by impulse. He was not set on fire by it, but used it.1142 As well in this as in ruling and restraining all the motions both of his inner and his outer man1143 his judgement was careful, his caution great. For he did not give so much attention to all, as to leave himself alone out of account, as, in his universal solicitude, to disregard only himself. He was careful of himself also. He *guarded himself.*1144 In fact, he was so wholly his own, so wholly also belonged to all, that his love seemed in no degree to hinder or delay him from his guardianship of himself, nor his concern for his own person from the common good.1145 If you saw the man busied in the midst of crowds, involved in cares, you would say he was born for his country, *not for himself.*1146 If you saw the man alone and dwelling by himself, you would suppose that he lived for God alone and for himself.

4. Without tumult he went about among tumults; without ease he spent the time which he gave to ease. How could he be taking his ease1147 when he *was occupied in the statutes of the Lord*?1148 For though he had time free from the necessities of the peoples, yet had he none unoccupied by holy meditations, by the work of prayer, by the ease itself of contemplation. In the time of ease he spoke gravely or not at all. His mien was either courteous, or humble and self-restrained. Assuredly—a trait which is counted worthy of much praise among the wise—*his eye was in his head,*1149 never flying forth except when it was obedient to power. His laughter displayed love, or provoked it: but even so it was rare. Sometimes indeed, it came forth, but it was never forced, intimating the gladness of his heart in such a way that his mouth did not lose but gained in grace.1150 So modest was it that it could not be suspected of levity; so gentle,1151 however, that it sufficed to free his joyous countenance from every trace and shadow of sadness.1152 O perfect gift! O *rich burnt sacrifice!*1153 O pleasing service in mind and hand! How *sweet unto God is the savour*1154 of him who employs his leisure in prayers, how sweet unto men of him who is occupied in fatiguing labours.

5. Because he was such an one, then, *beloved of God*1155 and men, not undeservedly was Malachy received this day into the company of angels, having attained in fact what his name denoted.1156 And indeed, already he was an angel not less in purity than in name. But now more happily is the significance of his glorious name fulfilled in him, since he is glad with a glory and happiness equal to that of the angels.1157 Let us also, dearly beloved, be glad because our *angel ascended*1158 to his fellow-citizens, acting as an ambassador for *the children of the captivity,*1159 winning for us the favour of the blessed ones, declaring to them the desires of the wretched. Let us *be glad,* I say, *and rejoice,*1160 because in that heavenly court1161 there is one who went

forth from us to take care of us,1162 to protect us by his merits,1163 whom he instructed1164 by his example and strengthened1165 by his miracles.

6. The holy pontiff, who *in a humble spirit*1166 often brought peace-offerings to the heavens, to-day in his own person has *gone unto the altar of God*,1167 himself the victim and the priest. With the departure of the priest the rite of sacrifice is changed into a better thing. The *fountain of tears*1168 is dried up, every burnt sacrifice is made *with gladness and rejoicing.*1169 *Blessed be the Lord God of* Malachy, who by the ministry of so great a pontiff *hath visited his people,*1170 and now, *taking him up into the holy city,*1171 ceaseth not, by the remembrance of so great sweetness to *comfort our captivity.*1172 Let *the spirit of* Malachy *rejoice in the Lord,*1173 because he is freed from the heavy load of the body, and is no longer hindered, by the weight of impure and earthly matter, from passing with all eagerness and fullness of life, through the whole creation, corporeal and incorporeal, that he may enter entirely into God, and *joined to* Him may with Him *be one spirit*1174 for ever.1175

7. *Holiness becometh* that *house*1176 in *which the remembrance of* so great *holiness*1177 is celebrated. Holy Malachy, preserve it *in holiness and righteousness*1178 pitying us who in the midst of so many and great miseries *utter the memory of thine abundant goodness.*1179 Great is the dispensation of the mercy of God upon thee, who made thee *little in thine own sight,*1180 great in His; who *did* great things by thee, in saving thy country, *great things to thee,*1181 in bringing thee into His glory. May thy festival, which is deservedly devoted to thy virtues, have a saving efficacy for us by thy merits and prayers. *May the glory of thy holiness,*1182 which is celebrated by us, be continued by angels: so shall it meetly be pleasant for us, if it be also fruitful. While thou departest be it allowed to us, who are met together to-day in thy so delicious feast, to preserve some remnants of the fruits of the Spirit, loaded with which thou ascendest.

8. Be to us, we beseech thee, holy Malachy, another Moses, or another Elijah, like them imparting *of thy spirit*1183 to us, for thou hast come *in their* spirit *and power.*1184 Thy life was *a law of life and knowledge,*1185 thy death the port of death and the portal of life,1186 thy memory the delight of sweetness and grace, thy presence *a crown of glory in the hand of the Lord*1187 thy God. O *fruitful olive tree in the house of God!*1188 O *oil of gladness,*1189 giving both anointing and light, cherishing with favours, *resplendent with miracles,*1190 make us partakers of that light and graciousness which thou enjoyest.1191 O sweet-smelling *lily, blossoming and budding* evermore before the Lord, and spreading everywhere a *sweet* and life-giving *savour,*1192 *whose memorial is blessed*1193 with us, whose presence is in honour with those who are above, grant to those who sing of thee that they may not be deprived of their share in so great *an assembly.*1194 O *great luminary*1195 and *light* that *shinest in darkness,*1196 illuminating the prison, *making glad the city*1197 by the rays of thy signs and merits, by the lustre of virtues put to flight from our hearts the darkness of vices. O *morning star,*1198 more brilliant than the rest because thou art nearer the day, more like to the sun, deign to go before us, that we also may *walk in the light as children of light*, and *not* children *of darkness.*1199 O thou who art the dawn breaking into day upon the earth, but *the noon light*1200 illumining the higher regions of heaven, receive us in the fellowship of light, by which illuminated thou sheddest light far without, and sweetly burnest within, by the gift of our Lord Jesus Christ, who with the Father and the Holy Spirit reigneth One God, world without end.—Amen.

[1005] The evidence that this discourse was delivered on the day of Malachy's death is cumulative. (1) The opening words of § 1, and the closing sentences of § 8 (note "this day"). (2) The statement in § 5, "He said *to us*, 'With desire I have desired,'" etc., implies that those who tended Malachy in his sickness were present (see *Life*, § 73). The first person plural in § 2 suggests the same conclusion. (3) In § 6, "dwelling among them *up to this time*" implies that his death was not long past. (4) The striking parallels with Letter iv.; for which see the notes on it. (5) The tone of the sermon—in marked contrast to that of Sermon ii.—indicates that the community was crushed with sorrow for a recent bereavement. See *R.I.A.* xxxv. 255 ff.

[1006] *damnum uestrum ... damnationem meam.*

[1007] Lam. iv. 4 (inexact quotation).

[1008] Acts ii. 23.

[1009] Cp. Matt. x. 29.

[1010] Cp. St. Bernard, *De Laud. Virg.* i. 1 (*P.L.* clxxxiii. 56): "For if neither a leaf from a tree falls on the earth without cause, nor one of the sparrows without the heavenly Father, am I to suppose that a superfluous word flows from the mouth of the holy evangelist?"

[1011] Matt. xii. 42.

[1012] See *Life*, § 67.

[1013] See *Life*, § 69.

[1014] Gal. iv. 14 (inexact quotation).

[1015] Cp. Eph. iv. 2.

[1016] He was evidently in haste to resume his journey. And no wonder, for the winter was drawing near, and the sooner the passage of the Alps was made the better for his comfort and safety. Cp. *R.I.A.* xxxv. 248. "Alpine passes ... become impassable usually about the commencement or middle of October, and remain closed until May" (Sennett, *Great St. Bernard*, p. 369).

[1017] Heb. xi. 40.

[1018] See *Life*, § 71.

[1019] Ps. xxi. 2.

[1020] See *Life*, §§ 67, 71.

[1021] The translation is supposed by Henriquez, *Fasciculus Sanctorum Ordinis Cisterciensis*, ii. 41. 6 (*P.L.* lxxxv. 1559) to have been made on All Saints' Day, the bones being reburied on All Souls' Day. But Vacandard (*R.Q.H.* lii. 41 f.) thinks that the date of the translation was Saturday, October 30. This event probably marked the end of the construction of the new monastery of Clairvaux, which began before Malachy's first visit. See p. 71, n. 4.

[1022] Gal. ii. 9.

[1023] Ps. lxxxvi. 17 (vg.).

[1024] Matt. xii. 42.

[1025] 2 Macc. iii. 32 (vg.).

[1026] 1 Tim. ii. 8.

[1027] Rom. x. 15.

[1028] Cp. Luke vii. 38.—Perhaps a reference to St. Bernard's own action just before this sermon was preached. See p. 129, n. 6.

[1029] Mal. ii. 7.

[1030] Ps. xxxvii. 30.

[1031] Ps. ci. 1.

[1032] Jas. i. 15.

[1033] Cp. 2 Cor. xi. 3; 1 Tim. ii. 14.—See J. H. Bernard on 2 Cor. xi. 3 (*Expositor's Greek Testament*).

[1034] 1 Tim. ii. 14.

[1035] Rev. xii. 9; xx. 2.

[1036] 1 Cor. vi. 15, etc.

[1037] Eph. iv. 15, etc.

[1038] 1 Cor. xv. 54, combined with 2 Cor. v. 4.

[1039] Cp. *Cant.* xxvi. 11: "Thou art dead, O death, and pierced by the hook thou hast imprudently swallowed, which saith in the words of the prophet, 'O death, I will be thy death! O hell, I will be thy bite.' Pierced, I say, by that hook, to the faithful who go through the midst of thee thou offerest a broad and pleasant path-way into life" (Morison's translation). A very old metaphor. It is thus explained by Rufinus (a.d. 400) in his Commentary on the Apostles' Creed (§ 16, Heurtley's translation): "The object of that mystery of the Incarnation ... was that the divine virtue of the Son of God, as though it were a hook concealed beneath the form and fashion of human flesh, ... might lure on the prince of this world to a conflict, to whom offering His flesh as a bait, His divinity underneath might secure him, caught with a hook by the shedding of His immaculate blood.... As, if a fish seizes a baited hook, it not only does not take the bait off the hook, but is drawn out of the water to be itself food for others, so he who had the power of death seized the body of Jesus in death, not being aware of the hook of divinity enclosed within it, but, having swallowed it, he was caught forthwith, and the bars of hell being burst asunder, he was drawn forth as it were from the abyss to become food for others."

[1040] Ps. lxxxix. 48 (vg.).

[1041] 1 John iii. 8.

[1042] 1 John ii. 13, 14.

[1043] Matt. xxv. 41.

[1044] Rev. xii. 12.

[1045] Jer. l. 23.

[1046] 1 Cor. xii. 7 (vg.).

[1047] Matt. x. 25.

[1048] Col. ii. 14.

[1049] Rom. vi. 12.

[1050] Rom. vii. 17.

[1051] 1 Cor. xv. 55 (vg.).

[1052] 1 Cor. xv. 26.

[1053] Heb. ii. 14; Tobit ii. 8.

[1054] Ps. cxxvii. 2, 3 (vg.).

[1055] Ps. xxxiv. 21 (vg.).

[1056] Ps. cxvi. 15.

[1057] Communio for All Saints (Wisd. iii. 2, 3).

[1058] Eph. ii. 19 (with variant).

[1059] Ps. lxvi. 12.

[1060] Hos. x. 15 (vg.: xi. 1).

[1061] Luke xxii. 15.—See *Life*, § 73, where for "he said to us" we have "lifting up his eyes on *those who stood round him*, he said."

[1062] Ps. lxvi. 12.

[1063] Luke xvi. 24, 25.

[1064] Ps. xlvi. 4.

[1065] Ps. xxxvi. 8 (vg.).

[1066] Ps. xxiii. 5 (vg.).

[1067] Gen. ii. 9.

[1068] 2 Cor. viii. 2.

[1069] Rev. xxi. 25; xxii. 5.

[1070] Eph. iii. 13.

[1071] Ps. lxvi. 12.

[1072] Ps. lxxxiii 12 (vg.).

[1073] 1 Sam. xix. 5.

[1074] See *Life*, §§ 19-31.

[1075] See p. 82, n. 5.

[1076] Ps. lxvi. 10, 11.

[1077] *Examinauit, non exinaniuit.*

[1078] Ecclus. xlv. 4 (vg.).

[1079] 1 John v. 4.

[1080] Gal. vi. 1.

[1081] 1 Kings xxi. 7 (vg.).

[1082] Cp. Matt. xiv. 25; John vi. 19.

[1083] Luke xxi. 19.

[1084] Ps. xci. 7.

[1085] That is, the sea. The details of the imagery are not clear. But evidently the sea represents the pleasures, and the hills and rocks the adversities, of life.

[1086] 2 Cor. vi. 7.

[1087] Ps. lxvi. 12.

[1088] Ps. cxvi. 7, 8 (vg.).—The printed text has, in place of the bracketed words, "and so forth." The threefold deliverance obviously corresponds to the threefold rejoicing mentioned below, sin being substituted for death in the description of it, because "the death of the soul is sin."

[1089] Luke xxiv. 29.

[1090] Cp. Ps. cxvi. 8.

[1091] Ezek. xviii. 4.

[1092] Rom. vii. 17, 20.

[1093] Ps. cxvi. 8.

[1094] For other comparisons of Malachy with Elijah, see *Life*, § 23; Serm. ii. § 8.

[1095] 2 Kings ii. 13.

[1096] Gen. xxxix. 12, 15 (vg.).

[1097] 2 Kings ii. 11.

[1098] Cant. i. 3, 4.

[1099] It is plain from § 7 that this sermon was preached on an anniversary of Malachy's death, *i.e.* on November 2, in a year later than 1148. I put it in 1149 because of its striking coincidences with the *Life*, which was written early in that year (see p. lxv).

There is also a possible echo (§ 3) of *De Cons.* i. which belongs to the same year (*P.L.* clxxxii. 723). These, together with two coincidences of phrase with other writings of St. Bernard, are pointed out in the notes. See *R.I.A.* xxxv. 260 ff.

[1100] 2 Cor. v. 6.

[1101] Rom. xii. 15.

[1102] Ps. lxviii. 3.

[1103] Ecclus. xliv. 7.

[1104] Ecclus. xliv. 16 (vg.).

[1105] Ecclus. xliv. 17.

[1106] Luke i. 75.

[1107] 1 Cor. ix. 18.—Cp. *Life*, § 43 (p. 84).

[1108] Eph. vi. 17.

[1109] Matt. xi. 30.

[1110] Ps. xvi. 5 (vg.).

[1111] Isa. xlviii. 20; Jer. xxv. 31.

[1112] Ps. ii. 8.

[1113] 2 Pet. ii. 1.

[1114] 1 Cor. vi. 20.

[1115] Acts xx. 28.

[1116] 2 Cor. xi. 7.

[1117] *Gratum erat munus gratuitum.*

[1118] Matt. vi. 22; Luke xi. 34.

[1119] Hab. iii. 13.

[1120] Matt. vi. 22, 23; Luke xi. 34, 35.

[1121] Ps. cxi. 2 (vg.).

[1122] Gen. i. 31.

[1123] Ps. lxviii. 5.

[1124] 2 Cor. ix. 7.

[1125] 1 Cor. ix. 22.

[1126] Jas. iv. 6; 1 Pet. v. 5.

[1127] See *Life*, § 60.

[1128] 1 John iv. 6.

[1129] Printed text, *Ipse enim est.* With A I omit *enim.*

[1130] Josh. vii. 15, etc.

[1131] So A: *cicius* (= *citius*) *ibat* for *riuus ibat* of the printed text.

[1132] The story is told much more fully in *Life*, §§ 58, 59; where there are many similarities in phraseology to the present passage. In both places it is connected with the miraculous blinding of the king, immediately preceding it here, immediately following it there.

[1133] Ps. lxxxvi. 5 (vg.).

[1134] Cp. the description of Malchus, *Life*, § 8: "He was reverenced by all, as the one father of all"; and of Malachy, § 33: "the loving father of all."

[1135] Matt. xxiii. 37.

[1136] Ps. lxi. 4 (vg.).

[1137] Cp. *Life*, § 42: "Neither sex nor age, nor condition nor profession, is held in account."

[1138] Ps. xxxv. 10

[1139] Ps. iv. 4 (vg.).

[1140] Prov. xvi. 32.

[1141] Job xxxvi. 18 (vg.).

[1142] *Non urebatur illa, sed utebatur.*

[1143] *Utriusque hominis sui.*

[1144] 1 Tim. v. 22.

[1145] Cp. *De Cons.* i. 6: "If you desire wholly to belong to all ... I praise your humility, but only if it is complete. But how can it be complete if you exclude yourself? And you are a man. Then, that your humanity also may be complete, let the bosom which receives all gather you also within itself ... wherefore, where all possess you let you yourself also be one of those who possess."

[1146] Lucan, *Phars.* ii. 383.

[1147] Cp. *De Cons.* iv. 12, "In ease not taking ease;" *Life,* § 43, "Quiet often, but by no means at any time taking ease."

[1148] Ps. cxix. 23.

[1149] Eccles. ii. 14 (inexact quotation).

[1150] Cp. Luke iv. 22.

[1151] *Tantillus.* The text seems to be corrupt. Read *tam laetus?*

[1152] Cp. *Life,* § 43: "Yea, what was there that was not edifying," etc.

[1153] Ps. xx. 3 (vg.).

[1154] 2 Cor. ii. 15.

[1155] 1 Thess. i. 4 (vg.); 2 Thess. ii. 13.

[1156] That is, Malachias, the Hebrew for *my angel*, with a Latin termination. For its origin see *Life,* § 12.

[1157] At this point, with A, I omit a passage which is identical with the first half of Serm. i. § 5, and interrupts the argument. With A, also, in the following sentence I read *Laetemur et nos dilectissimi quod* for *Laetemur quod* of the printed text. See *R.I.A.* xxxv. 260-262.

[1158] Judg. xiii. 20.

[1159] Dan. vi. 13; Ezra iv. 1.

[1160] Ps. ix. 2.

[1161] *Curia.*

[1162] *Cui sit cura nostri.*

[1163] Cp. Lett. iv. § 2.

[1164] *Informauit.*

[1165] *Confirmauit.*

[1166] Song of Three Children, 16.

[1167] Ps. xliii. 4.

[1168] Jer. ix. 1.

[1169] Ps. xlv. 15.

[1170] Luke i. 68.

[1171] Matt. iv. 5.

[1172] Ps. cxxvi. 1, 4 (vg.).

[1173] Luke i. 47.

[1174] 1 Cor. vi. 17.

[1175] See *De Cons.* v. 2, quoted p. 127, n. 13, and the sermon on the Marriage of the Soul with the Word (*Cant.* lxxxiii. 6), in which St. Bernard, quoting 1 Cor. vi. 17, says, "Love ... joins the two in one spirit, makes them no longer two but one." Cp. also *Cant.* xxvi. 5: "He that is joined to God is one spirit, and is wholly changed into a certain divine feeling, and cannot think of or mind anything but God, and that which God thinks and minds, being full of God." For the last phrase see Ignatius, *Magn.* 14.

[1176] Ps. xciii. 5.

[1177] Ps. xxx. 4.

[1178] Luke i. 75.

[1179] Ps. cxlv. 7 (vg.).

[1180] 1 Sam. xv. 17 (inexact quotation).

[1181] Luke i. 49.

[1182] Ps. cxlv. 5 (vg.).

[1183] Num. xi. 25; 2 Kings ii. 9, 15.

[1184] Luke i. 17.—See p. 151, n. 3.

[1185] Ecclus. xlv. 5.

[1186] The same phrase occurs in *Life*, § 75, similarly applied.

[1187] Isa. lxii. 3.

[1188] Ps. lii. 8 (vg.).

[1189] Ps. xlv. 7 (vg.).

[1190] Epiphany Collect.

[1191] Cp. *Life*, § 47 (p. 88).

[1192] Isa. xxvii. 6, combined with Hos. xiv. 5, and Ecclus. xxxix. 14.

[1193] Ecclus. xlv. 1.

[1194] Ecclus. xxiv. 2, 12 (vg.). The clauses containing the word assembly (*plenitudo*) are omitted in R.V.

[1195] Ps. cxxxvi. 7.

[1196] John i. 4.

[1197] Ps. xlvi. 4.

[1198] Ecclus. l. 6.

[1199] 1 John i. 7, combined with 1 Thess. v. 5.

[1200] Isa. xviii. 4 (vg.).

ADDITIONAL NOTES

A.—St. Bernard's Description of the State of the Irish Church.

Life, §§ 7, 16, 17.

In two passages of the *Life* serious charges are made against the Irish Church of the early years of the twelfth century. These charges refer primarily to the dioceses of

Armagh and Connor; but it is probable that those dioceses were typical of many other districts throughout the country. If St. Bernard's statements are true of them, they may be applied with little reserve to the greater part of Ireland. Indeed he himself gives us more than a hint that the abuses which he condemns were by no means confined to eastern Ulster (§ 19). It may be well, therefore, to bring them together and to discuss them.

1. There was no such thing as chanting at the canonical hours. In the whole bishopric of Armagh "there was none who could or would sing" (§ 7). "In the churches [of Connor] there was not heard the voice either of preacher or singer" (§ 16). We may suspect that there is some exaggeration here; for if church song was absolutely unknown, how could Malachy have "learnt singing in his youth" (§ 7)? But that St. Bernard's remarks are substantially correct need not be questioned. He is not speaking of the Irish Church as it was in its earlier period, but of its state at the time when it had probably fallen to its lowest depth. His assertion, therefore, is not disposed of by references to the chanting at the funerals of Brian Boroimhe in 1014 and Maelsechlainn in 1022 (O'Hanlon, p. 34). Indeed in the notices of those events in *A.F.M.* there is no express mention of ecclesiastical song.

2. At Armagh Confession was not practised (§ 7); in the diocese of Connor "nowhere could be found any who would either seek penance or impose it" (§ 16). It may be true that Confession had been much neglected among some classes of the people: Malachy on one occasion met a woman who had never confessed (§ 54), and the very fact that he put the question to her "whether she had ever confessed her sins" suggests that she was not singular in this respect. But it is remarkable that the *anmchara* (soul-friend), or Confessor, is frequently mentioned in Irish literature. The obits of several persons to whom that title is given are recorded in the Annals in the twelfth century. And penance is often alluded to in the obituary notices of distinguished persons, clerical and lay. In his sweeping statement St. Bernard may have had in mind some differences of method in penitential discipline between the Roman and Irish Churches.

3. The sacrament of Confirmation was not celebrated, at any rate in Armagh (§ 7). This rite has always been used in the Irish Church, though possibly neglected locally at some periods. St. Patrick tells us that he "confirmed in Christ" those whom he had "begotten to God" (*Epistle*, 2; cp. *Confession*, 38, 51)—thus giving us one of the earliest instances in literature of the application to the rite of its present familiar name. But in his practice (*Epistle*, § 3), as in the Stowe Missal, about a.d. 800 (ed. Sir G. F. Warner, vol. ii. p. 31), it seems to have consisted of an anointing with chrism without laying on, or raising, of hand, or a direct prayer for the Holy Spirit. According to the Stowe Missal it was administered by a presbyter. It is improbable that St. Bernard or his romanizing friends would recognize the rite so performed as true Confirmation.

4. One of the things which was neglected at Armagh was "the marriage contract" (§ 7). In the diocese of Connor there was "no entry into lawful marriages" (§ 16). By the labours of Malachy this abuse disappeared. In Armagh he "instituted anew" the marriage contract; in Connor it came to pass that "the celebration of marriage" was revived (§ 17). Putting these statements together we may conclude that St. Bernard's meaning is that marriages had ceased to be celebrated in the face of the Church, and that in consequence the vow of a life-long union was often evaded. Now contemporary writers charge the Irish of this period with loose sexual morality, especially in regard of arbitrary divorce, matrimony within the prohibited degrees, exchange of wives, and other breaches of the

law of marriage. Such accusations are made, for example, by Pope Gregory VII. (Haddan and Stubbs, *Eccl. Docs.* ii. 160), Lanfranc (Ussher, 490; *P.L.* cl. 535, 536), Anselm (Ussher 521, 523; *P.L.* clix. 173, 178) and Giraldus Cambrensis (*Gest.* ii. 14; *Top.* iii. 19). Their evidence is the more worthy of credence because the usages to which they refer were characteristic of the Irish at an earlier period (*Encycl. of Religion and Ethics*, v. 456, 460), and might be expected to recur in an age of spiritual decline. But both Lanfranc and Anselm testify to the existence of marriage as an institution among the Irish. The former speaks of the divorce of a wife "lawfully joined to her husband," and the latter uses terms of similar import. So also does St. Bernard himself. His praise of Malachy's mother (*Life*, § 1) is inconceivable if she did not live in wedlock; and he expressly states that eight "metropolitans" of Armagh were "married men" (§ 19). But if there was nevertheless a revival among large sections of the people of pagan ideas of marriage, which tolerated polygamy, concubinage, incest and easy termination of unions, it can be understood that marriage in the face of the Church, which included a vow absolutely prohibitive of all these things, would be commonly avoided. Malachy's anxiety to restore the marriage ceremony was no doubt due to a desire to purge the nation of immoral customs of which St. Bernard makes no express mention. But, however that may be, we have contemporary native evidence that the rite of marriage had fallen into desuetude, and that Malachy was successful in his effort to restore it. For in the document quoted on p. 170, we are told that in a district which was part of the diocese of Armagh when he was Cellach's vicar (*L.A.J.* iv. 37), and under the rule of his patron, Donough O'Carroll, "marriage was assented to."

5. "There was no giving of tithes or firstfruits," writes St. Bernard (§ 16). He is speaking of the diocese of Connor. But there is no doubt that the remark might have been made of other districts. There was no such custom as the payment of tithes in Ireland before the twelfth century. They are first mentioned by Gilbert of Limerick, about 1108, in his *De Statu Ecclesiae* (Ussher, 507); and they were enjoined at the Synods of Kells in 1152 (Keating, iii. 315) and Cashel in 1172 (Can. 3, Giraldus, *Expug.*, i. 35). From the document quoted above we learn that in Oriel, under Donough O'Carroll, "tithes were received"—evidently a new impost.

6. "Ministers of the altar were exceeding few" in the diocese of Connor (§ 16); and accordingly it is observed that Malachy provided his new churches with clergy (§ 17). This is not proved, nor is it in any great degree corroborated by the statement of *A.F.M.* (1148) that Malachy "ordained bishops and priests and men of every order"; but the parallel is perhaps worth noting.

7. The voice of the preacher was not heard in the churches (§ 16). This statement cannot, so far as I know, be checked.

8. The same remark must be made about the statements that the people would not come to church (§ 16), and that Malachy's exertions at length induced them to do so (§ 17), though they are sufficiently probable.

9. That "churches were rebuilt" (§ 17) cannot be questioned. No doubt the monasteries of Bangor and Saul would be counted among the number. We have explicit and independent evidence of the fact. The foundation of churches and re-edifying of monasteries were a conspicuous feature of the reign of Donough O'Carroll (see p. 170). And *A.F.M.* (1148) lay great stress on Malachy's activities in this direction. He "consecrated many churches and cemeteries," and "founded churches and monasteries,

for by him was repaired every church in Ireland which had been consigned to decay and neglect, and they had been neglected from time remote."

On the whole it appears that St. Bernard's strictures are at least not without foundation in fact, in so far as they can be tested. But he can scarcely be acquitted of some measure of exaggeration in the rhetorical passages in which they occur.

B.—The Hereditary Succession of the Coarbs Of Patrick.

Life, §§ 19. 20, 30.

The assertions of St. Bernard in *Life*, § 19, concerning the coarbs of Patrick are controlled by *A.U.* The ninth predecessor of Cellach, Cathasach II. († 957) is described in them (*s.a.* 956) as "coarb of Patrick, learned bishop of the Goidhil." None of the following eight is said to have been a bishop, though all are called coarbs of Patrick. Moreover Cellach himself was appointed abbot before he "received holy orders," and the record of his ordination on St. Adamnan's Day (September 23) 1105, several weeks after his "institution," seems to indicate that it was unusual for the abbots to be ordained. All this corroborates the statement that his eight predecessors were "without orders." It is true, indeed, that according to *A.F.M.* Amalgaid, one of the eight, anointed Maelsechlainn king of Ireland, on his deathbed in 1022. But it does not follow from this that he was a priest. In early times, as is well known, unction was administered to the sick by laymen; and there appears to be no evidence that this office was confined to the priesthood till well on in the ninth century (*Dict. of Christ. Antiquities*, ii. 2004). It is at least possible that the older usage lingered on in Ireland to a much later date than on the Continent. But the statement of *A.F.M.* as to the anointing of Maelsechlainn is not confirmed by the more reliable authority of *A.U.*

That at least five of the eight were, as St. Bernard says, "married men" is shown by the following table, compiled from *A.U.* and MacFirbis (*R.I.A.*, MS. 23 P. 1, p. 308). The persons whose names are printed in italics were coarbs of Patrick.

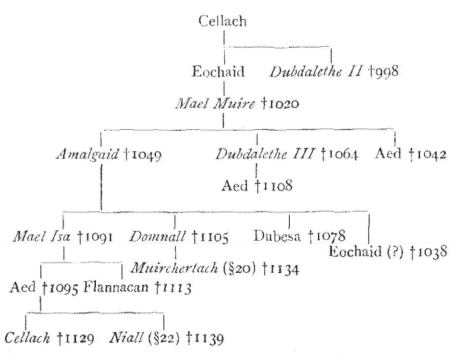

Cellach

Eochaid   *Dubdalethe II* †998

Mael Muire †1020

Amalgaid †1049   *Dubdalethe III* †1064   Aed †1042

Aed †1108

Mael Isa †1091   *Domnall* †1105   Dubesa †1078

Eochaid (?) †1038

Muirchertach (§20) †1134

Aed †1095 Flannacan †1113

Cellach †1129   *Niall* (§22) †1139

This table also confirms the statement that the abbots all belonged to the same family, and so obtained office by a sort of hereditary right. St. Bernard gives no hint which would enable us to identify this family. But the genealogy given by MacFirbis enumerates the ancestors of Cellach in a direct line up to Fiachrach, son of Colla fo Crich, and is headed "Genealogy of Ui Sinaich, *i.e.* the coarbs of Patrick." The Bodleian MS., Rawl. B. 502,1201 has the same genealogy, and entitles it "Genealogy of Clann Sinaich." The family then from which the abbots of Armagh were taken was the principal branch of that sept. From the genealogy it appears that the sept was derived from Sinach, from whom the fifth in descent was the Cellach whose name appears at the head of foregoing table.

St. Bernard represents Malachy to have said in 1132, when he was induced to oppose Murtough, that the system of hereditary succession had already lasted nearly two centuries (§ 20). This statement is in accord with known facts. The genealogical table gives sufficient evidence that it began not earlier than the accession of Dubdalethe II. (965), and continued to the accession of Murtough. If there is no evidence that the three predecessors of Dubdalethe were of the Clann Sinaich, neither is there anything to disprove it. But their immediate predecessor, Joseph, was certainly not of that sept; for *A.U.* (ms. A, 935) tells us that he was of the Clann Gairb-gaela, and the list of coarbs in the Book of Leinster notes in addition that he came from Dalriada (*R.I.A.* xxxv. 327, 359). Thus the succession cannot have been established before the death of Joseph (936). Hence it lasted for a period of between 167 and 196 years. A period of 167 years, or a period of 196 years, might be described as "well-nigh two hundred years" (*annos ferme ducentos*), though the latter suits St. Bernard's language better than the former.

But how can this be harmonized with the statement that "fifteen quasi-generations had passed in this wickedness" (§ 19)? Obviously a "quasi-generation" is not a generation of human life: apart from the facts just mentioned, the very word *quasi* forbids the supposition. Colgan (*Trias*, p. 301) suggested that the word indicates the period of office of a coarb; and this is very probable. The figure of generations, so applied, is in line with

St. Bernard's conception of a bishop as "the seed" of his predecessor (§ 34). But the first of a series of coarbs, of which Murtough was the fifteenth, was Maelcoba, the second predecessor of Joseph. So that, even on Colgan's hypothesis, St. Bernard's two statements are irreconcilable. Yet it is difficult to believe that an error so manifest was in his source. I suggest that he wrote "fifteen" in error for "twelve": in other words his document had *xii*, and he misread it *xu*. The confusion of *u* with *ii* is very common in manuscripts. If this explanation is accepted, St. Bernard's authority implied that the hereditary succession was upheld without interruption from the death of Joseph to the accession of Murtough, which is "well-nigh two hundred years."

This investigation may convince us that St. Bernard depended on an excellent document for his knowledge of the history of Armagh. But he certainly went astray in the interpretation of the document when he styled the predecessors of Cellach metropolitans (see p. 45, n. 1). And he goes further when he asserts that none were allowed to be bishops who were not of their family (§ 19); thus leaving the impression that under the rule of the eight lay abbots—that is, for a century and a half—Armagh was deprived of episcopal ministrations. But this is wholly unhistorical. The Ulster Annals mention six bishops of Armagh, contemporary with the lay abbots. They seem to have followed one another in regular succession, and there is no indication that any one of them belonged to the Clann Sinaich. They were no doubt monastic bishops, such as are found in the Irish Church from the sixth century onwards, who exercised the functions of their order at the bidding of the abbots. They were probably not referred to in St. Bernard's document; and if they were, one who had been trained in an entirely different ecclesiastical system would have been at a loss to understand their position.

Thus we conclude that St. Bernard, in the passage which we are considering, used good material with conscientious care, but that he was misled by lack of knowledge of Irish ecclesiastical methods. This result is important because it may apparently be applied to the whole of his memoir of St. Malachy. His statements, as a rule, stand well the test of comparison with the native records; and when he is at fault we can usually explain his errors as misunderstandings, due to ignorance of conditions of which he had no experience.

St. Bernard has been charged with gross exaggeration in another passage. "A great miracle to-day," he writes (§ 30), "is the extinction of that generation, so quickly wrought, especially for those who knew their pride and power." It is an extravagant hyperbole to say that either the O'Neills, or the great tribe of the Oirgialla, represented to this day by the Maguires, the O'Hanlons and the MacMahons, was blotted out when the *Life of St. Malachy* was written. So argued some in the time of Colgan (*Trias*, p. 302). But they misrepresented St. Bernard. The word "generation" obviously means in the sentence before us what it meant in § 19 ("adulterous generation")—not an extensive tribe, nor even the Clann Sinaich as a whole, but the branch of that sept which provided abbots for Armagh. The speedy extinction of a single family is not a thing incredible. And it is worthy of remark that neither the Clann Sinaich, nor any person described as ua Sinaich or mac Sinaich is mentioned in the Annals after 1135 (see p. 58, n. 9).

For a more detailed treatment of the subjects discussed in this note reference may be made to *R.I.A.* xxxv. 232-238, 340-353.

C.—Malachy's Contest with Niall.

Life, §§ 22-31.

The narrative of the series of events between the death of Murtough and the consecration of Gelasius, both in St. Bernard's *Life* and in *A.F.M.*, is obscure, and our two main authorities contradict each other in some particulars. In this note, I propose to attempt a reconstruction of the story.

1. Among the native authorities *A.F.M.* stand alone in giving what approximates to a full account of the struggle between the rival abbots. *A.T.* record only three incidents; the *Chronicon Scotorum* also records three incidents belonging to the year 1134, and then breaks off, to be resumed in 1142; in *A.U.* and *A.I.* there are hiatus which cover the whole period; the other Annals ignore the events with which we are concerned. The information supplied by *A.F.M.* runs as follows:

1134.(1) Malachy O'Morgair made a visitation of Munster and obtained his tribute.

(2) A chapel, which was erected by Cormac Mac Carthy, king of Cashel, was consecrated by a synod of clergy assembled at that place.

(3) Murtough died 17 September.

(4) Niall was installed in the coarbate of Patrick.

(5) A change of abbots at Armagh, *i.e.* Malachy O'Morgair in place of Niall.

(6) Malachy afterwards made a visitation of Munster and received his tribute.

1135.(7) Flann Ua Sinaich, keeper of the Staff of Jesus, died after good penance.

(8) Malachy O'Morgair purchased the Staff of Jesus, and took it from its cave 7 July.

1136.(9) A visitation of Munster was made by Malachy O'Morgair, coarb of Patrick.

(10) A change of abbots at Armagh, *i.e.* Niall in place of Malachy.

(11) Malachy O'Morgair resigned the coarbate of Patrick for the sake of God.

1137.(12) A change of abbots at Armagh, *i.e.* the erenach (*recte* abbot) of Derry in place of Niall.

1138.(13) Christian O'Morgair died.

A.T. record the second and fifth of the above events, and subjoin to the latter notice the passage quoted p. 51, n. 4. The *Chronicon Scotorum* records, the second, third and fifth.

There is obvious confusion in the narrative of the Masters. They put the death of Christian O'Morgair under 1138, which is a year too early (see p. 66, n. 1), and they credit Malachy with having made three visitations of Munster within three years, which he is very unlikely to have done. But it is to be observed that the notices of the visitations are not mere repetitions, for they differ from each other verbally. Thus we may suspect that the Masters copied those entries from three different sources, and that they refer to the same visitation, which, in at least one of the sources, appeared under the wrong year. Now the consecutive sentences 9, 10 are probably connected with each other: the absence of Malachy in Munster would give his opponents opportunity to reinstate his rival. In like manner entries 1, 2 (not consecutive) may be connected. It would not be surprising if Malachy, even at some risk to the security of his tenure of the abbacy at Armagh, took part in the consecration of his patron's church at Cashel. And it may be added that he would not improbably make this visit to the south the occasion of a circuit in Munster. The visitation, on that hypothesis, must have taken place in 1134 or early in 1135. Again, the note of time in entry 6 implies that it was made not very long after the appointment of Malachy, recorded in the immediately preceding entry 5. Finally, entry 8 mentions an event which must have greatly strengthened his hands. Having possessed himself of the more important and revered of the abbatial insignia he was at length more than a match for his antagonist. Probably, therefore, the restoration of Niall (10) should be placed rather before than after it. For these reasons we seem to be justified in placing the recorded incidents in the following order. When Malachy secured possession of the see (5) he remained long enough in Armagh to establish himself in the abbacy. During this time may have occurred the abortive conspiracy against him related in *A.T.*, but not alluded to in *A.F.M.* He then went to Cashel for the consecration of the Chapel (2), and held his visitation of Munster (1, 6, 9). When he returned he found that Niall had once more entered Armagh (10). By July 1135 the power of his rival had considerably decreased, and Malachy got possession of the Staff of Jesus (8). Finally he resigned his office (11) and Gelasius was appointed to it (12). If this is a true account of the course of events, one statement of the Annals needs correction. They tell us that Gelasius succeeded Niall; on our hypothesis he succeeded Malachy. But that the Masters should have substituted the former for the latter was to be expected; for according to their previous (as I believe misplaced) statement Niall, not Malachy, was in possession in the latter part of 1136.

2. We now turn to St. Bernard's narrative of these transactions. Sections 22 and 23 present no difficulty. They are simply an amplification, with differences in detail, of what we learn from *A.T.* In the early part of § 24 it is stated that Malachy remained in Armagh after the king, with whose aid he had "ascended the chair of Patrick," had returned home; and in the succeeding narrative it is implied that he never left it till he went to Down. That is to say, the visitation of Munster is ignored. This need cause no surprise. It is quite possible that St. Bernard had never heard of it. Again, there is no explicit mention of the reinstatement of Niall. But it seems to be implied in § 24 (see p. 53, n. 9). The whole story becomes more intelligible if we assume that Niall was in possession for a short time, and then fled, but continued to exercise his functions outside the city, as Malachy himself had done in a previous period (§ 21). If we suppose that the visit to Munster took place shortly after the episode of § 23 we can explain the only difficulty in the narrative, the return of Niall after he had been driven out. The latter part of § 24 seems to intimate a lessening of opposition to Malachy's rule. The whole passage, §§ 24-27, with the exception of the last two sentences of § 27, must relate to the period before July 1135, inasmuch as Niall is represented as carrying about with him the Staff of Jesus as well as the Book of Armagh.

Up to this point St. Bernard's narrative harmonizes admirably with the story as it has been reconstructed above from the Annals. But we must carry our comparison of the two accounts a little further. They agree in giving 1137 as the date of the appointment of Gelasius as coarb of Patrick; but while St. Bernard puts the resignation of Malachy in the same year the Masters record it under 1136 (p. 61, n. 7). Now their phrase (11), that he "resigned for the sake of God," in its present context (10) can have only one meaning. Malachy, seeing that his contest with Niall was hopeless, determined to retire rather than continue the strife, and left Niall in possession. But apart from entry 10, which seems to have been misplaced, the words have no such implication, and are in harmony with the reason given by St. Bernard for Malachy's return to his former diocese (§§ 20, 21). Since the dates of the Masters for this period are already suspect we need not hesitate to follow St. Bernard's guidance here. But we may go further. The annalists were compelled, if they would be consistent, to suppose that there was a considerable interval between the retirement of Malachy and the accession of Gelasius. How was it possible that when Niall had finally routed his formidable rival, who was in possession of the Staff of Jesus, another should at once step in and, apparently without any difficulty, deprive him of the fruits of his victory? The difficulty is increased if we accept the statement of St. Bernard —not contradicted by the Annals, and not easy to dispute—that Gelasius was nominated by Malachy himself, and was therefore presumably favourable to his cause. Thus we perceive that there was good reason that the annalists should separate the two events as far as possible, by antedating Malachy's resignation, and by connecting it rather with Niall's restoration than with the appointment of Gelasius.

3. In weighing the respective claims of St. Bernard and the annalists to credence in this part of Malachy's life it is well to remember that of it St. Bernard may be assumed to have had full and first-hand information. The main facts were probably communicated to him by Malachy himself, though some particulars were no doubt added by other Irish informants. It is true, we must also allow for bias on St. Bernard's part in favour of his friend. Such bias in fact displays itself in §§ 25, 26. But bias, apart from sheer dishonesty, could not distort the whole narrative, as it certainly must have been distorted in the *Life*, if the narrative of *A.F.M.* is to be accepted as it stands.

4. It is important to observe that in the earlier stages of Malachy's conflict with Niall the lord of Oriel was Conor O'Loughlin, who was apparently not friendly to the reformers of the Irish Church (cp. §§ 18, 20, p. 40, n. 2, and p. 46, n. 5). No doubt his defeat by O'Brien and Mac Carthy in 1134 (p. 43, n. 5) made him a less ardent supporter of Niall than he had been of Murtough; but it is not likely that he entirely discouraged his attempts to seize the abbacy. The ultimate success of Malachy was in fact probably due to O'Loughlin's murder at the end of May 1136 and the rise to power of Donough O'Carroll (see p. 58, n. 11), his successor in the kingdom of Oriel. St. Bernard never mentions O'Carroll by name, though he possibly alludes to him in one passage (§ 28: see note there). But we may infer from other sources that he was a zealous friend and helper of Malachy. The most important of these is a contemporary document, part of which has been copied on a blank page of a fourteenth-century Antiphonary of Armagh (T.C.D. ms. B. 1. 1.) opposite the first page of the Calendar. Unfortunately the scribe laid down his pen at the end of a line and in the middle of a sentence. The document was first published by Petrie (p. 389) with a translation. As it is referred to several times in the notes to the *Life* it may be well to print here, with a few slight alterations, Dr. Whitley Stokes' revised rendering (Gorman, p. xx.).

"*Kalend. Januar. v feria, lun. x. Anno Domini mclxx.* A prayer for Donnchad Ua Cerbhaill, supreme King of Oirgialla, by whom were made the book of Cnoc na nApstal at Louth and the chief books of the order of the year, and the chief books of the Mass. It is this illustrious king who founded the entire monastery both [as to] stone and wood, and gave territory and land to it for the prosperity of his soul in honour of Paul and Peter. By him the church throughout the land of Oirgialla was reformed, and a regular bishopric was made, and the church was placed under the jurisdiction of the bishop. In his time tithes were received and marriage was assented to, and churches were founded and temples and bell-houses [round towers] were made, and monasteries of monks and canons and nuns were re-edified, and *nemheds* were made. These are especially the works which he performed for the prosperity [of his soul] and reign in the land of Oirgialla, namely, the monastery of monks on the banks of the Boyne [as to] stone and wood, implements and books, and territory and land, in which there are one hundred monks and three hundred conventuals, and the monastery of canons of Termann Feichin, and the monastery of nuns, and the great church of Termann Feichin, and the church of Lepadh Feichin, and the church of...."

O'Carroll, then, was an ardent supporter of Malachy. Is it likely that after his long struggle to secure the Chair of Patrick, and when he was in actual possession of it, Malachy should voluntarily surrender his claim to Niall at the very moment when the new king of Oriel had come to his aid? Yet, unless we are prepared to place his resignation before June 1136, that is the assumption we must make if we adhere to the statements of *A.F.M.*

5. There are other documents of high authority which must be taken into account: the contemporary record of the succession of coarbs of Patrick in the Book of Leinster, and the copy of a similar record in the Yellow Book of Lecan. The former of these seems to have been written by a partizan of Malachy, since it ignores Murtough. The latter assigns to that abbot a rule of three years, in agreement with St. Bernard (§§ 20, 21). But neither of them so much as mentions Niall; and both make Gelasius the successor of Malachy. Thus they contradict *A.F.M.* and corroborate the narrative of St. Bernard. See *R.I.A.* xxxv. 355 f.

[1201] See Kuno Meyer's Facsimile edition, p. 146, e. The genealogy there begins with Amalgaid, not with Cellach.

APPENDIX.

The Portion of § 41 of the Life omitted in Translation.

Alia quaedam ibidem *pernoctabat in oratione*,1202 quam forte reperiens solam homo barbarus, accensus libidine et sui minime compos, irruit rabiosus in eam. Conuersa illa et tremefacta, suspiciens aduertit hominem plenum diabolico spiritu. "Heu," inquit, "miser, quid agis? Considera ubi es, reuerere haec sancta, defer Deo, defer seruo eius Malachiæ, parce et tibi ipsi." Non destitit ille, furiis agitatus iniquis.1203 Et ecce (quod horribile dictu est) uenenatum et tumidum animal quod bufonem uocant uisum est reptans exire de inter femora mulieris. Quid plura? Terrefactus resiliit homo, et datis saltibus festinus oratorio exsilit. Ille confusus abscessit, et illa intacta remansit, magno quidem et Dei miraculo et merito Malachiae. Et pulchre operi foedo et abominando foedum interuenit et abominabile monstrum. Non prorsus aliter decuit bestialem extingui libidinem quam per frigidissimum uermem, nec aliter temerarium frenari ausum frustrari conatum quam per uilem inutilemque bestiolam.

[1202] Luke vi. 12.
[1203] In hexameter rhythm. Cp. Virg., *Aen.* iii. 331; Ov., *Art. Am.* ii. 27.

Made in the USA
Coppell, TX
30 December 2021

70419005R00081